The American Woman 1988-89

Edited by Sara E. Rix for the
Women's Research & Education
Institute

W · W · NORTON & COMPANY
NEW YORK · LONDON

The American Woman 1988-89

A Status Report

First Edition

THE TEXT OF *this book is composed in Goudy old style, with display type set in Bodoni Bold Condensed. Composition and manufacturing by the Haddon Craftsmen. Book design by Marjorie J. Flock.*

ISBN 0-393-02530-6

ISBN 0-393-30441-8 PBK.

W. W. Norton & Company, Inc., 500 Fifth Avenue, New York, N. Y. 10110
W. W. Norton & Company Ltd., 37 Great Russell Street, London WC1B 3NU

1 2 3 4 5 6 7 8 9 0

Contents

Women in Brief

Appendices

Tables and Figures

Appendix · American Women Today: A Statistical Portrait

Editor's Note

IN JULY 1987, the Women's Research and Education Institute (WREI) released the first edition of *The American Woman*, a report designed to bring together in a single accessible publication some of the latest research and thinking on the status of American women and their families. The scholars, applied researchers, policy analysts, and women's activists who contributed to *The American Woman 1987–88* documented and analyzed the extent and nature of changes in the roles of women over the past two to three decades and commented on the consequences of those changes.

In many respects, the picture painted in that first edition of *The American Woman* was a gloomy one. Congresswoman Barbara Kennelly called it "a nightmare documented." And, certainly, the book described in detail the bleak situation of many women in contemporary America. The more than 10 million women heading families on their own were, and remain, a group warranting particular concern. Foremost among the problems of this growing group, as *The American Woman 1987–88* made startlingly clear, is low income. Many of these women—whose median family income is less than half that of their married-couple counterparts—have incomes well below the poverty level. Many are or will become what is known as "persistently poor."

The first edition of *The American Woman* noted that although there is no single explanation for the poverty of female-headed families, high divorce rates are a contributing factor. Half of all new marriages will end in divorce, and divorce propels many women and their children into poverty. In addition, the number of families whose members have always been poor has been rising, as has the number of unmarried teenage mothers with few of the skills needed for self-supporting work. Over half of all children living in female-headed families were poor when *The American Woman 1987–88* was released; for those children with black mothers, the percentage jumped to more than two-thirds. Sad to say, the situation is no less disturbing as the second edition of *The American Woman* goes to press.

The first edition of the book documented the dramatic increase in women's labor force participation in the past few decades. Over 29 million more women were working or looking for work in 1986 than in 1960, and in the past year the number of women entering or remaining in the paid labor force has continued to grow. However, women remain concentrated in female-dominated jobs characterized by low wages and little job security. Women are still, as the first edition of *The American Woman* stressed, far more likely than men to be part-time workers, typically earning low wages, entitled to few fringe benefits, and offered little opportunity for advancement.

Even the narrowing of the male/female wage gap discussed by Nancy Barrett in *The American Woman 1987–88* was not necessarily the positive development that it appeared to be. According to Dr. Barrett, the gap narrowed not only because women were moving into higher-paying jobs but because the recession of the early 1980s had a disproportionate impact on the better-paying male jobs.

Women who work for pay retain most of their traditional

unpaid responsibilities in the home. *The American Woman 1987–88* pointed out that formal or group child care is nonexistent at any price for millions of working women, forcing many mothers to juggle several informal and often unreliable arrangements in their search for safe, affordable care for their children while they are at work.

But the news in *The American Woman 1987–88* was by no means all bad. The book also documented considerable progress for women. Their representation in many relatively lucrative professions once exclusively or primarily the domain of men—e.g., law, economics, and medicine—has increased dramatically. Women have also made inroads in nonprofessional occupations as well: they are a growing proportion of telephone installers, mail carriers, and bus drivers. Women have been claiming a far greater share of first professional degrees in such fields as law, veterinary medicine, and dentistry than was the case 20 or even 10 years ago.

As was evident in *The American Woman 1987–88*, 1986 was a year of notable "firsts" for U.S. women. Terrie McLaughlin was named the Air Force Academy's outstanding cadet—the first woman to achieve that distinction. Jeana Yeager copiloted the first plane ever to fly around the world without landing or refueling. At the other end of the technological spectrum, Ann Bancroft with a dogsled became the first woman to reach the North Pole without mechanical transportation.

The accomplishments of such exceptional women—the "headliners"—are important because they weaken stereotypes and undermine barriers that militate against progress for women as a whole. Nevertheless, the "firsts" should not overshadow the really big story documented in *The American Woman 1987–88*: how change over the past 25 years has affected the lives of millions of women in ordinary circumstances—the women who won't ever attend a military academy, who have no desire to fly a plane of their own, who aren't angling to get to the North Pole by any means, mechanical or otherwise. It is when we look at these women that we really get a sense of how much things have changed in a single generation.

Persistent inequities and repeated setbacks are as much a part of the story of the past quarter-century as advancement has been. Nevertheless, if there is any one hopeful conclusion to be drawn from the diverse articles in the first edition of *The American Woman*, it is that women have many more choices about what to do with their lives than they had just 25 years ago.

The reader of *The American Woman 1988–89* may reach the same conclusion, although this book is different from its predecessor. *The American Woman 1988–89* is not a revised or updated version of the first edition. With the exception of a few key statistical tables that reappear with updated figures, all of the material in *The American Woman 1988–89* was prepared specifically for the 1988–89 edition.

Since, as Senator Barbara Mikulski once said, "Every issue is a woman's issue," winnowing the topics for inclusion in a book on the status of women is difficult, and some explanation of the choices for this edition seems called for.

As the twenty-fifth anniversary year of Betty Friedan's *The Feminine Mystique*, the book that some say launched the modern feminist movement, 1988 seems a particularly appropriate time to reflect on what women have gained—and perhaps given up—since the modern women's movement began. Historian Cynthia Harrison, author of a new book on the politics of women's issues from 1945 to 1968, was therefore invited to consider the more recent past in an essay that evaluates women's success in gaining freedom to control their lives.

The fact that 1988 is a presidential election year played its part in the decision to include a critical examination by Ruth Mandel, director of the Center for the American Woman and Politics, of the advances that women have made in seeking and gaining elective office. What encourages women to run for elective office, especially in view of the financial costs of campaigning today? Where have women been most successful? What obstacles have they encountered on the way? Do women candidates differ from male candidates? From male officeholders?

Dr. Mandel's chapter is complemented by a special section featuring 18 women who have succeeded in gaining elective office at the federal level where, as she points out, women are rarest. The two U.S. senators and 16 U.S. representatives who constitute the executive committee of the Congressional Caucus for Women's Issues report on their efforts on behalf of women and families in the first half of the 100th Congress.

The past several years have been marked by increasing media and political interest in family issues. Last year's *American Woman* noted almost in passing that married-couple families with a wife in the paid labor force had a median income that was nearly 50 percent higher than the median income of families in which the wife stayed at home. Such summary statistics can merely hint at the effect that women's increased labor force participation has really had on the economic situation and overall well-being of American households. Princeton economist Rebecca Blank considers the implications of women's paid work for three types of households: never married women living alone, women supporting children as single mothers, and married-couple households.

One might be tempted to conclude that the higher median income of married-couple families is clear evidence that working wives improve their families' economic circumstances. But Blank demonstrates that the answer is not quite so simple. Although the incomes of married-couple families with working wives have increased substantially more than those of couples where the wife stays at home, there are tradeoffs to be made when a wife, particularly one with children, enters the labor force. As working women have always known, the more time they spend on paid work, the less time they have for their traditional family responsibilities, but those responsibilities do not evaporate when women go off to work. Nor do most husbands help pick up much of the slack. Some of what working wives earn is spent on goods and services that would not be necessary if the wives did not work, so the increase in family income is unlikely to mean an equivalent increase in the family's standard of living. Blank's chapter highlights numerous family-related issues that should be of interest to candidates and officeholders developing family policies for the 1990s and beyond.

As we pointed out in *The American Woman 1987–88,* no single volume could hope to be all-inclusive. We were sure to omit topics important to what we hoped would be a large and diverse readership. The virtue of a regularly published report such as *The American Woman* is that omissions and deficiencies can be corrected in subsequent editions. The absence from the first edition of any discussion of women's health issues—a gap noted by many readers—is remedied in this second edition, which includes several health-related chapters, including a major chapter by Karen Davis, a noted health care policy expert with the Department of Health Policy and Management at the Johns Hopkins University. Dr. Davis tackles with skill the subject of health status and access to health care, especially among poor and near-poor women, and pays particular attention to the needs of elderly women, most notably the 7.1 million who live alone.

Dr. Davis's chapter is indeed a timely one: as *The American Woman 1988–89* goes to press, Congress is grappling with the thorny issue of meeting the health care needs of an estimated 37 million uninsured men, women, and children in the face of mounting federal budget deficits. Catastrophic-care health insurance legislation for the elderly was approved by Congress in June. And long-term care will become a major campaign issue in 1988 if some 100 organizations lobbying to make it a high priority are successful.

Insurance coverage was by no means the only health issue in the news in 1988. Women with, or at risk of getting, AIDS are the subject of a chapter in this year's *American Woman*. The media has made most of the public aware of the AIDS epidemic, but far fewer people know that although women are a very small proportion of all AIDS cases, they constitute the fastest growing group of persons with AIDS. Most of these women are intravenous drug users or the partners of drug users and most are of childbearing age. Half of the babies born to AIDS-infected mothers appear likely to be infected with the deadly disease. Less often in the headlines than AIDS, but of undoubted importance to women, are the potential health hazards of working in high technology industries. A chapter in this book focuses on this topic, examining, for instance, the implications of mounting evidence that the chemicals used in making computer chips may have an adverse effect on women's reproductive health.

As was the case with the first edition of *The American Woman*, this edition highlights women's continued march into occupations once virtually closed to them; this year's edition looks at women in law enforcement, in road construction, and in the clergy. Women's progress in these fields has not been without its problems, as the authors of several of the chapters stress. Moreover, with occupational integration comes concern about occupational *resegregation.* For example, women were 48 percent of the graduates of schools of veterinary medicine in 1985–86, up from 11 percent in 1964–65. Is this cause for wholehearted rejoicing? Maybe not: according to the executive director of the American Veterinary Medicine Association, "... the economic rewards of a veterinary practice have not kept pace with other professions such as law and medicine. In addition, once a profession becomes identified as female oriented, many men look elsewhere for their careers" (*New York Times,* February 21, 1988). The conclusions of this chapter about what happens as women make inroads in traditionally male-dominated occupations are not encouraging.

The status of workers in traditionally female occupations is of great importance as well, because it is in those occupations that the vast majority of employed women are found. This edition of the book includes a chapter examining the status and prospects of registered nurses, of whom 94 percent are female.

Ideas for some of the chapters in the book originated in queries from the media, recommendations from readers, or our own identification of issues of vital concern to women.

Calls to WREI about women in the clergy, for example, are fairly common: Who are they? Where are they? How many are there? The chapter on farm women was a direct outgrowth of a reader's suggestion. The press made much of a recent study reporting that women of a certain age, if unmarried, could give up hope of ever finding a spouse. Were the authors of that report correct, or was a subsequent study with more hopeful conclusions the "right" one? *The American Woman 1988–89* seemed just the place to attempt to answer those questions.

The contributors to this book were asked to include information about minority women in their assessments wherever possible, and such information is found in many of the chapters. Two chapters focus on minority women in particular: one on the educational attainment of black women, and another on the findings from a survey of young Hispanic women. More chapters on minority women and their families are scheduled for the next edition.

The section "1987 in Review" highlights "firsts" and significant accomplishments by individual American women during the year—the first black female astronaut appointed by NASA and the appointment of first female president of the American Society of Newspaper Editors. But more important, this section briefly summarizes some of the major legislative, judicial, economic, and other decisions and developments that could have an impact on the lives of millions of American women for years to come.

We have sought to be as comprehensive as a single volume allows, but of course, many important aspects of the status of women in the United States remain to be addressed. Future editions of *The American Woman* will include chapters on such topics as homeless women, women and disability, women in the judicial system, and women in the peace movement. That many issues are discussed in short chapters in this edition of *The American Woman* is by no means a reflection of the importance assigned to those issues. The subjects of some of these short chapters will be revisited at greater length in future years.

When the first edition of this report on the status of American women was released, Representative Claudine Schneider said: "Statistics have to be one of the tools we use to change the system . . . Clearly [*The American Woman*] provides us with the facts, the figures, the statistics, absolutely everything we need" (*New York Times*, July 22, 1987). Each edition of *The American Woman* has been designed as a resource for persons working—whether by changing the system or in other ways—to improve the status of American women and their families.

SARA E. RIX

Acknowledgments

THIS SECOND EDITION of *The American Woman* owes its existence in large part to several foundations and many individuals who have provided financial assistance, advice, and encouragement over the past several months.

At the top of the list is the Ford Foundation, which has expressed its confidence in us with a grant that has underwritten a large portion of both the first and second editions of *The American Woman*. We are extremely grateful to the foundation for its generous assistance in this endeavor and, in particular, to June Zeitlin and Alison Bernstein, who have not only been supportive of the project every step of the way, but have made creative and practical suggestions and recommendations for broadening the book's appeal and use to readers.

The other funders without whose assistance we could not have completed this book are AT&T; Sears, Roebuck and Company; Chevron U.S.A. Inc.; and the George Gund Foundation. We are indeed grateful to each of them for their invaluable support.

For a second year, we received guidance from an advisory board of individuals who represent potential users of *The American Woman 1988–89*: scholars, the media, government officials, policymakers, and librarians, among others. These advisors provided valuable suggestions about content, design, and how to best meet the needs of various readers. Our thanks to Jessie Bernard, Mariam Chamberlain, Jane Chapman, Beverly Ellerman, Gordon Green, Harriette McAdoo, Brenda Pillors, Sara Pritchard, Anne Radigan, Ida Ruben, Ann Schmidt, Elizabeth Waldman, and Franklin Wallick.

We wish to thank Kathleen Anderson, our first editor at W. W. Norton and Company, for having faith in our ability to produce *The American Woman* and providing us with expert editorial advice. Mary Cunane, our present Norton editor, also deserves our thanks, as does Donald Lamm, Norton's president.

Jean Stapleton, the unfailingly supportive president of WREI's board, has gone out of her way to promote *The American Woman* in conversations with newspaper reporters and television interviewers all across this country. We are especially grateful to Ms. Stapleton, as well as to Representatives Lindy Boggs, Barbara Kennelly, and Claudine Schneider, for making time in busy schedules to launch the first edition of the book in July 1987.

Mary Emrick of Chevron U.S.A. Inc. has been enthusiastic and tireless in her support and encouragement. Her initiatives on behalf of the first edition of the book have significantly increased its distribution. She has also assisted in obtaining materials for the second edition. Margaret Adams, national affairs editor of *Good Housekeeping* magazine, has worked diligently to promote the book both here and abroad. Maryland State Senator Ida Ruben has done much to get the book in the hands of state legislators and other policymakers around the country. Anne Bryant of the American Association of University Women, Jill Miller of the Displaced Homemakers Association, and Irene Natividad of the National Women's Political Caucus also deserve our gratitude for their practical efforts to promote the first edition. We would be remiss if we did not acknowledge the expert advice and assistance of Susan Bales of Public Affairs Research and Communications Inc. (PARC) and her colleagues, Lisa Lederer and Kathleen Sullivan. The success of the first edition of *The American Woman* owes much to PARC's efforts on behalf of the book.

The editorial and writing assistance of Celia Ekhardt, Allison Porter, Simon Cordery, and Wayne Welch has been invaluable. Mandana Dehghanian competently handled many of the proofreading and confirmation tasks associated with putting this book together.

Other individuals deserve our thanks for furnishing information, recommending authors, reviewing chapters, critiquing our approach, and/or keeping us apprised of new developments: Miriam Abrams, Lt. Cathy Atwell, Laurie Bassi, William Chafe, Kevin Dougherty, Lisa Garratt, Irwin Gertzog, Janet Heinrich, Lamont Johnson, Azar Kattan, Ruth Kobell, Dottie Lay, Donna Lenhoff, Lora Liss, Cynthia Marano, Marcelle Martin, Susan Martin, Stephanie Minor-Harper, Edward Morris, Carol Nechemias, Diann Neu, Phyllis Palmer, Marc Rosenblum, Alisa Shapiro, Ralph Smith, Thomas Snyder, and Christine Workentine. Laura Loeb of the Congressional Caucus for Women's Issues deserves special mention for her continuing assistance. In addition, we wish to thank the many people from the Bureau of Labor Statistics and Census Bureau—Howard Fullerton and Earl Mellor, in particular—who so generously shared their time and expertise.

As always, I want to express my appreciation to the dedicated staff at WREI, most notably the editor, Sara Rix, and the associate editor, Anne Stone, who devoted much of the past year to *The American Woman.* Thanks are also due to Kate McGuinness for, among other things, the many weeks she spent carefully preparing tables for the statistical appendix. Alison Dineen and Terry Walker also deserve my thanks for their many substantive contributions to the book and for their efforts at promotion and dissemination.

Finally, it should go without saying that our funders and advisors are not responsible for any errors or misstatements that may be found in the book. The opinions expressed herein do not necessarily represent the opinions of anyone other than the authors of the chapters.

BETTY PARSONS DOOLEY
Executive Director
Women's Research and Education Institute

Introduction

THE HONORABLE BARBARA B. KENNELLY *and*
THE HONORABLE CLAUDINE SCHNEIDER

WHEN THOMAS JEFFERSON wrote the Declaration of Independence, he claimed for Americans the "self-evident" truth that all men are created equal. It occurred neither to Jefferson nor to the other men who signed his document in 1776—as idealistic and forward-looking as they took themselves to be—that equality might apply to black men, or to women whatever their color. But the power of a truly great idea cannot be contained by the vision of one man, one group of men, or one historical period. The concept of a polity whose members are created equal has been one of the distinctive American contributions to Western civilization, and has also generated continuing political ferment in this country as one disenfranchised group after another has struggled to make the vision of equality their reality.

In the 1820s and 1830s, Frances Wright inflamed audiences from Cincinnati to Boston by applying Jefferson's maxim to her own experience and arguing that women were properly men's equals. No true affection is possible between men and women, she said, "until power is annihilated on one side, fear and obedience on the other, and both [men and women] restored to their birthright—equality" (D'Arusmont, 1972: 31–32). For publicly taking so radical a stand—and for trying to imagine social conditions that could make her vision real—Wright and her supporters were mobbed and stoned, and she became the most notorious woman in Jacksonian America.

The group of activists who met in 1966 to form the National Organization for Women (NOW) evoked essentially the same vision—and achieved no little notoriety—though they had the vision in somewhat sharper focus: "We believe that a true partnership between the sexes demands a different concept of marriage, an equitable sharing of the responsibilities of home and children and of the economic burdens of their support." The founding of NOW signaled the most recent surge of the American women's movement, and, as Cynthia Harrison puts it in this book, NOW offered one of the most politically radical agendas of the twentieth century: men and women would share equally in public and private responsibilities—in paid work and in the rearing of children.

Reality lags far behind that vision. The disjuncture between the two springs no doubt from the fact that until recently men monopolized the levers of political, financial, and cultural power in the United States of America: they have not only written our laws, they have interpreted and enforced them. The chapters in this book spell out a sobering truth: until the men who retain so disproportionate a share of power in this country commit themselves to sexual equality, we shall continue having to inch our way to progress, for the forces that work to deny equality are formidable and deeply embedded in our public and private institutions. The way jobs are organized and rewarded, the division of responsibility in households, child care arrangements—it is largely such unglamorous, day-to-day matters as these that determine how much equality between the sexes is actually possible. For instance, as Cynthia Harrison's chapter makes clear, equally shared responsibility for childrearing remains largely theoretical because few men have retreated from the world of paid work. The fact that almost half of all marriages entered into in the last 15 years end in divorce may reflect in part how intractable the old structures are.

But a strong argument can be made for the idea that today's women have been sowing the seed corn, that the harvest of equality between the sexes will be reaped by their children and their children's children ad infinitum. Women today are much better educated than earlier generations; women are now proportionately represented among those awarded bachelors' and masters' degrees, and they account for a rapidly increasing percentage (one-third) of Ph.Ds. Since the more education a woman has, the more likely she is to work and to keep her family small, the consequences of women's education radiate into the indefinite future.

Women are making their mark in American politics both at the polls and on the hustings. Not only do more women than men vote, but a larger proportion of eligible women vote. In addition, there are considerable differences by gender with respect to the issues voters think are most important. These factors add up to a formula for growing political influence.

And although, as Ruth Mandel's chapter cautions us, women's gains in elective office in the past 15 years have been incremental rather than meteoric, at every election more women are winning political office, especially at the state and local levels. The more women who hold public office, the more responsive our political institutions will be to reforms that encourage equality of the sexes. Findings cited in Mandel's chapter are consistent with our own experience that regardless of political party, women officials are more likely than their male colleagues to support measures to improve equity for women—although we know exceptions to this rule exist on both sides of the equation. There are some good male feminists in Congress, for example.

It is true, as Dr. Mandel's chapter says, that it can be tough for women to break into politics. Political parties have been for the most part run by men. The power of incumbency has contributed to women's inability to make greater inroads in Congress, since the overwhelming majority of incumbents are male. And it is generally harder for women to raise the staggering amounts of money typically needed to run for office. But women are honing their skills as campaign fundraisers and have developed networks and political action committees dedicated to electing women. Women are filling some powerful positions in major election campaigns these days. These signs bode well for accelerated gains for women in politics, although anything approaching equal representation seems a discouragingly distant prospect.

What are the prospects for equity in the workplace? Early in 1988, the Bureau of Labor Statistics reported that the wage gap in 1987 was narrower by eight-tenths of a percentage point than it had been in 1986. Women's wages had increased to 70 percent of men's. The question is whether we should celebrate: since 1979, the gap has shrunk by an average of only nine-tenths of a percentage point per year. At that rate, women workers won't have wage parity with men until 2020 or so.

Nevertheless, the money earned by women is increasingly important to the budgets of American families, according to Rebecca Blank's chapter. She characterizes as a "revolution" the dramatically increased presence in the paid workforce of wives—especially wives with children. In fact, a majority of women who have young children are in the labor force and a larger share of married couples' income is coming from wives' earnings. The difference a woman's paid work makes cannot be measured by numbers alone. Earnings of her own—no matter that the money may go mostly or entirely to the family budget—bring to a woman a sense of dignity, autonomy, and the possibility of choices. We understand better than we did a generation ago that healthy relations between men and women depend on their functional equality. We know that love and attention freely given weigh more than love and attention given because one's bread and butter depend on it.

For a family to be among the "haves" in this country seems increasingly to require two adults in the labor force. One earner may be enough if the earner is a man. But many families supported by a female earner are not making it: more than one in three of these families are poor and many more have incomes hovering just above the official poverty level. The odds are that these families lack many of the things other families take for granted, one of them being health insurance.

Karen Davis's chapter in this book points out that 37 million people—16 percent of the U.S. population—have no health insurance coverage of any kind. Millions of others have too little. These Americans not only live at great personal risk but represent a serious national problem.

Americans in general are healthier and live longer than they used to. Infant mortality has been cut in half over the past two decades, and life expectancy has increased dramatically. These are overall trends; for some groups of Americans the situation is not so rosy. Poverty is a life-threatening disease. You die earlier in this country if you live in poverty. And it is women and children who are disproportionately poor. Women who are not attached to men are poorer than those who are, and women of color are poorer than white women.

Lack of adequate prenatal care seems to be largely responsible for the high mortality rates for both black infants and black mothers. Black babies are twice as likely as white babies to die before their first birthdays. Black mothers are four times more likely than white mothers to die in childbirth. Black women in general have a greater need for health care than white women, but get less of it on a regular basis, in part because private-sector health insurance is less common among black women.

We tend to assume that most if not all children in poor families are covered by Medicaid. Not so: Karen Davis tells us that six million American children who live below the poverty level are not covered by Medicaid; one-third of these children are desperately poor, with family incomes below 50 percent of the poverty level. Most live in families headed by women.

Health care costs can be an especially heavy burden on older people. Women constitute the larger and poorer proportion of the elderly population and their overrepresentation increases among the oldest age groups. Thus, women are more likely than men to suffer hardship because Medicare covers neither long-term nursing home care nor such health needs as glasses, dental care, hearing aids, or prescription drugs. To qualify for Medicaid, which is generally tied to eligibility for public assistance, an elderly person must be—or become—impoverished.

In this country, we rely heavily on employers to provide health insurance. But women are more likely than men to have part-time or temporary jobs for which there is no health insurance coverage. About 80 percent of American women who are divorced or separated have no health insurance—

that's twice the comparable figure for men—and 24 percent of black women overall, as well as 16 percent of white women, remain uninsured.

Because in contemporary America people not only marry later but also have higher divorce rates, there are proportionately fewer married couples now than there were a quarter-century ago, and many more women are living alone or, as single parents, living with their children. Single mothers increasingly rely on their own earnings to support their families. Transfer payments—child support, AFDC, food stamps, welfare, and so on—accounted for only one-fourth of their income in 1985, down from 33 percent in 1969.

Thus, the question of women's wage-earning capability is even more important today. Though women earn more relative to men than they did eight years ago, the disparity in wages remains appalling. Moreover, education does not pay off for women in the way the American myth would lead us to expect: women with college degrees actually earn less than men who have only high school diplomas.

The statistics in this book demonstrate that the rich have been getting richer and the poor poorer—in short, that the economic profile of people in the United States over the past quarter-century has become more unequal rather than less. But more than that: those clustered in the poorest fifth of the nation's population are disproportionately female and disproportionately minority.

Despair, however, is not an option. As Juanita Kreps noted in last year's volume, *The American Woman 1987–88*, the measures we must support for the sake of women's economic progress include affirmative action policies to open up better jobs; pay equity to ensure that those women who remain—whether by choice or by lack of choice—in traditional "women's jobs" are well-paid; job-training and education for low-income women; good, affordable child care; and mandatory fringe benefits for part-time workers.

The pages that follow identify many specific problems crying out for creative solutions. For example, we need greater efforts to reduce occupational segregation, better preparation of young girls for economic self-reliance, more programs to encourage minority women to continue their education, appropriate training programs for women in prisons, and a much stronger and more dependable network of support for battered women. As for the spirit animating our work, we could do no better than to remember the words of Sojourner Truth, who said: "If the first woman God ever made was strong enough to turn the world upside down all alone, these women together ought to be able to get it rightside up again."

1987 in Review

ANNE J. STONE

January 8 / The settlement of a 10-year-old class action sex bias suit against the Sumitomo Corporation of America is filed in federal court in New York City. Under the landmark agreement, Sumitomo, a subsidiary of a Japanese-owned company, agrees to various measures to compensate past and present female employees for sex discrimination as well as to advance women in the company. In 1982 Sumitomo argued before the U.S. Supreme Court that as a foreign-owned company it was not required to comply with U.S. sex discrimination law (Title VII of the Civil Rights Act). The nation's highest court ruled otherwise (in *Aragliano v. Sumitomo Shoji America, Inc.*). The settlement filed today is an outcome of that 1982 ruling.

January 13 / The Supreme Court rules (in *California Savings & Loan Association v. Guerra*) that it is not discriminatory under federal law for a state to require employers to provide job-guaranteed pregnancy disability leave without requiring similar benefits for workers with other kinds of temporary disabilities. Rejecting the argument that the federal Pregnancy Disability Act (PDA) requires that pregnancy be treated no differently from any other disability, the Court holds that the PDA sought to establish "a floor beneath which pregnancy disability benefits may not drop—not a ceiling above which they may not rise."

January 21 / In *Wimberly v. Labor & Industrial Relations Commission of Missouri*, the Supreme Court rules that while a state "cannot single out pregnancy for disadvantageous treatment, it is not compelled to afford preferential treatment." The case involves Missouri's unemployment compensation law, which entitles workers to compensation only if they lose their jobs as the result of a work-related illness or disability, or an employer's decision to lay off workers. Since the Missouri law denies unemployment benefits to all workers who leave their jobs for nonwork-related disabilities, the Court finds that the state did not discriminate on the basis of pregnancy when it denied unemployment compensation to a woman whose employer refused to rehire her after she took pregnancy leave.

January 21 / Lois McCallin, pedaling the *Eagle*, sets a closed-course distance record for human-powered flight. Ms. McCallin kept the lightweight aircraft in the air for 37 minutes and 38 seconds.

February 2 / The Navy announces a five-year freeze on the number of women on active duty.

February 3 / Defense Secretary Caspar Weinberger, who was not consulted about the freeze, orders it rescinded.

February 3 / Gloria Molina is elected to the Los Angeles City Council. The first Latina ever to be elected to the Council, Ms. Molina has endorsed Lucille Roybal Allard—also a Latina—to fill her vacated California State Assembly seat.

February 4 / The first National Women in Sports Day is observed on Capitol Hill and across the country. The day seeks to spotlight both women's achievements in sports and the need for legislation—the Civil Rights Restoration Act—to ensure and encourage females' athletic opportunities in school and college.

March 2 / For the first time, young women take the top two prizes in the Westinghouse Science Talent Search. Winner of the first prize, a $20,000 scholarship, is Louise Chang, 17, a student at the high school of the University of Chicago Laboratory Schools. Winner of the second prize, a $15,000 scholarship, is Elizabeth Wilmer, of New York City's Stuyvesant High School.

March 18 / The City of San Francisco and the Service Employees International Union agree on a settlement providing $35.4 million in pay equity wage adjustments for 12,000 female and minority city and county workers concentrated in such relatively low-paid jobs as clerk-typist, licensed vocational nurse, hospital worker, school employee, and librarian. San Francisco voters approved a landmark pay equity referendum in 1986.

March 21 / Concerned that the Scholastic Aptitude Test (SAT) may be biased against women, the New York State Board of Regents asks the state to fund the design of a new test to replace the SAT as the basis for awarding state scholarships.

March 25 / The Supreme Court, ruling for the first time in an affirmative action case involving gender-based preference (*Johnson v. Transportation Agency, Santa Clara County* [California]), finds the use of affirmative action plans for women constitutional. In its broadest endorsement so far of voluntary affirmative action programs, the Court rules that in order to achieve a better-balanced workforce, employers may sometimes promote women and minorities ahead of better-qualified white males even if the employer in question has never intentionally discriminated.

March 30–31 / "Work and Family: Seeking a New Balance," a conference sponsored by the U.S. Department of

Dr. Mae Jemison, a California physician, is the first black woman ever selected for NASA's astronaut training corps. *Courtesy NASA*

Labor in cooperation with the AFL-CIO and the National Association of Manufacturers, attracts nearly 1,000 participants from across the country. This is the first major conference on work/family issues to be sponsored by the Labor Department.

March 31 / New Jersey Superior Court Judge Harvey Sorkow awards "Baby M" to her biological father, William Stern, and declares the rights of the biological mother, Mary Beth Whitehead, "terminated." Ruling in the first court test of a surrogate parenting contract, Judge Sorkow declares that the contract between Mr. Stern and Ms. Whitehead was "valid" and that Ms. Whitehead is obligated to give up all rights to the child.

April 7 / The National Museum of Women in the Arts opens in Washington, D.C.

April 10 / Katherine Fanning becomes the first woman president of the American Society of Newspaper Editors. Ms. Fanning has been the editor of the *Christian Science Monitor* since 1983.

April 16 / Rita Dove wins the Pulitzer Prize for poetry for *Thomas and Beulah*.

April 18 / In Texas, Annette Strauss is elected mayor of Dallas, and Betty Turner is elected mayor of Corpus Christi. Neither city has elected a woman mayor before.

May 4 / The Supreme Court rules that Rotary Clubs must admit women. The case, *Board of Directors of Rotary International v. Rotary Club of Duarte* (California), turned on whether Rotary clubs, with some 900,000 members worldwide, are public accommodations or whether they are, rather, "private" and selective enough in their membership to warrant constitutional protection under the First Amendment's guarantee of freedom of association.

May 12 / Lucille Roybal Allard is elected to succeed Gloria Molina in the California State Assembly.

May 20 / The Civil Rights Restoration Act (S. 557), which would reverse the Supreme Court's ruling in the *Grove City College* Title IX case, is approved by the Senate Labor and Human Resources Committee by a 12–4 vote.

May 26 / New Jersey's Division of Civil Rights rules that the remaining all-male eating clubs at Princeton University are places of public accommodation and must admit women. The state's order, which can be appealed, is the culmination of a sex-discrimination suit filed in 1979 against three Princeton eating clubs by Sally Frank, then a Princeton junior.

May 26 / NASA announces that Sally Ride, America's first woman astronaut, will leave the space program in the fall to join a Stanford University program training scientists in arms control policy and national security matters.

June 2 / Nancy Pelosi is elected to Congress from California's Fifth District, filling the seat left vacant by the death of Rep. Sala Burton on February 1. Ms. Pelosi is a former chair of the California Democratic party, but has not previously run for public office.

June 2 / Representatives Patricia Schroeder and Olympia Snowe, cochairs of the Congressional Caucus for Women's Issues, joined by Senators Alan Cranston and David Durenberger, announce the introduction of the Economic Equity Act (EEA) of 1987 (H.R. 2577/S. 1309). A package of bills embodying the caucus's legislative priorities, the EEA was first introduced in 1981 (first session of the 97th Congress) and has been reintroduced in each subsequent Congress. Its provisions change over time as some become law and new ones are added. The 1987 (100th Congress, first session)

EEA, designed to improve the economic status of American women by providing greater employment opportunities and child care options, contains 17 individual bills that fall under two titles, "Work" and "Family."

June 5 / Representative Patricia Schroeder says she may become a candidate for the Democratic presidential nomination. Rep. Schroeder, a Colorado Democrat and, in her eighth term, the most senior woman in the House, says that a crucial consideration will be whether she can raise enough money.

June 5 / Dr. Mae Jemison is among 15 new astronaut trainees named today by NASA. Dr. Jemison, a 30-year-old California physician, is the first black woman ever selected for the astronaut corps.

June 15 / Secretary of the Navy James Webb orders female civilian technicians allowed aboard submarines for sea trials to test new equipment. (This ruling does not affect the prohibition against civilian women or servicewomen serving on operational missions of submarines and other designated combat vessels.)

June 17 / The National Coalition of 100 Black Women presents its fifth annual Candace Awards to black women of achievement. In addition to Coretta Scott King and choreographer Katherine Dunham, both recipients of special awards, the group honors the Rev. Dr. Johnnie Colemon, founder of the Christ Universal Complex in Chicago; NASA aerospace engineer Christine Mann Darden; professional race-car driver Cheryl Linn Glass; newspaper publisher Pam McAllister Johnson; and automobile dealer Barbara J. Wilson.

June 23 / *Ms.* magazine's fifteenth anniversary issue goes on sale.

June 23 / A New York state appeals court, reversing the decision of a lower court, rules that it is not a violation of the state's human rights laws for insurance companies to set insurance rates on the basis of sex. The NOW Legal Defense and Education Fund (NOWLDEF), which brought a class-action suit against the Metropolitan Life Insurance Co., plans to appeal the decision.

June 25 / Two of the 20 winners of the National Medal of Science are women—Anne Anastasi, a Fordham University professor emeritus honored for her work "in the development of the discipline of differential psychology as a behavioral science," and Rita Levi-Montalcini, director of the Laboratory of Cell Biology in Rome, for her "discovery of the nerve growth factor, which set the stage for worldwide studies of the molecules involved in normal and malignant growth."

June 25 / Retiring Marine Commandant P.X. Kelley raises a storm of controversy when he blames mothers working outside the home for what he sees as a loss of moral fiber in the U.S.

July 2 / U.S. District Court Judge John Lewis Smith, ruling in *Palmer v. Shultz,* finds the U.S. State Department guilty of bias against female Foreign Service officers in job evaluations, job assignments—including assignments to key senior positions—and honor awards. (Judge Smith's earlier decision exonerating the State Department of sex bias was reversed on March 24 by the U.S. Court of Appeals for the District of Columbia.)

July 6 / Kiwanis International members vote overwhelmingly to allow women to join the organization.

July 18 / Wilma Mankiller is elected to head the Western Cherokee Nation, the country's second-largest Indian tribe.

Hulda Crooks, at 91, the oldest woman to reach the top of Mt. Fuji, July 24, 1987. *AP / Wide World Photos*

She is the first woman ever elected chief by the Cherokees.

July 18 / Molly Yard is elected president of the National Organization for Women (NOW).

July 22 / The Women's Research and Education Institute (WREI) releases *The American Woman 1987–88*, the first edition of its planned annual report on the status of American women.

July 24 / Hulda Crooks, a 91-year-old American, reaches the top of Japan's Mt. Fuji, more than 12,000 feet high. Ms. Crooks is the oldest woman ever to have climbed the peak.

August 1 / Effective today, all Minnesota companies with at least 21 employees are required by state law to offer up to six weeks of unpaid parental leave after the birth or adoption of a child. Both parents may go on leave at the same time.

August 1 / Mary Stout is elected president of the Vietnam Veterans of America. A former Army nurse, Ms. Stout is the first woman to become president of a major U.S. veterans' organization.

August 4 / The U.S. Court of Appeals for the District of Columbia upholds a lower court's decision that Price Waterhouse discriminated on the basis of sex when it denied a partnership to Ann Hopkins. According to the ruling, Price Waterhouse allowed sexual stereotyping to play a "significant role" in denying Ms. Hopkins a partnership.

August 7 / American Lynne Cox swims from Alaska's Little Diomede Island to the USSR's Big Diomede Island in the Bering Strait. To reach Big Diomede, where she finds a friendly greeting by Soviet officials, Ms. Cox covers at least four miles in 44-degree water.

August 24 / Massachusetts Insurance Commissioner Roger Singer issues regulations prohibiting sex-based discrimination in all forms of insurance. Insurance industry representatives say they will challenge the regulations in court.

August 26 / The Defense Advisory Committee on Women in the Services (DACOWITS) reports to Defense Secretary Weinberger that the Navy and Marine Corps in the Pacific condone sexual harassment, discrimination, and "morally repugnant behavior." DACOWITS cites as particularly egregious the behavior of Lt. Commander Kenneth Harvey, captain of the Navy salvage ship *Safeguard.*

September 1 / Catherine Rudder is appointed executive director of the American Political Science Association

(APSA). She is the first woman to hold this position since APSA was founded in 1903.

September 2 / President Reagan signs Executive Order 12606, "The Family," requiring a review of existing and proposed federal regulations and policies in terms of their impact on families. Policies will be assessed with respect to, for example, whether they "strengthen or erode the stability of the family and, particularly, the marital commitment."

September 14 / The Population Crisis Committee (PCC) announces completion of its study finding that the U.S. ranks seventh among developed countries in access to birth control. Ahead of the U.S. are the United Kingdom, West Germany, Australia, Canada, France, and Italy, according to the PCC.

September 15 / U.S. Secretary of Transportation Elizabeth Hanford Dole, the third woman to hold a cabinet-level job under President Reagan and the only woman currently in the cabinet, announces that she will resign on October 1 to devote full time to her husband's campaign for the presidency.

September 18 / Lt. Commander Kenneth Harvey is removed from command of the ship *Safeguard,* reprimanded, and fined for, among other things, sexually harassing female members of his ship's crew.

September 28 / Patricia Schroeder announces her decision not to seek the Democratic nomination for president in 1988.

October 1 / The National Coalition Against Domestic Violence toll-free hotline, 1–800-333-SAFE, is officially operational.

October 1 / Under a regulation that becomes final today, Californians will not be permitted state tax deductions for business expenses incurred at clubs that discriminate against women and/or minorities. California is believed to be the only state with such a regulation, which will be operational on January 1, 1988.

October 5 / The Supreme Court declines to review the legality of New York City's physical test for firefighters, thus allowing continued use of the test. Because women do not score as well as men on the test, which emphasizes immediate strength and speed rather than stamina, few if any females are likely to be hired as firefighters by New York City in the future.

October 9 / Clare Booth Luce dies at the age of 84. During her lifetime Mrs. Luce was, among other things, a successful playwright, a war correspondent, and a two-term member of the U.S. House of Representatives. As U.S. ambassador to Italy in the 1950s, she was the first woman to serve as America's ambassador to a major power.

October 21 / Ray Kinoshita and Ann Marshall jointly win the $15,000 first prize in a national, juried, design competition for the Wesleyan Chapel Block of the Women's Rights Historical Park in Seneca Falls, New York. The National Endowment for the Arts, which, with the National Park Service, sponsored the competition, reports that the two women designers "successfully interpreted the symbolic meaning" of the site.

October 22 / The Commission of Fine Arts votes down a proposal to honor nurses and other female Vietnam veterans with a statue at the Vietnam Veterans Memorial in Washington, D.C.

October 22 / Secretary of Defense Caspar Weinberger orders armed forces commanders not to interfere with the career decisions of military officers' spouses. Officers' wives have complained of pressure to quit their jobs or risk harming their husbands' careers.

November 5 / President Reagan nominates April Glaspie to be U.S. Ambassador to Iraq. If confirmed by the Senate, Ms. Glaspie, a career Foreign Service officer, would be the first woman ever appointed a U.S. ambassador to a Middle Eastern country.

November 13 / Carrie Saxon Perry is elected mayor of Hartford, Connecticut. Ms. Perry is the first black woman to be elected mayor of a major city in the Northeast.

November 17 / The House Education and Labor Committee reports out a revised version of the Family and Medical Leave Act (H.R. 925), legislation that would require employers to provide job-guaranteed (unpaid) leave to employees who need to care for a newborn, newly adopted, or seriously ill child, or for a seriously ill parent. The revised bill, which would cover fewer workers and provide fewer weeks of leave than the original bill, represents a bipartisan compromise believed to improve the measure's chances of passage by the full House.

December 11 / The Senate approves by a vote of 94 to 0 President Reagan's nomination of Ann Dore McLaughlin as U.S. Secretary of Labor. The only other woman ever to hold the top Labor post was Frances Perkins, appointed by President Franklin Roosevelt.

December 12 / As the Meadowlands Racetrack meeting closes, jockey Julie Krone is the meeting's leading rider with 124 winners (the second place rider had 104 winners). Ms. Krone was also the leading rider at Monmouth Park earlier this year (with 130 winners, compared to 78 for her nearest competitor). She is the first female jockey ever to be leading rider at any major racetrack.

Julie Krone, the first female jockey to be the leading rider at a major race track. *Ruby Washington / The New York Times*

December 16 / The U.S. House of Representatives passes a bill that would make sweeping changes in the nation's welfare system. The measure, which is expected to meet with difficulty in the Senate, stresses job training and employment for welfare mothers.

December 22 / Navy Secretary James Webb announces the opening of more seagoing jobs to women. When fully implemented, the new policy should triple Navy women's job opportunities at sea. Secretary Webb also orders a crackdown on sexual harassment in the Navy and Marine Corps.

December 27 / Gayle Sierens is the play-by-play announcer on NBC's regional telecast of the Seattle Seahawks-Kansas City Chiefs football game. She is the first woman to call a game on a network telecast of an NFL game.

The American Woman 1988-89

ONE A Richer Life: A Reflection on the Women's Movement

CYNTHIA HARRISON

Highlights

In 1966, the founders of the National Organization for Women (NOW) broke new ground with a "Statement of Purpose" that called for a true partnership between the sexes. This would require "an equitable sharing of the responsibilities of home and children and the economic burdens of their support." The feminist vision required reorganizing the way work gets done, so that no one has to choose between the rewards of paid work and the satisfactions of childrearing.

- Among the principal successes of the modern women's movement has been the opening of a public debate on the nature and extent of sex segregation in the workplace and the division between men's and women's "spheres" in public and private life.

- The women's movement has secured legal prohibitions against discrimination. Federal and state legislation now prohibits discrimination against women in employment, education, credit, and housing. In some occupations, women have established genuine and apparently permanent access denied to them before.

- Feminists established job rights as a top priority, and two pieces of legislation—the Equal Pay Act of 1963 and Title

VII of the Civil Rights Act—provided weapons with which to fight for those rights.

- Judicial decisions, legislation at the state level, and union negotiations have helped in the struggle for improved wages for women, most notably in recent decisions concerning pay equity.
- Women with their own income produce changes in families that are independent of feminist ideology. Women who earn income acquire more authority within their families, and those families make changes in the direction of equality.
- Not only are women with earnings more influential within the home, they are less vulnerable legally.
- Independent income gives a woman options about remaining in a marriage and provides a safety net for the woman whose marriage has ended.
- Mothers who have worked for pay have always known that costs and conflicts accompany entry into the labor force. Women feel pressed by the need both to do well at work and to maintain their commitment to their children.
- For working parents, child care is at least as pressing an issue as wages. Although few employers offer on-site or subsidized day care, a growing number recognize the importance of child care to firms' ability to attract and retain workers.
- In the public arena, feminists had a fundamental value—equal opportunity—to offer as a rationale for their demands. No similarly accepted ethos was available for changes they proposed in the family.

- Feminists have long recognized that merely granting women equal access to jobs would not represent an adequate solution to the problems facing women who hold jobs and raise families. Because of the inadequate response on the part of employers to family needs, the question persists of whether women for the present ought to have special privileges, such as special pregnancy leave. The feminists answer that giving only female parents special treatment produces workplace inequalities that militate against women; thus, the women's movement argues that working parents of both sexes should be entitled to the accommodations necessary for them to meet family responsibilities.
- Twenty years after the reinvigoration of the women's movement, the feminist agenda is far from fulfilled. In the 1960s, feminists argued from the premise that taking care of children was a valuable new opportunity for men. But while women today have attained the right to seek challenging jobs and have made substantial inroads in many occupational fields, they also continue to bear the primary responsibility for the care of children.
- Nevertheless, both women and men have more choices about how to shape their lives than they ever had before.

Introduction

In 1966, a group of women and men inaugurated a new era, one marked by an expansion of choices for women and new relationships between women and their children, their partners, and society. This group, the founders of the National Organization for Women (NOW), codified its goals in a "Statement of Purpose," adopted at the inaugural meeting of NOW in October 1966. The statement incorporated many concerns (including discrimination in the legal system, in employment, and in education) that prevented women from fully exercising freedom to control their lives. Most of the problems had a long history in the two-century struggle for equal rights for women. NOW promised a reinvigorated attack against these old obstructions.

But in one area the founders of NOW, the first avowedly feminist organization to appear since the suffrage fight, broke fresh ground. The statement of purpose declared: "We believe that a true partnership between the sexes demands a different concept of marriage, an equitable sharing of the responsibilities of home and children and of the economic burdens of their support." NOW recognized that full access for women to the public world required changes in their private lives as well. And if NOW supported a larger public life for women, NOW also argued from the premise that taking care of children was a valuable new opportunity for men. For men and women to have a wider range of options, both had to give up the notion that only the mothers of children could nurture them; men had to accept a central role in caring for children. Then the sharp boundaries between the roles of mother and father, between nurturer and breadwinner, with the limitations they imply, could fade.

NOW was only the first formal manifestation of a renaissance of feminist activism. Even as NOW was organizing, women in the civil rights, anti-war, and anti-poverty movements were taking a stand on their own behalf. By 1970, a multitude of groups, with differing perspectives and emphases, many national and many more local, arose to attack a wide array of problems women faced. Even women who didn't join a feminist group identified with the cause, so that the women's movement became a pervasive social phenomenon throughout the 1970s.

Before 1966, women struggling to gain access to the workplace had not questioned the norms that gave them the full responsibility for childrearing. Thus, at the same time they had asked for equal treatment as workers, they had to ask also for special consideration to allow them to take proper care of their children. Employers labeled the demands contradictory and argued that the preeminent responsibilities of motherhood justified discrimination against women employees. Women, they alleged, simply were not and could not be as committed to their jobs as their male counterparts.

The assertion by feminists in the 1960s that men and women should share responsibility for children and for wage earning meant that the new quest for women's rights would take place sustained by an innovative, internally consistent theory of equal treatment for men and women both at home and at work. Women arguing for equal employment opportunities would no longer have to ask for differential treatment because of their duties as mothers, and employers therefore would no longer be able to use motherhood as an excuse for discrimination.

But the feminist agenda was even more complicated than men and women sharing all of life's work. The new feminist vision required reordering priorities and reorganizing the way in which work got done, so that no one would be forced to choose between the rewards of work and the satisfactions of raising children. According to the feminist ethos, the demands of careers then imposed on men were unacceptable, cheating men out of the chance to have real relationships with their children. Under a new arrangement, women would commit more of themselves to paid work and men less. Good day care would be readily available and every job would pay a decent wage, so that all workers would have the opportunity for decent work and rewarding personal lives.

In 1988, the feminist agenda is far from fulfilled. The theoretical breakthrough in equal parenting remains to a large degree theoretical—women retain the major share of day-to-day responsibility for children. Women have earned for themselves the right to try for challenging jobs, but few men have retreated from their immersion in work. Unwilling to jeopardize new career opportunities, many professional women exhaust themselves meeting male standards of work performance. Few employers willingly alter the traditional patterns that separate work and home to accommodate workers who are also parents. Without adequate day care or an improvement in wages for women, single parents and working-class couples in particular juggle child care and manage household responsibilities by dint of sheer will.

Twenty years after the reinvigoration of the women's movement, many of the issues NOW confronted remain unresolved. Aware of the resistance to profound changes in the texture of American life, feminists are grappling to plot a strategy for the future. What have been the gains? Do women (and men) now have more choices in fact as well as in theory? What should be next on the agenda for the women's movement?

The Victories of the Women's Movement

One of the principal successes of the women's movement in the past twenty years has been the opening of a public debate on both the nature and extent of sex segregation in

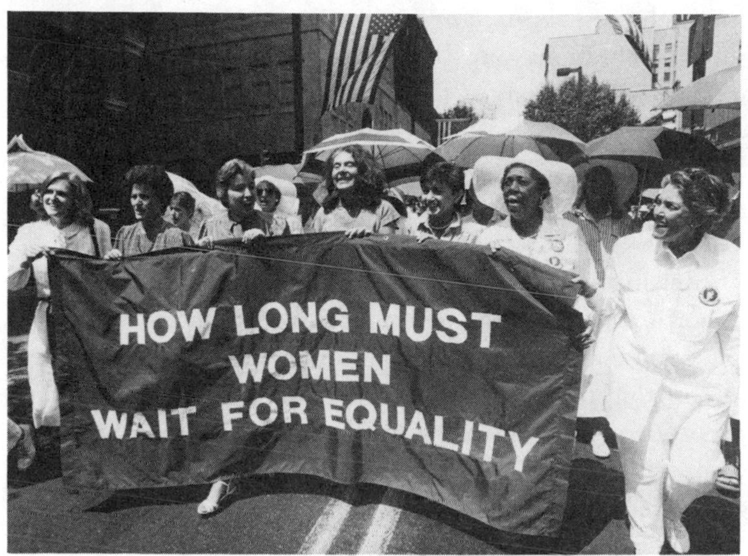

"March for Equality" during the NOW convention in July 1987.
Sara Krulwich / The New York Times

the workplace and the division between men's and women's "spheres" in public and private life. The women's movement has secured legal prohibitions against discrimination, obtained new provisions in the tax code permitting child care deductions, and achieved regulatory and statutory relief for some of the barriers to pension rights that beset women. In some occupations, especially ones requiring professional education, women have established genuine and apparently permanent access denied to them before. Feminist assertions that children are the responsibility of fathers as well as mothers and that women are entitled to a public life have made it easier for working women to press for child care assistance. A new acceptance of nontraditional family arrangements has permitted men and women more flexibility in making personal choices about living situations. Most important, although definitions may vary, women have become committed to the idea of equality. Their social and legal subordination as a matter of course has come to an end.

Women in the Public World

Relying upon an appeal to the fundamental value of equal opportunity, the women's movement was able to expand choices for women most readily in employment and professional education. In 1970, women represented a significant proportion—38 percent—of the workforce, albeit (as documented elsewhere in this book) squeezed by the sex-segregated character of the labor force into a handful of female-dominated occupations, virtually all of them low paying. In 1970, 42.6 percent of white women over the age of 16 and 49.5 percent of black and other women were in the labor force. Moreover, paid employment was not the pursuit of only single women or childless women. Thirty percent of married women with children under six years of age were in the labor force, as were 49 percent of mothers with children between the ages of six and 17 (Bureau of the Census, November 1986). Nearly 60 percent of women in the labor force were married and living with their husbands in 1970 (Bureau of the Census, 1987: 382).

The increasing number of never-married women with children and a rising rate of divorce in the 1960s meant that more women were the sole support of their families than in previous decades. In 1970, nine percent of white families and 28 percent of black families were headed by women. Access to better jobs was essential to the material well-being of these families.

Feminists established job rights as a top priority for both financial and strategic reasons. First, two pieces of federal legislation, the Equal Pay Act of 1963 and Title VII of the Civil Rights Act of 1964 (prohibiting sex discrimination in employment), provided weapons with which to fight. Second, no claim for change was so powerful as women's argument that they were entitled to compete for jobs for which they were objectively qualified. "Equal opportunity" was an American watchword. Since feminists now asserted that special consideration needed to be accorded to all working parents, not just female ones, they made it more difficult than in the past for employers to argue that discriminatory practices were justified by women's special role as nurturers.

In the two decades since this battle began anew, women have broken barriers in virtually all traditionally male occupations. Feminists have used litigation, administrative enforcement, publicity, and lobbying to win new legal protection against employment discrimination and to institute affirmative action programs.

Dramatic gains have been made in the professions. In 1964, not quite four percent of first-year law students were women; by 1984, the proportion had increased tenfold. In 1986, women made up 17.6 percent of physicians, nearly double the percentage in 1970. Even in resistant fields like engineering, the representation of women—though still low—more than tripled in 15 years.

Professional gains benefited mainly an elite group of women; progress was slower for women who might have wanted to do other kinds of nontraditional work. The proportion of women in the construction trades went from 1.7 percent to only 2.1 percent in the decade between 1970 and 1980. Among miners, women's representation remained stable at about 2.4 percent, while the proportion of women driving trucks went up one percentage point, from 2.2 to 3.3 percent. Women are, however, now familiar figures in many police departments and have fared well in the military, an important avenue to educational opportunities and a variety of civilian careers. Although women are still barred from combat, as of 1986 over 200,000 served in the armed forces—approximately 10 percent of the total force, up from 1.5 percent in the 1950s and 1960s (Becraft, 1987). The number of women in the service academies and in the ranks of officers continues to rise.

Overt discrimination in the workplace on the basis of sex is now illegal, and no occupation is as closed as it once was. Although anecdotal evidence and statistical analyses suggest that subtle barriers still exist, women whose resources permit them to make choices now have a wider range of options than in the past.

The collective outcome of these individual choices has ramifications for all women. Some previously female-dominated fields—teaching and nursing—face shortages as women take advantage of opportunities to move into better-paying jobs formerly closed to them. In 1982, the proportion of women college freshmen planning to become elementary and secondary school teachers stood at 7.4 percent, compared to 37.5 percent in 1968 (Astin et al., 1987: 70). Where public and private employers have resisted raising salaries, as in nursing, they have contributed to serious shortages.

Judicial decisions, legislation at the state level, and labor union initiatives have also helped in the struggle for improved wages for women, most notably in recent years in decisions concerning pay equity. In 1986, the state of Washington reached a $482 million pay-equity settlement with the

American Federation of State, County and Municipal Employees. Minnesota has completed implementation of its pay equity plan, and as of August 1987, 18 additional states (California, Connecticut, Florida, Illinois, Iowa, Massachusetts, Michigan, New Jersey, New Mexico, New York, Ohio, Oklahoma, Oregon, Pennsylvania, Rhode Island, South Dakota, Vermont, and Wisconsin) had made some pay equity adjustments (National Committee on Pay Equity, August 1987).

For working mothers and fathers, child care is at least as pressing an issue as wages. Although few employers offer on-site or subsidized day care programs, a growing number are recognizing the importance of such facilities and the need for business interest in this issue. In 1987, according to an estimate by the Conference Board (a business research organization), 3,000 companies were offering some kind of child care assistance, either through on-site centers or through the administration of a federal tax subsidy program (Skrzycki and Swoboda, 1988). Other firms offer help in the form of information or referrals. In 1988, the National Association of Manufacturers for the first time backed federal legislation that would encourage the establishment of child care centers. Other employers, including the federal government, were enabling their employees to exercise some control over their work schedules. Although this opportunity is available to only one worker in eight, "flex-time" is becoming more prevalent (Mellor, 1986), and work-family issues have become increasingly a matter of political attention.

As with employment, the range of opportunities in education expanded sharply for girls and women. As a result of feminist actions, barriers to admission have fallen and access to financial aid has improved. Data from the U.S. Department of Education (1987: 172) reveal that in 1965–66, women earned 42 percent of all bachelor's degrees, 34 percent of master's degrees, and 12 percent of doctoral degrees. Encouraged by the message of the women's movement, women earned half of the bachelor's and master's degrees and just over one-third of doctoral degrees in 1986–87.

The expansion of women's activity in electoral politics ensures further changes built on these earlier victories. In 1980, a political gender gap emerged. Women were not only voting in equal proportions to men, they were voting differently from men. Women were also running for office. Although their number has remained fairly stable in Congress, twice as many women are now in state legislatures as in 1975.

In 1971, the Supreme Court found in the Fourteenth Amendment a prohibition against invidious forms of sex discrimination, establishing a new level of scrutiny for statutes distinguishing on the basis of sex. (The case, *Reed v. Reed*, concerned an Idaho law specifying that men had to be preferred over women in choosing the administrator of an estate.) Although the states did not ratify the Equal Rights Amendment to the Constitution, proposed by Congress in 1972, the 10-year discussion during the ratification campaign generated new attention to sex discrimination and led to state laws ameliorating the problems women identified. Feminists have won new legal protections for equal opportunity in almost every public arena. Such improvements should not be undervalued: American society regards the law as imperative and ethic—what must be done and what should be done. The changes in law and in legislative bodies mean that the gains of this feminist era in expanding the range of choices will be preserved and enhanced for future generations of women and men.

Women in Their Private Worlds

Feminists sought changes in the private world as extensive as those they looked for in the public spheres of employment, education, law, and government. In the public arena, feminists had a fundamental value—equal opportunity—to offer as a rationale for their demands. No similarly accepted ethos was available for the changes they proposed within the family. To the contrary, altering roles within the family struck at the heart of traditional national values.

Predictably, the nation proved less willing—at least initially—to adopt the new theory of family life that feminists proffered: that fathers and mothers would share equally in childrearing. Feminists found themselves in the often uncomfortable position of rejecting the argument that a unique bond existed between themselves and their children. Feminists were arguing for an enlarged role for fathers and for the larger community—more rather than fewer people concerned about the welfare of children. But their opponents stood ready to accuse them of being "unnatural" mothers.

Moreover, employers balked at the notion that their work arrangements would have to accommodate both men and women raising children. If they grudgingly conceded to laws prohibiting discrimination, they saw no reason to accord special privileges to some group of employees just because they were parents. Employers insisted on a single standard, but the standard they insisted on was based on traditional family arrangements. For a woman to get ahead at work, child care was vital, but Dad couldn't fill the gap because he was going to work as he always had. In 1971, Richard Nixon vetoed a child care bill, claiming it would "diminish both parental authority and parental involvement with children."

The government would not help working parents by providing day care.

Women nevertheless made it plain that in their view they would help their families more by being in the workforce than by staying at home full time. Faced with a lack of support from government and employers, families with two parents at work did the best they could to manage. Practically speaking, child care arrangements and schedule-juggling in the event of emergencies, not to mention routine household chores, continued to be the responsibilities of the woman of the house. The women's movement strove to help her out by fighting for community day care centers and by continuing to work for change. The women's movement thus gave working mothers at least moral support, if not the financial and practical help they really required. Working mothers also discovered that their decision to help their families by earning income yielded some additional, nonmonetary, benefits. If expanded choices outside the home permitted some women to decide upon work more likely to provide them financial, intellectual, and emotional satisfaction, flexible roles within the home allowed men and women to allocate family responsibilities according to reason, talent, and preference, rather than simple sex stereotyping.

A woman earning her own income produces changes within the family independent of, although supported by, feminist ideology. Studies reveal that women who earn income acquire more authority within their families, and that those families make changes in the direction of equality (Hood, 1983). Most married fathers with wives who work become more involved in child care (although not in housework). Moreover, when there are two earners, the family can better survive financially—at least for a brief period—when one spouse becomes unemployed.

Women who earn income are not only more influential in the home but also less vulnerable legally. A working wife is legally entitled to control her own income and she owns the goods or a proportion of the goods purchased with the money she earns. In community property states, both spouses share equally in the income of the marriage regardless of who earns it. Feminists succeeded in replacing statutes that had given husbands total control of community property so that homemakers now have equal management rights in these states (Ross and Barcher, 1983). Thus, members of happy families gain autonomy, flexibility, and stability by sharing both financial and family responsibilities; those caught in unhappy family situations acquire crucial freedoms by virtue of revised roles for women. With the advent of more humane divorce laws and the growing acceptance of alternative lifestyles and economic independence for women, both men and women have feasible and legitimate escape routes from unsatisfactory marriages. While it is true that women still earn less money than men and are therefore likely to suffer a decline in living standards as the result of divorce (Weitzman, 1986; Cherlin, 1987), and while it is also true that men frequently fail (now as in the past) to meet payments for child support, an independent income gives a woman options about remaining in a marriage and provides a safety net for the woman whose marriage is ended by her husband.

The consequences of adaptation and flexibility within families go beyond financial matters. With the acceptance of alternative lifestyles, women and men can live alone or together, singly with their children, and in extended families, blended families, or in traditional nuclear families. The women's movement did not result in a rejection of marriage: in 1983 the proportion of white women older than 35 who had never married was lower than it had been since 1950 and lower than the rate for white men. But women, now more able to earn reasonable incomes than in the past, did come to regard the single life as more of an option, and neither single nor divorced women confront the isolation that was once their lot.

As parents come to share child care and financial decisions, their children will find such arrangements commonplace, so that the next generation will be able to make an easier transition to equal roles in the home. Empathy, compassion, affection, tenderness, assertiveness, independence, and authority have been established as traits to value in all human beings, male as well as female. Daughters of women who work outside the home see themselves as having more options to choose from. For some families, the chief gains of the women's movement may be sown by the children of feminists (Bianchi and Spain, 1986; Mortimer and Sorensen, 1984).

The women's movement has made notable strides in ensuring women's rights to control their own fertility, making a choice available in having children. A Supreme Court decision in 1973 (*Roe v. Wade*) prohibited states from banning early abortions and established a woman's right to terminate a pregnancy. With the availability of new birth control technologies and new fertility treatments, women have gained more command over their childbearing decisions. The women's movement, through feminist health organizations, has supported and enhanced the right of women to use these opportunities to make choices most suited to the circumstances of their lives.

Setbacks: The Costs of a Revolution Half-won

The objective that women and men have equal opportunities for financial gain and self-expression through work, and equal joys and responsibilities within their families, represents one of the most radical political agendas of the twentieth century. It is therefore not surprising that the program is not yet fulfilled. More perplexing are the costs women have come to bear because these victories are only half-won.

Work

Legislation has made overt sex discrimination in employment illegal, but the sex-segregated character of the labor force remains intact. Women have gained access to low- and mid-level jobs, while the overwhelming majority of high-ranking positions continue to be filled by men. Most women labor as they always have in poorly paid job ghettos, as secretaries, nurses, teachers, and service workers. Full-time women workers earned only 70 percent of what full-time working men made in 1988 (Bureau of Labor Statistics, 1988). As of 1985, college-educated women employed full time, year round, earned only 59 cents for every dollar earned by college-educated men (Bureau of the Census, August 1987).

Neither experience nor training explains all of this wage gap. Some researchers have estimated that perhaps only half of the difference in earnings is due to work-related skills (Shaw, 1985). There is considerable speculation that persistent discrimination offers the real explanation. But sex discrimination complaints languish for years at enforcement agencies; private suits are expensive and difficult to win. To make matters worse, because many of the barriers of the past are now permeable and some women do break through them, the mythology has been recast to place the burden of personal responsibility on those women—still barred, although now tacitly—who fail to overcome these obstacles. Because the constraints are often disguised, women can be left to think that they indeed have no one to blame but themselves. But new laws, new "opportunities," without restructuring work and family life, in many cases offer the illusion of choice, not genuine options, especially for poor women and women of color.

Even women with responsible, well-paid jobs face acute problems, especially if, like the majority of women workers, they have children. Mothers who have worked for pay outside the home have always known that costs and conflicts accompany entry into the labor force. By emphasizing the role that paid work plays in women's lives, indeed by encouraging it, feminism—in the absence of any accommodation on the part of employers to the needs of workers' families—has exacerbated the conflicts women feel.

Earlier in this century, when women viewed paid work as auxiliary to their family responsibilities, the family came first. Now more women feel doubly pressed—wanting to do well at work while maintaining their commitment to their children (Coser and Rokoff, 1982; Bianchi and Spain, 1986). Resistance to meeting the need for child care has had especially grave consequences for women with limited resources, although its impact is felt by all working women. Professional women are beset by excessive demands on their time; working-class women are harassed both by time constraints and by inadequate financial resources to help them sort out their child care arrangements. The campaign to win men over to the notion that fathering includes nurturing as well as bread-winning has had limited success. More men are more actively engaged in child care than before the women's movement, but there are few institutional supports for men who want to care for their children at home. Because men still usually make more money than women, financial considerations dictate that it is mothers rather than fathers who give up their jobs, even temporarily, or take part-time work.

The options women now have for coping with the dual demands of work and family come with great costs. Many women have accepted part-time employment in order to spend more time with their children: in 1986, approximately 50 percent of working women worked part time or for part of the year. But part-time workers pay a price in professional advancement and career success and they deny themselves benefits and income. Other women delay childbearing in response to financial and career pressures: in 1980, 42 percent of young married women were childless, compared to 25 percent in 1960 (Bianchi and Spain, 1986). Women who deal with constraints simply by sacrificing their careers to their families, or vice versa, can confront disappointment and regret (Shreve, 1986; Basler, 1986).

In addition to juggling the roles of mother and worker, women encounter barriers created by the culture of male-dominated workplaces. In the sex-segregated world of the past, women were expected to espouse cooperation, deference, and assistance. In the "male" world of work, women may be either denigrated for timidity or castigated for "inappropriate" (which is to say characteristically male) behavior. Working women continue to be subjected to judgments that they attained their positions by illegitimate preferential treatment—either legal or sexual (McGlen and O'Connor, 1983). Some men (and women) do not disguise their objections to women in traditionally male positions; women have won sex discrimination cases against private and public employers, including academic institutions. Few enterprises have been invulnerable to these charges.

As far as employers are concerned, women are still on probation in the "male" work world, and women still feel uneasy. Eighty percent of the more than 56,000 respondents in a *Woman's Day* magazine survey in 1985 believed that men underestimated women's abilities in the workplace (*Washington Post*, June 11, 1986). This sense of not being comfortable at work—with employers still holding views that women are the "different" ones—constitutes a burden women carry with them through the day. A female six-year veteran of the FBI observed that acceptance comes only with extra effort and "never at the beginning" ("14 Years of Women as Federal Agents," 1986).

Feminists have long recognized that merely granting women equal access to jobs—without making serious changes within the workplace and without society's assuming some responsibility for the care of children—would not represent an adequate solution to the problems facing women who hold jobs and raise families. Because of the inadequate response to family needs, the question persists of whether women therefore ought for the present to have special privileges—special leaves for pregnancy disability, for example, an approach validated by the Supreme Court in *California Federal Savings & Loan v. Guerra* (1987).

Feminists respond that the argument is both unnecessary and potentially dangerous to women. A mother (or father) temporarily disabled by a broken leg or cancer needs her (or his) job as much as a mother disabled by pregnancy. Singling out pregnancy disability (the case did not, it should be emphasized, protect the right either to leave for a normal pregnancy or to leave to take care of an infant) makes women once again "special" workers, prey to all the prejudices that go with that label. All working parents need disability leave; all parents need to have time to care for their children. No obstacle exists to making benefits available to parents; women may be more likely to take advantage of such opportunities, but as long as these benefits are couched in sex-neutral terminology, they assist women without excluding men.

Economic Status

Historical experience leaves little doubt that labeling women as different workers results in financial inequity. Women continue to be most disadvantaged by their lack of money. The women's movement has been able to do little to change the fact that by and large women who are not attached to men are poorer than single men and also poorer than married women. The advantage of maintaining a household with two incomes pertains to both men and women. But the feminization of poverty grows more pronounced as increasing numbers of single women support children. Most women do marry (in 1983, 95 percent of white women and 91 percent of black women under the age of 35 had been married at least once), and most divorced women remarry (75 percent of white women and 67 percent of black women in the 1970s [Bianchi and Spain, 1987: 12, 37]), but conditions are hard for those who are single mothers.

The women's movement sought changes in divorce laws that would make it easier for women to get out of bad marriages with more economic security in return for their services as homemakers. In some cases, the results have been paradoxical. No-fault divorce made leaving marriages easier but resulted in fewer alimony awards for women. Because men had rarely met alimony requirements in the past, feminists advised seeking property, pension, and employment rights to make women independent of former spouses, rather than having them rely on the good will of antagonistic ex-husbands.

But laws prohibiting discrimination in employment have been used against women by husbands' attorneys who claim that women's capacity to earn is now equal to that of men—this despite the reality of persistent income disparities between men and women. The continuing refusal of some men to support their children means that the newly formed female-headed families often have trouble supporting themselves. As of 1985, only 61 percent of divorced, separated, or never married women raising children under the age of 21 had been awarded child support. Of those entitled to such payments, more than half (52 percent) failed to receive the full amount. More than a quarter who should have received payments got nothing. The average amount of child support received in 1985 was about $2,200 (Bureau of the Census, August 1987a). Moreover, recognition in the courts of a legitimate nurturing role for fathers has resulted in painful losses for women in custody battles.

Summing Up and Looking Forward

Since its reemergence in the 1960s, the women's movement has recorded an important slate of achievements; more work remains in pursuit of the agenda of integrated work and private lives for women and for men, one that will meet the needs of children and permit both parents to carry out their responsibilities to their employers and to themselves. The absence of a national child care policy and continuing inequalities in the domestic and public division of labor are crucial areas where change is needed.

A firm legal foundation has been laid upon which further action can be taken. Federal and state legislation now protects women against discrimination in employment, education, credit, housing, and the use of public accommodations. Statutes enacted in the last two decades prohibit pregnancy discrimination and sexual harassment; court decisions have, so far, sustained these protections and the right of women to equal opportunity and to control of reproduction.

The women's movement has provided support for women as they have rearranged their lives in response to economic exigencies and the need for intellectual growth and personal autonomy. By articulating an ideology that children are the responsibility of fathers and communities as well as of mothers, and by insisting that women's needs are as important as those of other family members, the women's movement helped women, men, and social agencies adapt to the demographic developments and the new circumstances of the late twentieth century. Support for feminist ideas stays strong: a 1986 Gallup poll reported that 56 percent of women respondents stated that they considered themselves feminists, including 57 percent of women with family incomes of less than $20,000 a year and 64 percent of women of color (Ehrenreich, 1987).

The energy devoted to women's issues has led to continuing congressional response, not the least in the shape of the Economic Equity Act (see "The Congressional Caucus for Women's Issues" in this volume). In a further initiative at the end of 1987, 126 representatives and 23 senators cosponsored a $2.5 billion child care bill. Despite the overwhelming preoccupation with budget cutting, even fiscally conservative members of Congress have advocated allocating new funds to child care. Sen. Orrin Hatch (R-Utah) called his $375 million package for child care services his "number one priority." At the same time, the House Education and Labor Committee approved by a vote of 21 to 11 a family and medical leave bill, despite opposition from the U.S. Chamber of Commerce and the National Association of Manufacturers. Although the federal bill would offer only minimal leave rights—10 weeks of parental and 15 weeks of unpaid medical leave to employees working in businesses with more than 50 employees (which would drop to 35 employees after three years)—this small first step is an acknowledgment of the essential need for such protections. Four states enacted parental leave laws in 1987, and 27 more states were considering either parental or maternity leave legislation that year.

Economic objectives like child care and pay equity require substantial investments of public and private funds; they are therefore much harder to attain than legal prohibitions against discrimination that have helped women with the means to take advantage of them. Federal and state legislators have accepted claims based upon the fundamental value of equal opportunity, like employment and credit discrimination laws. These kinds of laws require only enforcement mechanisms. Social programs that would assist those in greater need, such as the creation and maintenance of child care centers, require not only large allocations of public funds but also the assumption of new responsibilities by government; they thus have met far more resistance.

In its early life, the women's movement chose to devote its limited resources to those objectives that would elicit the readiest response from the political system. The outcomes of those decisions were not as relevant to the concerns of some groups of women as to others. Black and Hispanic women more often chose to attack racism and to work within cultural norms different from the mainstream women's movement. But to the extent that women are united by sex, all women—poor women, women of color, and elderly women and their families—profit from expanded employment and education options. Protection against sexual harassment, access to abortion, rights to credit, entry to on-the-job training programs, support for rape victims, and spousal entitlement to pensions and health insurance reach women across lines of race or class.

In a society that does not integrate the raising of children with the performance of productive physical or intellectual work, painful choices are inevitable. The agenda is far from completed; the last two decades constitute only a moment in the course of its pursuit. But as a result of that moment, and despite the continuing difficulties and constraints, women (and men) do now have more choices about how to shape their lives than nature and society have ever allowed them before.

TWO The Political Woman

RUTH B. MANDEL

Highlights

CONTEMPORARY FEMINISM can claim credit for changes in perceptions about the sexes as well as for shifts in Americans' social, economic, and political lives. Over the last 15 years feminism has caused an enormous change in women's patterns of political participation.

- Before the early 1970s, while American women had long been active as volunteers in civic and political efforts, their involvement had not been regarded by political scientists or practitioners as political behavior.

- The turning point in women's political lives occurred in 1971, the year the National Women's Political Caucus (NWPC) was founded. NWPC was the first national membership organization to promote women's entry into politics at leadership levels.

- Many women entered electoral politics in the 1970s, when the feminist announcement that the country needed women in positions of political power coincided with women's growing belief in their political efficacy and in their own potential as leaders.

- The change in women's self-concept went hand in hand with a shift in public attitudes. Opinion polls revealed a gradual growth in approval even for the idea of women seeking the highest offices.

- In numerical terms, women's progress in achieving public office has been slowest at the federal level: of 100 U.S. senators, only two are women in 1988, no more than in 1960. Progress has been slightly better in the House of Representatives, but even there women have captured no more than five percent of the seats, although some modest headway is apparent in the rising numbers of women presenting themselves as candidates for Congress and getting major party nominations.

- The United States is among the nations with the smallest proportions of women in their national legislative bodies.

- The picture is brighter at other levels of government. In state legislatures, for example, women's representation has more than tripled since 1971. As of 1988, women account for nearly 16 percent of state legislators nationwide.

- Until 1974, no woman had been elected governor in her own right; since then, five have achieved this distinction. As of 1988, the elected incumbent governors of two states (Vermont and Nebraska) are women.

- Black women constitute a minute proportion of America's elected officials overall, and only a very small proportion of its elected women, but they represent a distinctive group of political women in several respects. Elected black women are more likely than their white counterparts to belong to feminist organizations as well as to acknowledge the importance of various types of organizations in developing and supporting their candidacies. Among female and male officeholders at all levels, black women were the most liberal.

- In the aggregate, women and men in elected office fit a similar demographic profile, but elected women are less likely than elected men to be married or to have young children at home. Conflicts between the demands of public and private life are more likely to affect the political woman than the political man.

- The growing population of women in politics is more diverse than it used to be; nevertheless, elected women typically have more in common with each other than with men when it comes to political background.

- In many ways the newly elected woman is at an advantage; as a newcomer she can bring a fresh perspective to an old process. However, her inexperience can be a liability—and her gender usually makes her an outsider—in a tough, competitive, and male-dominated environment.

- For newcomer women candidates with no established base, raising money can be an onerous burden.

- As long as men hold the overwhelming majority of all elective offices—especially high-level offices—and remain in them, and as long as incumbency continues to confer an overwhelming reelection advantage, women will remain in the position of challengers and outsiders.

- The pioneer elected women of the 1970s brought to public office perspectives different from those of men. As more women enter politics, the characteristics of political women will become more diverse. Nevertheless, elected women's attitudes on a number of key issues—especially "women's issues"—have differed from men's at all levels of office, within both political parties, and across the ideological spectrum.

- Political women make a point of hiring and promoting women, and take the trouble to encourage other women to enter politics.
- Many of the differences between political women and political men may disappear as women work their way into the mainstream of party politics. However, the evidence so far supports the view that women have special contributions to make to public life: that women officials will not only represent women's interests and concerns better than men have to date, but will also affect the political system by bringing more women into public positions.

Introduction

The first wave of American feminism, surfacing in the mid-nineteenth century, gave rise to the suffrage movement and, after seven decades, the vote for women. The reemergence of American feminism almost 50 years after suffrage arose most directly from two sources: (1) the experience of sexism and the training in activism gained by women in the civil rights, peace, and student movements of the 1960s, and (2) the thwarted expectations and experience of discrimination and powerlessness encountered by highly educated professional women (Evans, 1980; Freeman, 1975). This time feminism burst forth upon a communications- and media-wired America with great speed and force, its power due in no small part to a public receptiveness produced by several decades of significant change in patterns of education, labor force participation, marriage, and fertility (Freeman, 1975; Baxter and Lansing, 1983; Klein, 1984). Not only did the burgeoning women's movement of the 1970s demand changes in law and reforms in public policy to grant women equity in employment, education, credit, housing, and other areas, but it also stimulated a fundamental and far-reaching reexamination of sex roles, gender identity, individual lifestyles, family arrangements, and women's proper place in society. If contemporary feminism has not managed to produce a complete social revolution, it certainly can claim credit for changes in perceptions about the sexes as well as for shifts in Americans' social, economic, and political lives. It is in this context that over 15 years of enormous change in women's patterns of political participation must be examined.

Beginning in the 1970s, American women have sought and entered both elective and appointive public office in unprecedented numbers. By word and deed, women signaled their intention to seek a place in the public world, to share responsibility and power with men in governing. Women were ready to leave the relative calm of private life and behind-the-scenes political activity for the rough contest for public power.

The most useful chronological signpost marking this turning point in women's political lives bears the date July 1971, when the National Women's Political Caucus (NWPC) was founded. Regardless of how much credit historians ultimately give NWPC itself for influencing women's political behavior, its very establishment was highly significant. NWPC was the first national membership organization to promote women's entry into politics at leadership levels. The political arm of the women's movement, it was created by feminist activists (many of whom belonged to the National Organization for Women

[NOW] and had been active in electoral politics) who believed that to effect real and lasting progress on their agenda, women would have to seek political leadership in their own right, on behalf of their own issues. The time had come to focus women's attention on achieving political power for women.

In justifying as well as encouraging women's political advancement throughout the 1970s, several reasons were cited repeatedly by feminists and others sympathetic to the idea of full and equal political participation. First, there was the simple matter of equity: a representative democracy should not de facto exclude the majority of its population from leadership. Second, a pragmatic country could hardly afford to ignore the skills, intelligence, and energies of over half its citizens, especially in the domain of public service, where more talent was urgently needed. Third, women in politics would bring a different perspective, and perhaps different values and priorities (derived from varying combinations of biology, socialization, and gender-based experiences), to a broad range of public issues; moreover, they would advance a set of special concerns, or women's issues, that had not received attention from men. Also, by virtue of their presence in the public arena, women in politics would be role models, inspiring and influencing other women to follow their example. A balance of sexes in government might just carry the hope of more balance all around: more fairness and equity in society; more representativeness in experience, interests, and outlook; more willingness among more people to share responsibilities for the larger community.

American women had traditionally been active as volunteers in civic and social community efforts, and in electoral politics as political wives, party loyalists, and—since 1920—as voters; but women's involvement had not been regarded by political scientists or practitioners as political behavior, and women's political status had been understood as subordinate. While a few unusual women had sought and won elective office, the overwhelming majority of politically minded women had accepted their place as secondary and auxiliary to the real politicians and leaders, the men (Gruberg, 1968). The vast majority of women interested in electoral politics had worked at party housekeeping tasks or had joined campaigns behind the scenes. They staffed campaign storefronts, performed the well-known licking and sticking duties, and organized candidates' evenings and fundraising parties. Virtually all of them worked on a volunteer basis for male party leaders and male candidates.

In the 1970s, some of these women with years of service and valuable experience in electoral politics, as well as in civic and community volunteer activities, responded to the feminist movement's call. Many of them began to apply their skills to building their own political careers, competing and risking themselves in public, dealing with public success or defeat, and eventually—after some hesitation—even acknowledging ambition for power (Mandel, 1983).

The feminist announcement that the country needed women in positions of political power coincided with women's growing belief in their political efficacy and in their own potential as leaders (Kirkpatrick, 1974). Women granted themselves permission to climb over fences erected by culture and custom and to head toward the door marked "candidate," "elected official," "leader"—the door traditionally reserved for politically ambitious men. Underlying the move into new areas of political activity was a change in self-concept whereby women now envisioned themselves as seeking the "number one spot," becoming the people in charge of the public good. After a centuries-old history of understanding the terms "woman" and "leader" as contradictory and the private and public domains as separated by gender as well as by function, women challenged these accepted dichotomies.

The change in women's self-concept went hand in hand with a shift in public attitudes. Surveys of public opinion demonstrated that the populace increasingly accepted women's political participation. Poll data revealed a gradual growth in approval even for the idea of women seeking the highest offices (McGlen and O'Connor, 1983). For example, the percentage of people who told Gallup pollsters that they would vote for a qualified woman for president if their party nominated her rose from 31 percent in 1937 to 80 percent in 1983 (Gallup, 1985).

Those who sounded the call for women to enter politics and those who answered it believed there was some value to working within the U.S. two-party system. Whether partisan liberals or feminist activists in the mainstream branch of the women's movement, or both at once, they held a reformist view of American politics, confident that its institutions and practices were basically sound and worth preserving, and capable of responding constructively to pressures for timely change.

Many women entered the electoral fray in the 1970s. Some emerged from years of homemaking, or from the League of Women Voters where they had learned the issues, or from local grassroots organizations and activism in various movements for social change (Johnson and Stanwick, 1976; Johnson and Carroll, 1978). Many had been active in their communities, working on problems ranging from getting potholes filled and streetlights installed to fights for state income taxes. For some, the launching pad was issue politics—nuclear disarmament and freeze campaigns, school busing, the Equal Rights Amendment (ERA). An increasing number of women moved into electoral politics from female-dominated fields such as nursing and social work that were organizing to have an impact on the political system.

Sometimes the connection between the feminist call to get involved and the decision to try was direct. Kathy Whitmire, now in her fourth term as mayor of Houston, Texas, remembers when she first thought of running. She "recalls coming back into town from a business trip one night and finding a copy of the newspaper her husband had marked for her—circled was a story about the coming meeting in Houston of the National Women's Political Caucus. It was the Caucus that gave her the idea she could run for office and the courage to try" (Ivins, 1987: 124).

The election years of 1972 and 1974 demonstrated the strong appeal of the call to political action. An early NWPC project called Women's Education for Delegate Selection (WEDS) informed women about party rules and procedures and encouraged them to become delegates to the 1972 presidential nominating conventions. That year women comprised an unprecedented 40 percent of the Democratic delegates and 30 percent of the Republican delegates, whereas in the previous two decades, women's representation as delegates to the two national party conventions had remained between 10 and 18 percent (Lynn, 1979). The year 1972 also saw a record number of women (32) running as major-party nominees for the U.S. House of Representatives (just two years later a new record of 45 was set). Congresswoman Shirley Chisholm of New York ran for the Democratic nomination for president in 1972. Although her candidacy was controversial among women and blacks who thought she could not win the nomination, many women worked enthusiastically on her grassroots, people's campaign (Chisholm, 1973). Despite not being taken seriously, Chisholm remained in the race until the Democratic convention, where she won 151.95 delegate votes on the first ballot. Frances ("Sissy") Farenthold, a former Texas legislator, received the second highest number of votes for the vice presidential nomination at the 1972 Democratic national convention after her name was placed in nomination by feminist leader Gloria Steinem. While male party leaders never took Farenthold's nomination seriously, her vote count signaled that a new voice was emerging in national politics (Chisholm, 1973; Tolchin and Tolchin, 1974).

Ann Armstrong delivered the keynote address at the 1972 Republican National Convention—the first woman ever to perform that function. In 1974, Mary Louise Smith of Iowa became the first woman to chair the Republican National Committee. Also in 1974, Ella Grasso was elected governor of Connecticut, the first woman ever to be elected a state governor in her own right.[1] "Firsts" for women in partisan and electoral politics dotted the 1970s and 1980s (see "Milestones for Women in Politics, 1971–87" at the end of this chapter). Since women had no significant representation in leadership anywhere in the political system, each new appointment, nomination, or victory was a breakthrough.

Some firsts remain to be achieved for women in the hierarchies of the political parties, campaign staff positions, staff jobs in the offices of powerful government officials, media consulting, polling, and, of course, candidacy and officeholding for both elective and appointive positions. But the atmosphere has changed drastically in a little over 15

Statue of Ella T. Grasso, governor of Connecticut from 1975 to 1980, dedicated on February 5, 1985. The statue was installed in a niche in the State Capitol in Hartford. *The Hartford Courant*

years. No longer a matter of a society rethinking its concepts of "leader" and "woman," the situation today is more a matter of keeping the list of firsts going and moving on to seconds, thirds, and parity. This is neither easy nor inevitable. Nevertheless, the challenge in the late 1980s is quite different from that faced in the early 1970s.

The New Political Woman[2]

The turning point in American women's political participation occurred when a social movement's call to action encountered a condition of readiness among women; actually moving women into positions throughout the political system, however, loomed as a formidable challenge. Having accepted the challenge, how successful have women been? Who were the pioneers and where did they come from? What routes have they taken? What support systems have they used? What obstacles have they encountered? And have they found their sex to be an advantage?[3]

Numbers

Women's representation in federal, state, county, and municipal elective offices increased significantly between the mid-1970s and the late 1980s (Table 2.1). Until 1974, no woman had been elected a state governor in her own right; since then, five have gained governorships: the late Ella Grasso, governor of Connecticut from 1975 to 1980 (she resigned on account of illness halfway through her second term); Dixy Lee Ray, governor of Washington from 1977 to 1981; Martha Layne Collins, governor of Kentucky from 1984 to 1988; Madeleine Kunin, first elected governor of Vermont in 1984 and currently in her second term; and Kay Orr, incumbent governor of Nebraska (and the first Republican woman governor ever), elected in 1986.

In 1970, no state had an incumbent female lieutenant governor, and only one state had ever elected a woman to that office (Gruberg, 1968). By 1988, 15 women had been elected lieutenant governors; two of these (Collins and Kunin) went on to win their states' governorships.

Women's recent history in state legislatures is indicative of the overall national pattern of change for women in politics. State legislatures are important arenas for the politically

Table 2.1 • WOMEN AS A PERCENT OF ELECTED OFFICEHOLDERS, SELECTED OFFICES, 1975–88

Officeholders	*1975*	*1977*	*1979*	*1981*	*1983*	*1985*	*1987*	*1988*
Members of U.S. Congress	4	3	3	3	4	5	5	5
Statewide elective officials	10	8	11	11	13	14	15	14
Members of state legislatures	8	9	10	12	13	15	16	16
Members of county governing boards[1]	3	4	5	6	8	8(1984)	9	NA
Mayors & members of municipal/township governing boards	4	8	10	10	NA[2]	4[3]	NA[2]	NA[3]

[1]Three states (Connecticut, Rhode Island, and Vermont) do not have county governing boards and were not included in calculating this figure. Data for 1988 are not yet available.

[2]CAWP currently updates municipal figures every four years.

[3]Data are incomplete for the following states: Illinois, Indiana, Kentucky, Missouri, Pennsylvania, and Wisconsin.

Source: Center for the American Woman and Politics, 1988.

ambitious. Although the size of constituencies, competition for seats, availability of staff support and offices, salary levels, length and frequency of legislative sessions, and distances to state capitals vary greatly across the country, in every state the legislature is often both a base for building a political career and a springboard to higher office. Women's share of seats in state legislatures has more than tripled since 1971; in late 1988, the 1,176 women state legislators represented 15.8 percent of the total (7,461) (Table 2.2). Every state counts at least five women in its state house in 1988; only one state (Louisiana) still has no woman in its senate. Representation by minority women remains quite low; the 98 black women and 13 Hispanic women accounted, respectively, for 8.3 percent and 1.1 percent of all female state lawmakers.

Table 2.2 • WOMEN IN STATE LEGISLATURES, 1971–88

Year	*Total Number of Women Legislators*	*Women as a Percent of All Legislators*
1971	344	4.5
1973	424	5.6
1975	604	8.0
1977	688	9.1
1979	770	10.3
1981	908	12.1
1983	991	13.3
1985	1,103	14.8
1987	1,168	15.7
1988	1,176[1]	15.8

[1]The party breakdown for women serving in all state legislatures in 1988 is 685 Democrats (58 percent), 482 Republicans (41 percent), and 9 nonpartisans (1 percent).

Source: Center for the American Woman and Politics, 1988.

At local levels, too, women began the climb into elective office from a position of virtual invisibility, pushing their representation upward over the years to what are still small shares of the total. The proportion of women in elected county office rose from three to nine percent between 1975 and 1987; and among municipal officials from four to 14 percent in the decade between 1975 and 1985 (Table 2.1). As of January 1988, 102 cities with populations over 30,000 (nearly 12 percent of all such cities) had women mayors, according to the U.S. Conference of Mayors. In early 1988, women were also mayors of eleven of the 100 largest U.S. cities: Houston, Dallas, San Diego, Toledo, Charlotte, Sacramento, Tampa, Corpus Christi, Spokane, Stockton, and Little Rock.

Significant progress notwithstanding, women occupy proportionately few positions throughout the hierarchy of electoral politics, and the rate of change has been quite slow. In numerical terms, at any rate, progress has been slowest at the federal level. A very high percentage of elections for the U.S. House and Senate involve incumbents, and incumbents can nearly always prevail over challengers, regardless of gender. Competition is intense for nominations in races where there is a reasonable chance for a newcomer to win—generally this means one of the few open seats—and women simply do not acquire enough of these "good" nominations to swell the ranks of women on Capitol Hill. Of 100 U.S. senators, only two are women—no more than in 1960 (Table 2.3). Progress

Table 2.3 • NUMBER OF WOMEN IN THE U.S. CONGRESS, 1917–88[1]

Congress	*Dates*	*House of Representatives*	*Senate*	*Total*
65th	1917–1919	1	0	1
66th	1919–1921	0	0	0
67th	1921–1923	3	1	4
68th	1923–1925	1	0	1

Congress	*Dates*	*House of Representatives*	*Senate*	*Total*
69th	1925–1927	3	0	3
70th	1927–1929	5	0	5
71st	1929–1931	9	0	9
72nd	1931–1933	7	1	8
73rd[2]	1933–1934	7	1	8
74th	1935–1936	6	2	8
75th	1937–1938	6	3	9
76th	1939–1940	8	1	9
77th	1941–1942	9	1	10
78th	1943–1944	8	1	9
79th	1945–1946	11	0	11
80th	1947–1948	7	1	8
81st	1949–1950	9	1	10
82nd	1951–1952	10	1	11
83rd	1953–1954	12	3	15
84th	1955–1956	17	1	18
85th	1957–1958	15	1	16
86th	1959–1960	17	2	19
87th	1961–1962	18	2	20
88th	1963–1964	12	2	14
89th	1965–1966	11	2	13
90th	1967–1968	11	1	12
91st	1969–1970	10	1	11
92nd	1971–1972	13	2	15
93rd	1973–1974	16	0	16
94th	1975–1976	19	0	19
95th	1977–1978	18	2	20
96th	1979–1980	16	1	17
97th	1981–1982	21	2	23
98th	1983–1984	22	2	24
99th	1985–1986	23	2	25
100th	1987–1988	23	2	25

[1]Number shown is the maximum number of women who served in that Congress. Not all served full terms; some were elected or appointed to fill out the unexpired terms of others.

[2]Beginning with the 73rd Congress, the terminating date listed is the date that Congress adjourned.

Source: Center for the American Woman and Politics, 1988.

has been slightly better on the House side, but even there women have only achieved a high of five percent representation. While these numbers are discouraging for those interested in women and men sharing leadership, it is important to emphasize that in recent years the women entering the House and Senate are less likely than before to be widows inheriting their husbands' seats, and more likely to be ambitious politicians pursuing office in their own right.

With so few women in Congress, the U.S. compares poorly with other countries, placing among the nations with the smallest proportions of women in national legislative bodies (Sivard, 1985; Douglass College/Center for the American Woman and Politics, 1987). It should be said, however, that some modest headway is apparent in the rising numbers of women presenting themselves as candidates for Congress and getting major party nominations (Table 2.4). Not only do women nominees for high office increase the visibility and plausibility of women as influential players in the political process, but the growing number of female nominees represents an expanding base of women entering politics and gaining experience at lower or less visible levels.

More time will be required to produce scores of victories by women with viable combinations of experience, ambition, readiness, political and financial support, and the luck of finding open seats or vulnerable incumbents at the right moment. In the meantime, as long as lists of female potential candidates lengthen and the numbers of actual female nominees continue to mount, the odds increase for making further significant gains at the ballot box, even for high-level offices.

Table 2.4 • NUMBER OF MAJOR-PARTY[1] FEMALE CANDIDATES FOR THE U.S. CONGRESS, 1970–86

Year	*House of Representatives*	*Senate*
1970	25 (15D, 10R)	1 (0D, 1R)
1972	32 (24D, 8R)	1 (0D, 1R)
1974	44 (30D, 14R)	3 (2D, 1R)
1976	51 (33D, 18R)	1 (1D, 0R)
1978	43 (25D, 18R)	2 (1D, 1R)
1980	52 (27D, 25R)	5 (2D, 3R)
1982	55 (27D, 28R)	3 (1D, 2R)
1984	65 (30D, 35R)	10 (6D, 4R)
1986	64 (30D, 34R)	6 (3D, 3R)

[1]D = Democrat; R = Republican.

Source: Center for the American Woman and Politics, 1986.

By the late 1980s, then, the optimist can certainly point to a cup half-full, with a record of enormous expansion in women's participation in a blink of the historical eye: women almost quadrupling their numbers in elective offices since the early 1970s; women moving to the center of the political stage. In 1972, Gloria Steinem's placing Sissy Farenthold's name in nomination for the vice presidency was understood to be a symbolic gesture. Only 12 years later Geraldine Ferraro was the actual Democratic nominee for vice president.

The pessimist, on the other hand, can point out that the cup is more than half-empty if the goal is parity with men: in 1988 women still hold no more than 16 percent of elected legislative or executive political positions at any level of the system (see Table 2.1).[4] Wherever one looks in electoral politics, one finds women advancing to leadership in a pattern perhaps mostly aptly labeled "incremental progress."

Profile

As noted earlier in this chapter, many of the female candidates who came forward in the 1970s had experience in either the political system—generally working for male politicians—or in community projects and charitable causes, or both. The majority of these pioneer political women shared a number of demographic characteristics: they tended to be middle-aged, of middle-class socioeconomic status, relatively well educated, and with occupational experience in traditionally female fields. Elected women then, as now, were typically white, married, and the mothers of children over 12 years old (Kirkpatrick, 1974; Johnson and Carroll, 1978; Mandel, 1983; Carroll and Strimling, 1983; Carroll, 1985). Substantial proportions of women holding elective office in the 1980s are members of women's organizations; in proportions ranging from one-third among women local council members to over three-fourths of women state legislators, elected women belong to at least one of the following five national organizations: the American Association of University Women, the Federation of Business and Professional Women's Clubs, the League of Women Voters, NOW, and NWPC. The higher her office, the more likely a woman official is to belong to such feminist groups as NOW and NWPC; for example, 58 percent of state senators and 46 percent of state representatives, but only 29 percent of county commissioners and seven percent of local council members, were members of feminist groups in 1981 (Carroll and Strimling, 1983).

Black women constitute a very small proportion of America's elected officials,[5] yet they represent a distinctive, vanguard group of political women in several respects. Larger proportions of black elected women than of women officeholders overall acknowledge the important role played by various organizations (including civil rights groups, church groups, community groups, and women's groups) in developing their political candidacies (Table 2.5). Indeed, elected black women are more likely than women officeholders overall to be members of women's organizations; moreover, they are substantially more likely to belong to feminist organizations. Black women more often than white women report that women's organizations encouraged them to run and supported their candidacies.

Table 2.5 • THE ROLE OF WOMEN'S ORGANIZATIONS IN THE POLITICAL CAREERS OF BLACK WOMEN AND ALL WOMEN, 1981 (in percentages)

	State Representatives		*County Commissioners*		*Local Council Members*	
Role	*Black Women*	*All Women*	*Black Women*	*All Women*	*Black Women*	*All Women*
Member of a major women's organization	84	77	63	58	47	37
Member of a feminist organization	68	46	47	29	30	7
Encouraged by a women's organization to run for office	59	27	32	24	18	15
Received campaign support from a women's organization	54	54	32	18	13	7

Source: Center for the American Woman and Politics, 1985.

In the aggregate, women and men in elected office fit a similar demographic profile with respect to socioeconomic status, educational attainment, race, ethnicity, and median age. However, some differences by gender are apparent in background and experience. While the great majority of elected men and women are married and are parents, elected women are more likely than elected men to be widowed, separated, or divorced, and they are less likely to have young children at home. Furthermore, elected women are more likely than elected men to report that the age of their children was an important factor in their decision to run for office (Carroll and Strimling, 1983). Among married officeholders, women are more likely than men to report strong spousal support for their political activities (Johnson and Carroll, 1978; Carroll and Strimling, 1983). It seems to be more necessary for a successful woman politician to have her husband's encouragement for her political ambitions than it is for her male counterpart to have his wife's support.

Among elected officials at municipal, county, state, and federal levels overall, women are more likely than their male colleagues to have attended college, but less likely than men to hold law or other graduate degrees (ibid.). A smaller proportion of elected women than of elected men have paid jobs in addition to their elected offices. Not surprisingly, those women who are employed are concentrated in traditionally female occupations: the four most often cited by elected women are secretarial/clerical, elementary/secondary teaching, nursing/health technical, and social work (ibid.).

Even though the growing population of women in politics is also more diverse than it used to be, elected women typically have more in common with each other than with elected men when it comes to political background. For example, among state legislators serving in 1981, women were less likely than their male counterparts to have had previous experience in elective office but more likely to have held appointed office. The women more often than the men had worked in someone else's political campaign before becoming candidates themselves (Table 2.6).

Table 2.6 • PREVIOUS POLITICAL EXPERIENCE OF WOMEN AND MEN IN STATE LEGISLATURES, 1981 (in percentages)

	State Senators		*State Representatives*	
Experience	*Women*	*Men*	*Women*	*Men*
Held one or more previous elective offices	47	49	25	34
Held one or more appointive government positions	55	43	42	26
Worked in a campaign	84	72	82	74
Worked on the staff of an elected official	25	12	24	16

Source: Center for the American Woman and Politics, 1984.

As to the routes they took to political office, women are more likely than their male colleagues to give an organization credit as an important factor in getting them to seek office. In addition to citing help and encouragement from women's organizations, political women often attribute inspiration or assistance with their political careers to female role models, mentors, and the campaigns of other female candidates for whom they worked (ibid.). There were notable differences, at least as of 1981, between female and male elected officials with respect to the organizations to which they belonged. By and large women were less likely to belong to business groups and commercial associations. Few women elected officials belonged to veterans' organizations and, needless to say, none to fraternal organizations. Political women and men have much in common, but a gender-segregated and stratified society means that they depend on different professional connections and political bases of support.

Support Systems—A Women's Political Community

The conviction among women candidates and women voters continues to be that considerations of the candidate's gender should come after values, issues, and ideologies. Nonetheless, there also appears to be a new sense of purpose about electing and appointing women to positions of leadership, a growing belief that having women in leadership positions is in itself important to other women.

Many women entering politics are connected to a women's political community that began to develop in the 1970s and has continued to grow in the 1980s. While still neither large nor wealthy, its very existence and continued expansion are significant. In addition to the encouragement and support political women receive from membership in various women's organizations, the efforts of independent, as well as partisan, women's groups have produced recruitment and training projects, contributions of money, technical assistance, and volunteer support for women's campaigns.[6]

Beginning in 1974, when the Women's Campaign Fund was founded in Washington, D.C., women have established political action committees (PACs) to raise and distribute campaign money for female candidates, and, in some cases, for male candidates who support a feminist agenda. As of the 1986 elections, there were 27 women's PACs or campaign funds. Among these were several affiliated with feminist organizations or women's professional associations, some affiliated with the major political parties, some independent, and some whose activities were limited to a particular state or locality. In 1984 and 1986, a few of the national women's PACs were able to raise and distribute over $250,000 each to various races. State and local groups distributed much less, but the candidates they supported usually had smaller campaign budgets than those required for statewide or federal offices (Center for the American Woman and Politics, 1986). While insignificant measured against the size and wealth of older political networks on which male candidates have traditionally depended, the women's political community has made a difference for female candidates.

At all levels of government, female officeholders have also formed and joined a variety of organizations for elected and appointed women. By 1988, cross-jurisdictional statewide associations for elected women had been established in 12 states. The oldest of these is the California Elected Women's Association for Education and Research, formed in 1974. The Congresswomen's Caucus, established in 1977 for women only, became the Congressional Caucus for Women's Issues in 1981 and admitted congressmen to its membership, while retaining its primary goal of advocating a policy agenda of issues particularly important to women. (Gertzog [1984] describes the history of the caucus.) For high-level officeholders in the states, Women in State Government was formed in 1985. Associations of women officials also formed within such existing national groups as the National Conference of State Legislatures (the Women's Network), the National Association of Counties (Women Officials of NACo), and the National League of Cities (Women in Municipal Government). Organizations of women officials are not large, and by no means all eligible women belong to them, but their very establishment is evidence of a felt need among women officials to convene for purposes of mutual support and advancement, and to promote public policy and political issues of special concern to them. The issue agendas for which they lobby are most likely to be about matters of rights, justice, and equity for women.

The various educational, funding, issue advocacy, partisan, and professional networks of the women's political community have developed over only a few years. Still very modest in number and size, they nevertheless represent a recognition that women need other women in order to succeed in American politics.

Obstacles and Advantages

The main assets a woman brings to politics are simultaneously some of her greatest liabilities. The fact that she has grown up and lived her life as a woman, played women's roles in her family and community, and functioned in women's networks, means that she has some perspectives and is responsive to some constituencies less familiar to, and possibly neglected by, men. Difficulty arises because at the same time a woman feels a responsibility to represent those constituencies and perhaps champion new issues, she must also show that she is able to fit into the political system as it is presently structured. Although elected women may have a keen sense of being different from their male colleagues, most women believe they must prove themselves in the eyes of the men in power because it is men who still control politics and distribute the rewards that help to enhance elected women's influence and effectiveness.

In many ways it is an advantage to be a newcomer. A newcomer can bring a fresh perspective to an old process, a new outlook to an ancient institution, a set of concerns different from the familiar litany of policy issues. To some extent, this is what the public wants from political women: something different, an untainted approach, new ideas for solving old problems. Unrealistic expectations about women's potential for bringing about ameliorative change may arise from stereotypes that have served in the past both to elevate and to limit women: the notion that women are more pure than men, more dutiful, less interested in self-promotion and personal gain, more conscientious and hard-working. These are sometimes men's perceptions of women, but they have also been women's perceptions of themselves.

Often enough the woman campaigning for office, or the new official fresh from her swearing-in ceremony, hears someone say "The men have been in charge long enough, and they've made a fine mess of things. Let's see what she can do!" Perhaps she can do better: she arrives in office with much of the energy, enthusiasm, and even idealism reserved for those who have not been jaded, worn down, or simply desensitized by years of routine frustrations.

Soon, however, the newcomer woman, alone or nearly so in a political institution, realizes how heavy is the weight of expectation with which she is saddled. As a newcomer she must contend with inexperience, which can be a great liability in a tough, competitive political environment. And as a newcomer woman in surroundings controlled by men, she feels isolated—even, sometimes, like a misfit.

As in any traditionally male-dominated line of work, high visibility is an aspect of newcomer status for women. It is at once an advantage for any ambitious person desiring to be noticed and a liability, in that one's mistakes are conspicuous. High visibility can make the newcomer an easy target for political attack. Being the first woman this or that virtually guarantees that when she does make a mistake, or even when her performance is merely unremarkable, the judgments made about her will be generalized to all women, one woman's "ordinariness" projected as all women's weakness. The pressure to perform perfectly is added to other burdens the new political woman shoulders above and beyond the duties of office.

Because women are such a small minority among elected officials, elected women are special. But this "specialness" is less often a blessing than a liability, because it does not compensate for the disadvantages facing the outsider, who is perceived as lacking in knowledge and experience of the "way things work," and thus perhaps not trusted; who is excluded—more by habit than by malice—when the inner circle gathers; who is treated as less serious, less potentially powerful, less in need of being informed and consulted; who is ghettoized by stereotyped assumptions about what she knows, what she cares about, how she will behave; who is, in short, made less effective by her very specialness.

The political woman faces yet another mixed blessing not shared by her male colleagues. Especially if she is in Congress or other high-level office, a newly elected woman is likely to receive a flood of requests for her participation in programs and activities far beyond the legal boundaries of her constituency. She feels honored and needed because she is one among so few women for so many women to call on, but she is also overtaxed by the extra demands inherent in this special status.

Finally, conflicts between the demands of public life and private life, specifically family life, still appear more likely to affect the political woman than the political man. This is particularly true in the case of women with young children, which may explain why so few elected women have children under age 12. The fact is that during the present period of societal transition, or perhaps for the indefinite future, a woman's obligations in the domestic sphere and her commitments to it (perhaps somewhat modified) usually continue when she enters public life. This situation makes for a double set of major responsibilities that often conflict with one another, resulting in strain and guilt. Whether or not she has a supportive husband, whether or not she has paid housekeeping help, whether or not her children understand her ambitions, a woman whose life outside the home is a demanding political life is less likely than her male colleagues to see a week go by without a clash between her private and public worlds.

Individually or in combination, then, four sociocultural factors—lack of experience and control over institutions and resources created by and for men, the effect of stereotypes, the fact and effect of being in the minority, and the conflicts between professional and family roles and responsibilities—present a formidable force against which the new political woman contends.

Within the electoral system itself are at least three additional barriers: the power of incumbency, the high cost of a political campaign, and candidate recruitment patterns. As long as men hold the overwhelming majority of all elective offices—especially high-level offices—and remain in them, and as long as incumbency continues to confer such an overwhelming reelection advantage, women will remain in the unenviable position of challengers and outsiders (Mandel, 1983; Carroll, 1985).

Related to the power of incumbency is the power of money. As campaign costs continue to rise exponentially, no one can make a serious run for most political offices without spending enormous amounts of time in fundraising. Incumbents, whether male or female, find the task easier because they begin with a base of support already in place and with the odds favoring their victory on election day. For newcomers with no established base, especially those who are challenging incumbents, raising money is an onerous burden.

Women are still less likely than men to be recruited as candidates by the political parties or elected officials, and less likely too to be part of the business and community networks that breed potential candidates and ease their way into the system. Not yet integrated into the interlocking institutions and informal networks that serve as feeders for the electoral system, women still must rely on independent methods and organizations for recruiting female candidates and supporting their campaigns. Unless a systematic grassroots effort is made to develop the women's political community further, and especially to enhance its ability to search out and recruit new candidates, women will most likely continue to enter elective office only in a trickle.

The Impact of Women in Politics

Do public policies, political processes, and governmental institutions change when women enter politics? Do women approach public leadership differently? Do they view issues differently? Do the agendas of political women differ from those of political men? How can differences best be measured? How do views about women as well as women's self-perceptions affect expectations and assessments of their impact? How are proportional representation and the notion of reaching a critical mass related to impact? These types of questions cannot be answered well until women fill many more leadership positions throughout the political system. Preliminary research and some informed observations offer food for thought, but no comprehensive or conclusive answers. Ideas about impact and questions of difference are intriguing areas for future inquiry.

Early information about whether and how the post-1970s generation of political women is making its mark comes from surveys of female candidates and women and men holding office. In her study of women running for congressional, statewide, and state legislative offices in 1976, Susan Carroll (1985: 156) found that "an overwhelming majority of women candidates, and of those elected, feel that they can do a better job of representing women's interests than their male counterparts."

In surveying elected women and men at local, state, and federal levels in 1977 and again in 1981, the Center for the American Woman and Politics (CAWP) found women's views to be more liberal and more feminist than men's on a number of public policy issues (Johnson and Carroll, 1978; Stanwick and Kleeman, 1983). (A feminist attitude here, as in CAWP's surveys, refers to a position on an issue taken by the women's rights movement and endorsed by national feminist organizations such as NOW and NWPC.) In the 1981 survey, officeholders were asked about their views on eight issues. A "gender gap" emerged on matters as diverse as whether the Equal Rights Amendment (ERA) should be ratified, whether the private sector could resolve our economic problems, and whether there should be a death penalty for murderers. Although the gap was smallest at the municipal level, and largest at the state legislative level, women's attitudes differed from men's at all levels of office, within both political parties, and across the ideological spectrum. Republican women, for example, expressed more liberal and feminist views than Republican men, and women who called themselves conservative appeared to be somewhat more liberal about policy issues and more feminist about "women's issues" than men labeling themselves conservative. Differences were most pronounced in attitudes towards women's issues, for example whether there should be a constitutional ban on abortion and whether the ERA should be ratified. Across all levels of office, black women were the most liberal (Stanwick and Kleeman, 1983).

In the 15 states that did not ratify the ERA by the 1982 deadline, CAWP's survey of state legislators found an enormous 40-point gender gap. Seventy-six percent of the women legislators in these states, compared to 36 percent of their male counterparts, agreed that the ERA should be ratified.

Another piece of evidence suggesting that the new political woman brings something different to government and is having an impact on public policy emerges from agendas of the various caucuses and networks of women officials. At the federal level, the Congressional Caucus for Women's Issues has, since its founding, been concerned with the "rights, representation, and status of women." Over the years, this caucus has promoted such issues as the ERA, employment opportunities for women, women's health concerns, programs for displaced homemakers, assistance for women business owners, programs for victims of domestic violence, and dependent care and parental leave legislation (Mandel, 1983; Gertzog, 1984). Women in state legislatures have worked together across party lines on agendas of particular interest to them as women. Such alliances range from formal women's legislative caucuses to informal networks meeting on issues and legislation affecting the lives of women and children, including the ERA, child care, equity in pensions and insurance, rights of divorced women, pay equity, counseling services for displaced homemakers, rape law, marital law, and domestic violence (Kleeman and Mandel, 1987). A case in which women legislators worked together forcefully and successfully in West Virginia in 1987 resulted in getting the legislature to override the governor's veto of a bill providing medical care assistance for poor pregnant women and poor children. The women lawmakers won this victory over powerful opposition by "first, threatening to filibuster both houses of the legislature throughout the remaining week of the session; second, getting a resolution passed through the House on a unanimous voice vote calling on the Senate to reconsider the bill; and third, staging a quickly called candlelight vigil outside the Capitol by various advocacy groups . . . " ("Women Legislators Lead . . . ," 1987).

Similar signs of a political women's consciousness can be seen in towns and counties with women elected officials. Sometimes it is a county shelter for battered women, sometimes a park for children, or a local health care program for elderly women living alone. In 1985 the city of San Francisco, which had a woman mayor and several women supervisors, adopted an ordinance requiring developers building office space in central business areas to make provisions for on-site or nearby child care.

Elected and appointed women have also begun to make a difference by serving as role models for other women and, more directly, through their powers to hire and appoint. Because they are likely to belong to women's organizations and to have worked and socialized with other women, female officials know where to find qualified women to recommend for positions on boards and commissions, to hire for their own staffs, and to suggest to others with positions to fill in politics or government. Like men, women reach automatically into familiar networks for people with whom they share common experiences and can work comfortably. Moreover, political women in general make a point of hiring and promoting women. CAWP's 1981 national survey of officeholders found that large majorities of the women with staffs (state legislators, federal and state appointees) actively recruited women to fill staff openings. A large majority of women state legislators said that they specifically sought out women for staff positions (Stanwick and Kleeman, 1983).

Women officials also take the time and trouble to encourage, educate, and advise other women about political life. They speak frequently to women's groups, counsel individual women, and lend their support to various efforts to bring other women into politics. CAWP's study concluded that political women "show evidence of a strong commitment when they take the time to educate women about political opportunities and to encourage women's political involvement. Contrary to the notion of the 'Queen Bee'—the woman who wants to keep all of the attention and power for herself to the exclusion of other women—the women in our studies and at our consultations welcome the chance to support other women" (ibid.: 19).

The pioneer elected women of the 1970s brought to office perspectives different from those of men. Of late, however, murmurs of disappointment can be heard from active feminist officeholders and constituency groups about some women who have been coming into office more recently. Complaints include charges that these women are not feminists, not idealists committed to advancing women's issues and to social reform in general. Some of the recent entrants are described as being merely ambitious professional politicians, cautious game-players toeing the line, careful about alienating the men in power.

It is inevitable that as more women enter politics, the characteristics of political women will become more diverse. Many differences between them and political men may disappear as women work their way into the mainstreams of party politics. Nevertheless, preliminary evidence does bear out several claims that women make special contributions to the public world and does suggest the potential for significant long-term impact if current trends continue. First, it appears that women in government will represent women's interests better than men have to date. They will do so collectively in caucuses and organizations, consciously as advocates of women's concerns, unconsciously as people with a shared history and set of life experiences. Second, women in politics will affect the political system by bringing more women into positions in government and throughout public life. They will do so directly by hiring, promoting, and appointing women, and serving as mentors; indirectly by serving as role models and educators who encourage women's participation by example and admonition.

At a grander and more abstract level, questions about whether women will make fundamental differences in the public world must await a time when there are many more elected and appointed women establishing and implementing policy and expanding the public's image of an attorney general, an environmental commissioner, an insurance commissioner, a governor, a senator, a secretary of state, a secretary of defense, a president. Only then will it be possible to provide a sound analysis of whether or how a full partnership of women and men in leadership might reshape policies and institutions, transform issue agendas, and change the nature and conduct of public business. Of course, there is great skepticism about idealistic projections for women's potential for transforming society. Nonetheless, some inspiring, energetic voices maintain that a vision of powerful change is not unrealistic. Their challenge and their question cannot be ignored: "If women do not become leaders in order to make a difference," they ask, "why bother?" In 1983, former Congresswoman Bella Abzug stated that position forcefully in a documentary film about women in politics:

> There's no point of women getting into politics or getting into public office if they are going to imitate and ape the white, male, upper-class power structure which has failed to recognize the needs of the majority of the people. We might just as soon let them do it. I don't want women to substitute themselves for what the male power structure has done. Women have another responsibility . . . which is enormous, and that is to find a way to change the nature of power so that it's more reflective of our pluralism and diversity (*Not One of the Boys,* 1984).

Conclusion

When Margaret Chase Smith was elected to the U.S. Senate in 1948, she won that seat in a social and political environment not basically encouraging to women with political ambitions. To some degree, she and the few other exceptional women in office before the 1970s may have been accepted precisely because they were anomalies—viewed as individual cases of unusual behavior, unthreatening because their untraditional behavior did not symbolize vast changes in the given order of the male/female hierarchy. By 1978, when Nancy Landon Kassebaum won election to the Senate, it was assumed that she would not long remain the sole female senator elected to a full term. And, indeed, while there would not be a swell in female Senate membership, before long a next woman and then another would inch in. Indeed, this has been the case—Paula Hawkins served from 1981 to 1987 and Barbara Mikulski was elected in 1986, both women entering the Senate in their own right.

Jeannette Rankin entered the House of Representatives in 1917 as the first congresswoman. Margaret Chase Smith's election to the Senate in 1948 made her the first and, for nearly 40 years (until Barbara Mikulski's election), the only woman to have served in both houses of Congress. Because women had granted themselves permission to pursue political leadership and the social climate had changed by the time Margaret Chase Smith left the Senate in 1972, men and women were resettling the society in new "proper places." The extraordinariness of Rankin, Smith, and a handful of others has given way to the more ordinary struggle of many political women to increase their leadership ranks. The singularity of a vice presidential nomination, a governorship, a Supreme Court appointment, or a United Nations ambassadorship creates great excitement as it bursts forth; before long, however, it seems quite natural to have women in these powerful positions. Rather than facing resistance as examples of deviant behavior, women with power find relatively easy public acceptance. Long-held assumptions and certainties about women's lack of leadership abilities appear to diminish dramatically and almost instantaneously with the appearance of real women—Geraldine Ferraro, Ella Grasso, Sandra Day O'Connor, Jeane Kirkpatrick—in positions for which women had for centuries been considered unfit.

While the numbers of women and men in public office remain far from equal in the late 1980s, the possibilities for women's participation are far greater than ever before. For centuries, few had questioned the natural order of a world in which women were subordinate. Women's movement into politics represents a major difference in how society thinks about social roles and demonstrates that what is regarded as the natural order can change fundamentally. Even in 1960, it was virtually inconceivable for a young woman to imagine a career in political leadership. The odds still favor men, but in 1988, young women can and do take it as their equally rightful possibility to run the world, and perhaps to change it for the common good.

Milestones for Women in Politics, 1971–87

1971 The National Women's Political Caucus (NWPC) is formed in July at a Washington, D.C. meeting of more than 300 feminists. Its aims are to increase women's access to political power in the major parties and to encourage and support women committed to women's rights who seek elective and appointive office.

The Center for the American Woman and Politics (CAWP) is founded as part of the Eagleton Institute of Politics at Rutgers—The State University of New Jersey. For the first time, a university establishes a research and educational center to examine women's roles, status, and influence in politics and government.

Ann Armstrong of Texas is the first woman to cochair the Republican National Committee.

For the first time in the 150-year history of the U.S. Senate, girls are appointed as Senate pages.

1972 Congresswoman Shirley Chisholm of New York enters the presidential primaries and runs for the Democratic presidential nomination. She receives 151.95 delegate votes on the first ballot before Senator George McGovern is nominated at the national convention.

Frances ("Sissy") Farenthold, an attorney, former state legislator, and twice candidate for the Democratic gubernatorial nomination in Texas, receives over 400 votes to become runner-up in the balloting for the vice presidential nomination at the Democratic National Convention.

A record number of female delegates (40 percent) participate in the Democratic National Convention. These women press the party to support representation of women at future national conventions in proportions consistent with their numbers in the population.

The Women's Education for Delegate Selection (WEDS) project is started by the NWPC. Its purpose is to assist and train women in running for election as delegates to both major party conventions.

Jean Westwood is named by presidential nominee George McGovern to chair the Democratic National Committee. The first woman to hold that position, she serves until just after the election, when she is replaced by Robert Strauss.

Yvonne Braithwaite Burke, a Democrat from California, is the first black woman to cochair a national party convention.

Ann Armstrong, at the Republican National Convention, is the first woman keynote speaker at the national convention of any major political party.

Women comprise 30 percent of delegates at the Republican National Convention, a large increase over the 1968 figure of 17 percent. Republican women win approval of Rule 32, which requests each state to "endeavor" to have equal representation of men and women in delegations at future conventions.

1973 Sissy Farenthold is elected the first chair of the National Women's Political Caucus at its first biennial convention.

The National Women's Education Fund (NWEF) is founded in Washington, D.C. A nonpartisan resource organization, it offers training programs in campaign techniques and provides technical assistance and public information in order to increase the numbers and influence of women in politics.

Yvonne Braithwaite Burke becomes the first member of Congress to take maternity leave.

1974 Mary Louise Smith of Iowa is elected chair of the Republican National Committee. Smith is the first woman not to share the chair with a man.

Ella Grasso, a former Democratic congresswoman, is elected governor of Connecticut, the first woman ever elected governor of any state in her own right. (Three women had served before her as surrogates for or successors to their husbands.) Reelected in 1978, Grasso had to step down in 1980 because of a terminal illness. Since Grasso, four other women governors have been elected: Dixy Lee Ray (D-WA) in 1976, Martha Layne Collins (D-KY) in 1983, Madeleine Kunin (D-VT) in 1984 and 1986, and Kay Orr (R-NE) in 1986.

The Woman's Campaign Fund (WCF) is founded. It is the first national political action committee (PAC) established exclusively to fund women's campaigns. Its purpose is to elect "qualified progressive women of both parties" to national, state, and local offices. It provides both financial contributions and technical consultation to candidates.

1976 Lindy Boggs, a Democrat, is the first woman to chair a national presidential nominating convention of a major political party.

Barbara Jordan, a congresswoman from Texas, is the first woman and the first black person to keynote a Democratic national convention.

1977 Patricia R. Harris, the first black female cabinet member, is appointed by President Jimmy Carter as secretary of the U.S. Department of Housing and Urban Development.

The Congresswomen's Caucus is established by women in the U.S. House of Representatives to support legislation affecting women and to monitor federal government programs that influence opportunities available to women. In 1981, it is renamed the Congressional Caucus for Women's Issues and admits male members of Congress to its membership.

The National Women's Conference is held in Houston, Texas. This is the first time American women have come together in a federally sponsored meeting with elected delegates from every state and territory to discuss and vote on a national plan of action for women. The presiding officer of the conference is Congresswoman Bella Abzug from New York.

1978 Nancy Landon Kassebaum, a Kansas Republican, is elected to the U.S. Senate. Prior to Kassebaum's election, all of the women who served in the Senate had succeeded their husbands in Congress or had first been appointed to fill unexpired terms.

Dianne Feinstein, a Democrat, becomes mayor of San Francisco, California when Mayor George B. Moscone is killed by an assassin. She is elected mayor in her own right the following year.

1979 Jane M. Byrne, a Democrat, is elected mayor of Chicago. She is the first woman elected to lead one of the nation's three largest cities.

1980 For the first time, a national party's nominating convention delegates include equal numbers of men and women. At the convention in New York, the Democratic party added to its charter a requirement that future conventions also have equal numbers of female and male delegates.

1981 Sandra Day O'Connor, a former Republican state legislator from Arizona who had served on the state appeals court, is appointed by President Ronald Reagan as the first woman ever to sit on the U.S. Supreme Court.

Jeane J. Kirkpatrick, a professor of political science, becomes the first woman appointed as U.S. ambassador to the United Nations.

Kathy Whitmire, a Democrat, is elected as the first woman mayor of Houston, Texas.

1982 The Democratic National Committee establishes the Eleanor Roosevelt Fund to provide money to Democratic women running for office.

1983 The Campaign Fund for Republican Women is formed to provide Republican women candidates with financial support.

1984 Geraldine A. Ferraro, an attorney, three-term congresswoman from New York, and secretary of the House Democratic Caucus, becomes the first woman ever to run on a major party's national ticket when she is selected by Walter F. Mondale as his vice presidential running mate.

Ten women receive major party nominations for the U.S. Senate. While this is by far the largest number of female nominees ever to run for the Senate, nine are defeated in races where they challenge incumbents. The one who succeeds is Senator Nancy Landon Kassebaum of Kansas, an incumbent winning reelection.

Arlene Violet, a Republican, is elected attorney general of Rhode Island. She is the first woman elected to serve as a state's attorney general.

1986 Kay Orr of Nebraska is the first Republican woman elected governor of a state. Her opponent in the general election is Democrat Helen Boosalis, former mayor of Lincoln. This is the first time two women have run against each other as major party gubernatorial candidates.

Barbara Mikulski, five-term congresswoman from Maryland, is the first Democratic woman elected to

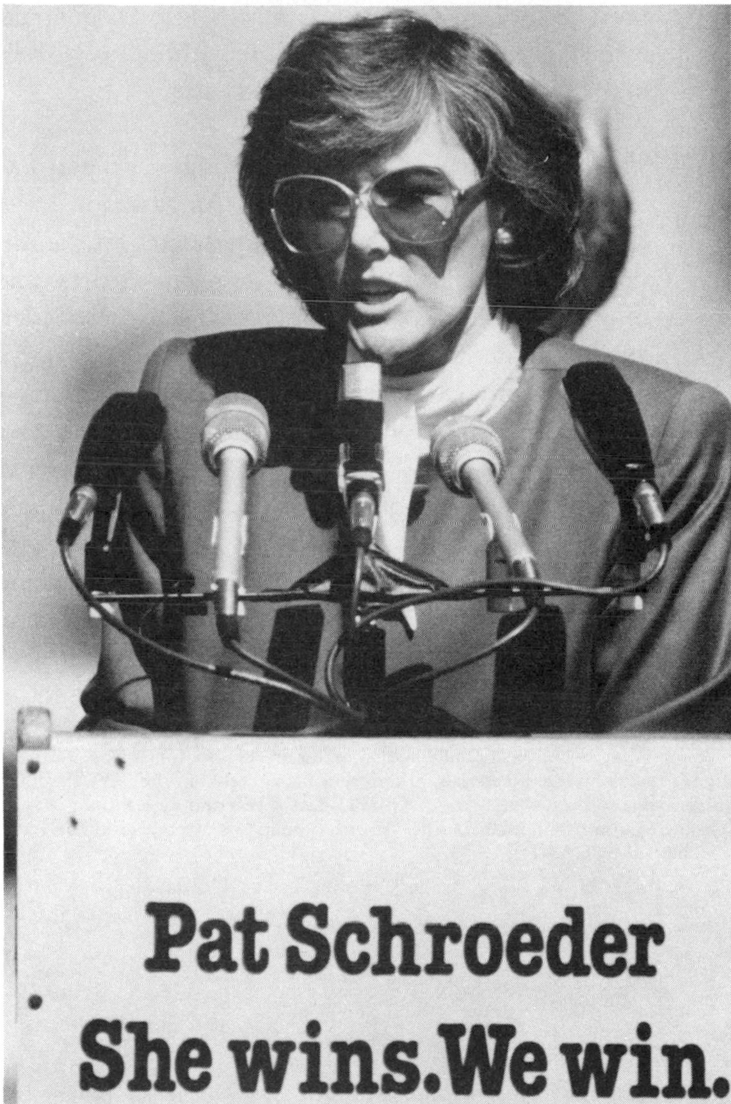

Rep. Patricia Schroeder announces she will not seek the Democratic nomination for president in 1988. *Damian Strohmeyer / The Denver Post*

the U.S. Senate since 1960 and the first Democratic woman ever elected to the Senate without previously filling out a husband's unexpired term.

1987 The national media treat both Congresswoman Patricia Schroeder and former U.N. Ambassador Jeane Kirkpatrick as serious potential candidates for the nation's highest office. While each woman considers running for president, and Congresswoman Schroeder explores a candidacy through a summer of nationwide public appearances, neither woman chooses to pursue her party's nomination through the primaries.

Susan Estrich, a professor at Harvard Law School, becomes the first woman to serve as campaign manager for a major party presidential candidate when Governor Michael Dukakis of Massachusetts appoints her in October 1987.

Source: Center for the American Woman and Politics (CAWP), Eagleton Institute of Politics, Rutgers University. Information in this chronology comes from a variety of news reports, printed materials, and documents collected in the CAWP library and available to the public through CAWP's fact sheets and monographs. A full time-line of women's participation in American politics is in preparation and will be published by CAWP in 1990.

THREE Women's Paid Work, Household Income, and Household Well-being[1]

REBECCA M. BLANK

Highlights

THE SO-CALLED TRADITIONAL American family, long pictured as a working husband with a wife who remained at home with the children, is becoming less and less common. In fact, married-couple households, with or without children, have become a much smaller proportion of the total: just over half (54 percent) of all households consisted of a married couple in 1985 versus nearly 70 percent in 1969. Married couples in which the wife did *not* work constituted a minority of both black and white married-couple households in 1985. The increase in the number of women working for pay has important implications for the family income, as well as strong effects on how both women and men spend their time when not on the job.

- The importance of earned income to households varies enormously, depending on the type or composition of the household. For example, close to 90 percent of all household income among nonelderly married couples comes from the wages and salaries of one or both partners. In contrast, over 25 percent of the total household income of female-headed families derives from income transfers, mainly welfare, while earnings account for little more than 70 percent.

- Transfer income—child support, welfare, and Social Security payments—has accounted for a decreasing proportion of the income of female-headed households. This trend reflects both an increase in work effort by these women and a reduction in transfer program benefits, especially welfare, over the last decade.

- Between 1969 and 1985, average real income (adjusted for inflation) of households with working wives rose 17 percent in the case of white households and 38 percent in the case of black households. In contrast, the average incomes of white and black married-couple households without working wives increased by only seven and 5.5 percent, respectively. Female-headed households with children, however, have seen little growth in real income over the past 16 years.

- White wives' earnings increased total household income by 39 percent in 1969 and by 42 percent in 1985; black wives' earnings increased their families' income by an average of 47 percent in 1969 and by 67 percent in 1985. Danzinger and Gottschalk have calculated that the presence of working wives decreases the poverty rate of married couples by 35 percent among whites, 39 percent among blacks, and 26 percent among Hispanics.

- The growth in real household income between 1973 and 1984 occurred largely because women worked more. However, more research is needed before questions about the full effect of wives' employment on the consumption patterns and economic well-being of their families can be answered.

- Single-adult households clearly are less well off than married couples in terms of income even when differences in household size are taken into account. But female single-parents, on average, have far less income than married couples in which the wife does not work, and less income than women who live alone without children. Still, the earnings of female household heads keep many of the relatively poor from being desperately poor.

- In 1985, married-couple households with working wives were almost twice as likely as households overall to be in the top fifth (the richest end) of the income distribution. Single-parent households, on the other hand, were more likely to be at or near the bottom of the income distribution.

- As women spend more time at work, they necessarily have fewer hours at home, and fewer hours at home mean less time for household tasks that have been traditionally considered "women's work." However, women still bear more of the responsibility for household tasks than men, but the disparity appears to be less dramatic than it was.

- Of all home responsibilities, the most critical for many householders is the care of children. Hill and Stafford found that when a woman increased her hours on the paid job, she typically decreased time spent on leisure activities or other household tasks so that she could maintain the same amount of time with her children.

- The patterns of child care for working mothers have changed markedly. Reliance on relatives for child care has become much less common, while the use of group care facilities has become much more common.
- Increased labor force participation by wives not only changes time demands and time allocation in a household, it changes the household's income needs and consumption patterns. Families with working wives are more likely to spend more resources on eating out or cleaning services, not to mention child care.
- According to one study, a household with two full-time labor market participants must earn at least 30 percent more income in order to purchase the goods and services that make their dual-earner household as well off as a one-earner household with a wife working full time in the home.

Introduction

One of the most dramatic economic changes of the last few decades has been the movement of American women into the labor market. Not only has the two-earner household become the norm among married couples, but the number of women who are the primary—or only—earners in their own households continues to grow. The trends since 1950 in labor force participation rates for women are summarized in Table 3.1. The numbers show that unmarried women have had relatively high labor force participation rates, at least as far back as 1950. Between 1950 and 1985, the labor force participation rate of never-married women drew increasingly close to that of all men, which fell steadily over this period. The

Table 3.1 • CIVILIAN LABOR FORCE PARTICIPATION RATES OF WOMEN BY MARITAL STATUS, MARRIED WOMEN BY AGE OF CHILDREN, AND MEN,[1] SELECTED YEARS, 1950–85

			Married Women				
Year	*All Women*	*All Men*	*No Children Under Age 18*	*Children Age 6 to 17*	*Children Under Age 6*	*Never Married*	*Widowed, Divorced, and Separated*
1950	33.9	86.4	30.3	28.3	11.9	50.5	37.8
1960	37.7	83.3	34.7	39.0	18.6	44.1	40.0
1970	43.3	79.7	42.2	49.2	30.3	53.0	39.1
1980	51.5	77.4	46.0	61.7	45.1	61.5	44.0
1985	54.5	76.3	48.2	67.8	53.4	65.2	42.8

[1]Persons age 14 and over for 1950 and 1960; persons age 16 and over for 1970, 1980, and 1985.

Source: Bureau of the Census, *Statistical Abstract 1986*, 1985, Tables 674 and 675; Bureau of Labor Statistics, *Handbook of Labor Statistics 1985*, 1985, Tables 5, 50, and 54; and *Employment and Earnings*, January 1986, Table 3.

real "revolution" in female labor force participation, however, occurred among married women, especially those with children. More than half of all mothers with preschool children, only 12 percent of whom were in the labor force in 1950, were working or looking for paid work by 1985. Particularly large increases in the labor force participation rate of mothers of very young children occurred between 1980 and 1985.

The increase in the number of women working for pay has important implications for the income of households, as well as strong effects on how both women and men spend their time when not on the job. This chapter discusses the effect that the increase in women's labor force participation has had on both the economic situation and the overall well-being of American households. The focus is on three aspects of women's labor market work: (1) its effect on household income, with particular attention to the distribution of income among households; (2) its effect on household behavior (that is, the roles and responsibilities of household members with respect to such tasks as caring for children and household work); and (3) its effect on the overall well-being of women and their families.

Sources of Household Income: The Importance of Earnings

The importance of earned income to households varies enormously, depending on the type or composition of the household. Married couples, single-parent households, and single-adult households without children typically rely on different mixes of income sources. For example, close to 90 percent of all household income among nonelderly married couples comes from the wages and salaries of one or both partners. Relatively little—five percent—of their income derives from transfer payments, which include payments from government programs (e.g., Social Security, unemployment compensation, and welfare) and payments from private sources such as pensions or child support. In contrast, transfer payments account for a much larger proportion of the income of women who head households as single parents: on average, over 25 percent of their total household income derives from transfers, mainly welfare, while earnings account for slightly more than 70 percent of their income.

Changes in the income sources of the average household occur in two ways. First, changes take place over time in the sources of income received by households of similar composition. For example, as more wives enter the labor force or increase their hours of paid work, the percentage of income the average married couple derives from earnings may increase. Second, demographic shifts and other societal changes may produce changes in the relative predominance among all households of particular household types; for example, an increase in divorce rates or in female life expectancy could decrease the married-couple proportion of all households and, concomitantly, increase the proportion of single-parent or single-person households. Much of the recent change in sources of household income discussed below has been due to the latter effect.

Changes in Household Composition

The traditional American family has long been pictured as a working husband, a nonworking wife, and their children. However, as many have noted in recent years, this particular family type is becoming less and less common.

As demonstrated in Table 3.2, married couples, who in 1969 accounted for over two-thirds (69 percent) of all households, composed only slightly more than half (54 percent) of all households by 1985. (The *number* of married couple families, however, has been increasing.) Over this period the proportion of married couples with wives in the labor force grew from 45 percent to 55 percent.

Table 3.2 • PERCENT DISTRIBUTION OF HOUSEHOLDS BY MARITAL STATUS OF HOUSEHOLDER, 1969, 1979, AND 1985

Type of Household	*1969*	*1979*	*1985*
Married-couple families	69.1	59.2	53.8
Wife in labor force	30.8	30.7	29.5
Wife not in labor force	38.3	28.5	24.3
Single householders	30.9	40.8	46.2
Female householders with children	4.3	6.4	7.1
Female householders without children	17.3	20.3	22.6
Male householders with children	0.5	0.7	1.0
Male householders without children	8.8	13.4	15.5

Source: Calculations from Bureau of the Census, Current Population Survey tapes.

There are many reasons for this change. Women's education, training, and wages have increased steadily, making paid employment more attractive. Family size has continued to shrink, decreasing household demands on women's time. And, after having increased for years, men's real earnings (that is, adjusted for inflation) were virtually stagnant throughout the 1970s, so that many women entered the labor market to maintain or improve their family's standard of living. (For a more extensive discussion of these issues, see Michael, 1985; Smith and Ward, 1985; Bergmann, 1986.)

As the married-couple proportion of all households has grown smaller, the proportion of single-adult households has grown larger (Table 3.2). Single-parent households (defined as households headed by a single adult and containing one or more children under age 18) have increased their proportion of all U.S. households from just under five percent in 1969 to over eight percent in 1985. And nonmarried women who head childless households now compose almost a quarter (23 percent) of all American households.

The formation of households headed by single adults, with or without children, has been spurred by a number of factors. First, rising divorce rates in the 1960s and 1970s left increased numbers of both women and men heading households on their own, often as single parents; a significant increase in the number of out-of-wedlock births has also added to the number of single-parent households. Second, both women and men are marrying later than they used to, and young single people are more likely than in the past to establish their own households. Third, as a result of women's lower mortality rates and longer life expectancy compared to men's, the number of elderly nonmarried females—particularly widows—has been increasing, and these women have shown a growing tendency to maintain independent households.

The rising number of single-adult households is also related to the increase in women in the labor market. The average woman today has spent more years in school as well as more time actually in the paid labor force than her counterparts in earlier generations. As women's employment opportunities and career expectations expand, it becomes easier for a woman to support herself in her own household. For the average woman, marriage is no longer the urgent economic necessity that it once was. Certainly, many women have very low earnings and face serious hardships when they are the primary support of a household, especially if they have children. Nevertheless, growing numbers of women are finding it more feasible to assume the role of primary household breadwinner.

Various studies have investigated the extent to which changes in composition and behavior of households are related to the increase in female labor force participation. Rising divorce rates appear to have led to some of the increase. However, there is little statistical support for the claim that rising labor force participation by women is responsible for increased divorce rates (Michael, 1985; Johnson and Skinner, 1986). Greater labor force participation by women does, however, appear to be a factor contributing to both increases in age at first marriage and rising education levels among women (Michael, 1985). Other research has found that increased labor market participation leads women both to delay childbearing and to have fewer children (Hofferth, 1984). Overall, the recent changes in household composition are clearly connected to the changes in the working lives of women, although the exact nature of that connection is complex and difficult to specify precisely.

Working Wives' Contribution to the Income of Married Couples

What effect does a working wife have on family income? Table 3.3 shows the average income level and the sources of income for nonelderly black and white married couples in 1969, 1979, and 1985. Households in which the wives worked in the paid labor force are shown separately from those in which they did not. The effects of inflation over this time period have been eliminated by calculating all dollar amounts in constant (1985) dollars.

Real income—that is, income adjusted for the effects of inflation—rose in all of these households between 1969 and 1985. By 1985, white households with working wives had total average (mean) incomes of $36,805 (an increase of 17 percent since 1969), while the average income of black households with employed wives was $30,777 (up 38 percent since 1969). In contrast, the average incomes of white and black married-couple households without working wives increased by only seven and 5.5 percent, respectively.

In the average household with a working wife, the percent of income that derived from the wife's earnings also rose over these years, especially in black households. In 1985, the wife's earnings accounted for over 40 percent of the income of black married couples with employed wives and nearly 30 percent of the income of white couples.

In 1969, husbands with working wives not only typically earned less than husbands whose wives did not work, but had less income from other sources as well. The average working wife in 1969 was helping her household catch up with higher-earning husbands whose wives typically did not work. In 1985, however, among all nonelderly married-couple families, husbands with working wives generally earned more than the husbands with nonworking wives. (These figures are not shown in Table 3.3, which presents black and white nonelderly couples separately.) Thus, in 1985, a working wife's earnings frequently gave an already "better-off" couple an additional advantage. Differences by race are apparent, however. Among white families, husbands with working wives still earned, on average, somewhat less than husbands whose

Table 3.3 • SOURCES OF INCOME FOR NONELDERLY MARRIED-COUPLE FAMILIES,[1] 1969, 1979, AND 1985 (in percentages)

	White								
	Working Wives[2]			*Nonworking Wives*			*All Nonelderly Couples*		
	1969	*1979*	*1985*	*1969*	*1979*	*1985*	*1969*	*1979*	*1985*
Total mean income (in 1985 dollars)	$31,367	$32,570	$36,805	$27,356	$27,571	$29,320	$29,228	$30,375	$33,856
Percent of income due to									
Husband's earnings	68.3	66.1	62.9	93.2	88.0	83.3	81.6	75.7	70.9
Wife's earnings	28.0	27.9	29.6	0.0	0.0	0.0	13.1	15.7	17.9
Transfers[3]	2.0	3.4	3.2	3.0	7.0	8.4	2.5	5.0	5.3
Dividends, interest, and other	1.7	2.6	4.3	3.8	5.0	8.3	2.8	3.6	5.9
Percent husbands employed	90.1	88.4	87.3	82.8	77.5	74.8	86.2	83.6	82.4
Total number of households (in thousands)	13,120	15,918	16,471	14,992	12,476	10,721	28,112	28,394	27,192

	Black								
	Working Wives[2]			*Nonworking Wives*			*All Nonelderly Couples*		
	1969	*1979*	*1985*	*1969*	*1979*	*1985*	*1969*	*1979*	*1985*
Total mean income (in 1985 dollars)	$22,229	$27,659	$30,777	$16,414	$18,218	$17,315	$20,101	$24,506	$26,913
Percent of income due to									
Husband's earnings	64.8	59.0	53.5	92.5	86.3	78.0	74.9	68.1	60.5
Wife's earnings	32.0	36.2	40.3	0.0	0.0	0.0	20.3	24.1	28.7
Transfers[3]	2.7	3.9	5.0	6.8	12.4	18.6	4.2	6.8	8.9
Dividends, interest, and other	0.5	0.9	1.2	0.7	1.3	3.4	0.6	1.0	1.8
Percent husbands employed	91.8	89.8	87.6	86.4	81.6	73.3	89.9	87.1	83.5
Total number of households (in thousands)	1,397	1,188	1,094	805	596	440	2,202	1,784	1,534

[1]Includes all married-couple families in which the husband is under age 65.

[2]Includes all married-couple families in which the wife ever worked during the year indicated.

[3]Includes government transfers (AFDC, Social Security, unemployment compensation, etc.), pension income, and child support.

Source: Calculations from Bureau of the Census, Current Population Survey tapes.

wives did not work, although the gap was substantially narrower than it had been in 1969. Among black married couples, on the other hand, the average husband with a working wife earned substantially more in 1985 than the average husband whose wife did not work.

In 1969, if all the employed black wives had quit work (thereby eliminating one-third of their families' average $22,229 income), their households' aggregate income would have been about eight percent less than that of households in which the wives had not been working. By 1985, if the black working wives had quit their jobs (their families thereby losing the 40 percent of income contributed by wives' earnings), the remaining income for these families would still average over $18,000—six percent higher than the $17,315 total income of their counterparts whose wives had not been working.

As noted, in 1985 couples in which the wife did *not* work constituted a distinct minority of white as well as of black married-couple households (where they were already a minority in 1969). The 1985 average aggregate earnings of the husbands in these households were lower than in 1969, in part because they were less likely to be working. Among white couples, 83 percent of husbands with nonworking wives were employed in 1969, but only 75 percent of the husbands were employed in 1985, and there was heavier reliance on transfers and other nonearned income sources. The comparable figures for blacks were 86 percent and 74 percent, respectively. (The increased percentage of income accounted for by transfer payments among couples without working wives in 1985 versus 1969 is largely due to increased early retirement among workers under age 65 combined with more generous Social Security benefits.)

The effect of working wives on married couples' average income is further documented in Table 3.4. White wives' earnings increased total household income by 39 percent in 1969 and by 42 percent in 1985; black wives' earnings increased their families' income by an average of 47 percent in 1969 and by more than two-thirds—67 percent—in 1985.

Table 3.4 • IMPACT OF WIVES' EARNINGS ON HOUSEHOLD INCOME OF NONELDERLY MARRIED-COUPLE FAMILIES, 1969, 1979, AND 1985 (in 1985 dollars)

	Average Total Income of Households with Working Wives	*Average Total Income If Wives' Earnings Set to Zero*	*Percent Increase in Income Due to Wives' Earnings*
White			
1969	31,367	22,596	38.8
1979	32,570	23,474	38.8
1985	36,805	25,908	42.1
Black			
1969	22,229	15,115	47.1
1979	27,659	17,655	56.7
1985	30,777	18,381	67.4

Source: Calculations from Bureau of the Census, Current Population Survey tapes.

Similar calculations have been made for other years by Danziger and Gottschalk (1986), who have also calculated that the presence of working wives decreases the poverty rate of white married couples by 35 percent, of black married couples by 39 percent, and of Hispanic couples by 26 percent.

There are, of course, problems with these simple calculations comparing married couples' average household income when the wife works for pay and when she does not. In particular, if the households in which wives currently work outside the home were to lose that source of income, one might expect that other household members (particularly husbands) would, if possible, increase their labor market work to replace some of the lost income. One might also expect that the loss of wives' earnings would make some households eligible for certain transfer programs—unemployment compensation, for example. Thus, the calculations in Table 3.4 are almost surely an overstatement of what would actually happen to family incomes should all working wives quit their jobs. Still, there would undoubtedly be a substantial effect.

The issue of how wives' earnings affect household income and consumption is one on which too little research has been done. It would be particularly useful to have more information on the extent to which wives' earnings contribute to necessary household consumption and help households maintain their standard of living, and the extent to which wives' earnings are used to provide extra income for less essential expenditures.

As Levy (1987) noted, the growth in real household income between 1973 and 1984 occurred largely because women worked more. Many have argued that wives went into the labor force during this period mainly to help their families purchase essentials. Others argue, however, that the average family in earlier decades had a far lower standard of living (for example, the average family's house was smaller and less elaborately equipped); thus, "economic need" is an extremely relative or subjective concept, which can be overemphasized as a cause of increased labor market involvement by wives (see Bergmann, 1986). Without better research on the effect of wives' employment on the consumption patterns and economic well-being of households, this argument cannot be resolved. For instance, it would be interesting to know what items women's earnings allow families to purchase that they could not otherwise buy—perhaps a house, a college education, a second car—and how important those items are, or are perceived to be, to the well-being of the family.

Women's Earnings in Single-adult Households

Women who head households and who are the primary wage-earner make up a rapidly growing part of the population. For these women, the major determinant of how well their household fares financially is their own earnings. Table 3.5 illustrates the income sources in 1969, 1979, and 1985 for four groups of single-adult households: female and male-headed households with children, and female and male-headed households without children.

Men as well as women head single-parent households, but few people worry about the situation of the small proportion of such households that are headed by men. In terms of income, at least, most of them are relatively well off compared to women who head families. It is the growing numbers of female-headed households with children that have generated great concern. As of 1985, 87 percent of all single-parent households were headed by women, and over one-third of them were poor. In fact, rising poverty rates of the early 1980s were at least partially due to the growth in female-headed families. If the proportion of female-headed families among the poor were the same in 1985 as in 1969, the overall poverty rate would have been only 12.2 percent instead of the actual 14 percent.

Female-headed households with children have seen little growth in real income over the last 16 years (Table 3.5). On average, those headed by white women had only $11,644 in

Table 3.5 • SOURCES OF INCOME FOR NONELDERLY SINGLE ADULT HOUSEHOLDERS,[1] 1969, 1979, AND 1985 (in percentages)

	White											
	Single Householders With Children						*Single Householders Without Children*					
	Female Householders			*Male Householders*			*Female Householders*			*Male Householders*		
	1969	*1979*	*1985*	*1969*	*1979*	*1985*	*1969*	*1979*	*1985*	*1969*	*1979*	*1985*
Total mean income (in 1985 dollars)	$11,468	$11,289	$11,644	$20,643	$23,368	$23,418	$11,801	$12,016	$14,333	$18,199	$17,630	$19,231
Percent of income due to												
Householder's earnings	63.7	65.7	70.6	95.0	92.6	92.2	83.0	81.9	80.8	92.6	90.2	87.9
Transfers[2]	33.1	31.5	25.5	3.8	5.8	5.4	9.5	11.4	10.3	3.9	6.5	6.5
Dividends, interest, and other	3.2	2.8	3.9	1.2	1.6	2.4	7.5	6.7	8.9	3.5	3.3	5.6
Percent householders employed	68.2	70.1	68.6	89.4	81.2	81.4	75.4	79.2	79.9	84.5	85.2	83.4
Total number of households (in thousands)	1,436	2,635	3,127	189	330	543	3,785	5,741	6,990	2,541	5,599	7,039

	Black											
	Single Householders With Children						*Single Householders Without Children*					
	Female Householders			*Male Householders*			*Female Householders*			*Male Householders*		
	1969	*1979*	*1985*	*1969*	*1979*	*1985*	*1969*	*1979*	*1985*	*1969*	*1979*	*1985*
Total mean income (in 1985 dollars)	$7,487	$8,063	$8,672	$13,998	$15,255	$14,070	$7,129	$8,789	$10,727	$11,695	$12,647	$13,121
Percent of income due to												
Householder's earnings	53.0	64.6	73.3	96.2	91.0	87.4	85.6	83.0	82.8	93.7	89.0	88.7
Transfers[2]	46.8	35.0	26.2	2.4	8.6	10.7	12.9	15.7	13.4	5.7	10.2	9.2
Dividends, interest and other	0.2	0.4	0.5	1.4	0.4	1.9	1.5	1.3	3.8	0.6	0.8	2.1
Percent householders employed	63.2	59.8	60.5	87.0	86.2	74.4	76.6	67.6	69.7	86.4	80.9	78.1
Total number of households (in thousands)	639	1,003	1,150	46	65	78	662	935	1,104	470	701	893

[1]Includes all households with single adult householders under age 65.

[2]Includes government transfers (AFDC, Social Security, unemployment compensation, etc.), pension income, and child support.

Source: Calculations from Bureau of the Census, Current Population Survey tapes.

income in 1985; those headed by black women had a low of $8,672. Over 70 percent of the income of these households came from their own earnings, a proportion that has increased since 1969, but these earnings were typically low. For instance, while two-thirds of the white women who headed families worked in 1985, they averaged just over $8,200 in earnings that year; their black counterparts averaged only $6,350.

Surprisingly, transfer income—a category which includes child support as well as welfare and Social Security payments—has accounted for a decreasing proportion of the income of these single-mother households. This trend reflects both an increase in work effort by these women and reductions in transfer program benefits, especially welfare, over the last decade. For instance, between 1975 and 1985, the maximum Aid to Families with Dependent Children (AFDC) benefit fell by an average of 24 percent across the states after adjusting for inflation (U.S. Congress, 1987: Table 13).

Single-adult households without children are a group less frequently discussed, although they constituted a large and growing proportion—38 percent—of American households in 1985. This is a very mixed group, ranging from young single adults living on their own to older divorced or widowed individuals who live alone. Elderly single-adult households are not illustrated in Table 3.5, but Census data show that there are far more women than men among this group. Households headed by elderly women account for over nine percent of all female-headed households without children. The comparable proportion for men is only 2.5 percent.

Nonelderly single men who head households without children derive 85 percent of their income from their own earnings. While their mean yearly income ($19,231 for whites in 1985 and $13,121 for blacks) may not seem large, it should be noted that many of these households include only one person. The per-person income in single male-headed households without children is four to five times larger than the per-person income of female single parents heading households.

In 1969, childless households headed by nonelderly single women—both black and white—had, on average, about the same total income as their counterparts with children. By 1985 this had changed dramatically, and female-headed childless households showed large real income gains, much of it coming from increased earnings, although there were also increases in transfers and dividend and interest income. (Again, the per-person income difference between households with and without children is even larger than the difference in overall average household income.)

Single-adult households clearly are less well off than married couples in terms of income even when differences in household size are taken into account. This is especially true in the case of single female parents. It is not at all surprising that female-headed families have less income than married-couple households in which the wife works. But such families, on average, also have far less income than married couples in which the wife does not work, and less income than women who live alone without children. Thus, single-mother households are under greater economic strain, as well as psychological and physical strain from being a single parent.

The Effect of Women's Earnings on Income Distribution in the U.S.

The preceding discussion has shown both that a larger share of married couples' income is coming from women's earnings, and that a growing number of single-adult households are headed by women who rely primarily on their own earnings. Among all white households—single adults as well as married couples—women contributed 21 percent of aggregate household income in 1969. By 1985, that proportion had reached over 28 percent. Among black households, the percent of income contributed by women rose from 34 percent in 1969 to 46 percent in 1985. As more women work and the share they contribute to household income rises, what has been the effect on the income distribution?

Table 3.6 looks at the aggregate income distribution for households of various types. Specifically, the income distribution is calculated by ordering all households from richest to poorest, and dividing them into fifths. Thus, the bottom fifth of the income distribution is composed of the poorest 20 percent of all households, the second fifth is the next poorest 20 percent, and so on to the richest 20 percent of all households in the top fifth.

Table 3.6 shows that different household types tend to cluster in very different locations in the income distribution. In 1985, married-couple households with working wives were almost twice as likely as households overall to be in the top fifth of the income distribution; that is, almost 40 percent of married-couples with working wives were in this category and only three percent of them were in the bottom fifth. In contrast, only four percent of single-headed households with children were in the top fifth, while 41 percent of them were in the bottom fifth. The top of the income distribution is disproportionately composed of married-couple households while the bottom is disproportionately composed of single-adult households.

Married couples improved their relative standing in the income distribution between 1969 and 1985. The likelihood

Table 3.6 • POPULATION DISTRIBUTION BY HOUSEHOLD TYPE AND RELATIVE LOCATION IN THE INCOME DISTRIBUTION, 1969 AND 1985 (in percentages)

	1969					
	All Households	*Married-Couple Families*		*Single Householders*		
					Without Children	
Households Ordered by Income		*Working Wife*[1]	*Nonworking Wife*	*With Children*[2]	*Female*	*Male*
Top fifth	20	35.0	20.1	4.5	3.4	7.7
Fourth fifth	20	28.8	22.8	7.5	5.8	12.3
Third fifth	20	20.8	23.7	15.7	12.1	17.1
Second fifth	20	12.3	21.4	34.2	25.1	24.9
Bottom fifth	20	3.2	12.0	38.1	53.6	37.9
	1985					
	All Households	*Married-Couple Families*		*Single Householders*		
					Without Children	
		Working Wife[1]	*Nonworking Wife*	*With Children*[2]	*Female*	*Male*
Top fifth	20	39.9	22.0	4.0	4.7	9.4
Fourth fifth	20	30.5	23.0	10.9	10.0	14.8
Third fifth	20	18.4	22.7	18.4	18.6	21.6
Second fifth	20	8.5	21.5	25.9	27.2	25.9
Bottom fifth	20	2.6	10.8	40.8	39.5	28.4

[1]Refers to wives working for pay.

[2]Includes both male and female householders.

Source: Calculations from Bureau of the Census, Current Population Survey tapes.

of being at or near the top increased, especially for couples with working wives. The same was true for single-headed households without children, who, although still disproportionately likely to be in the bottom ranges, did show some upward shift in their relative status. Single-parent households, on the other hand, did worse: they were more likely to be at or near the bottom of the income distribution in 1985 than they had been in 1969.

A number of studies have concluded that the increase in working wives has generally narrowed the income distribution among married couples (Smith, 1979; Danziger, 1980; Betson and van der Gaag, 1984; Lazear and Michael, 1986). This effect seems to occur primarily because women with low-wage husbands have been (1) more likely to work, and (2) more likely to work more hours, than the wives of high-wage husbands. Thus, the increasing work effort by the wives of low-wage husbands has raised their families' income relative to couples with higher-wage husbands. Offsetting this effect, there is generally a positive correlation between the wages a wife earns and the wages her husband earns; that is, high-wage husbands are more likely than low-wage husbands to be married to high-wage wives. During the last two decades, this second effect has been less important than the more rapidly growing work effort among wives of low-wage husbands in white households. Among blacks, most studies have concluded, working wives have increased income disparities among married couples. However, as more and more women enter the labor force, the relative size of these effects may change. Since it appears that by 1985 the income of married couples with employed wives was moving further and further ahead of the income of other married couples, continuing increases in work by wives might widen the income distribution among married couples more than it has in the past.

While much attention has been paid to married couples, far less research has looked at whether women's earnings alter the income distribution of married-couple and single-adult households. Danziger and Gottschalk (1986) found that increased work by female household heads with children has brought their household income closer to that of married couples than it would otherwise be and thus has narrowed the income distribution. No one has done a complete study of the income distribution effects of working women across all household types.

The question of how working women have affected the overall income distribution in this country is difficult to answer, largely because women's earnings affect not only the relative location of any particular household type within the income distribution, but also because these earnings may affect what proportion of the population is in particular categories. For instance, increased work by women heading households narrows the income distribution by providing these households with more income relative to married couples than would be the case if the female household head did not work. However, if the women heading households did not work, many of them would almost surely be unable to survive on their own, and there would be a decrease in the number of single-adult households. The earnings of female household heads keep many relatively poor households from being desperately poor. If these women stopped working, many female-headed households simply could no longer exist as independent households.

Allocating Time

While the impact of women's work on their households' income is an interesting and important issue, other significant household changes occur as more women enter the paid labor force. As women spend more time at work, they necessarily have fewer hours at home, and fewer hours at home mean less time for the household tasks that have traditionally been considered women's work.

Economic analysis of household behavior typically assumes that there are three ways to spend time: (1) working in the labor market to earn money; (2) working to produce "home goods" and services—the combination of housework, yardwork, cooking, shopping, and child care that are necessary to maintain a household; and (3) engaging in activities that are personally enjoyable rather than necessary or productive (leisure time). Under the division of labor by sex in so-called traditional American families, the husband was assigned the job of earning income in the labor market; the wife was responsible for most of the home work and home production. But that traditional family has been changing.

As more wives spend more of their time in the labor market, households can respond in two ways. First, both husbands and wives can change their allocation of time, decreasing the amount devoted to leisure and/or reducing the amount of time devoted to home work as labor market work increases. Second, the household can use the additional income from the wife's paid work to purchase more household assistance, thus decreasing the time the couple must spend on household tasks. Home goods purchased to substitute for the householders' time spent on household work can include everything from hiring cleaning help, to eating out more often, to hiring someone to look after the children when the parents are at work.

A major complaint by many working women is that their increased time in the labor market is not offset by an equivalent decrease in home work time. Table 3.7 shows results from tabulations of male and female time allocation in 1975–76 (Hill, 1984). Married women who worked full time for pay put an additional 25 hours a week into home-oriented work, while women who were not in the paid labor force spent 41 hours a week in home-oriented work. Married men who worked full time put only 13 hours a week into home-oriented work (although it should be noted that, on average, a full-time job involved more hours for men than for women).

What these data do not tell us is whether full-time working women spent fewer hours in the labor force so that they could spend more hours in the home, but that is probably the case in many instances. Single men and single women worked about the same number of hours in total, although the women spent a greater percentage of the total on home work. Looking at a variety of age and labor-market groups (not shown on Table 3.7), Hill concluded that married women who worked put in three to 18 more hours in the home than did married men with equal hours in the labor market. (See also Hartmann, 1981.)

It is discouraging that wives who enter the labor market must also do a disproportionate amount of the household work, but there are some signs of change, particularly among younger couples. Juster (1984), who compared time-use surveys for 1981–82 and 1975–76, found significant changes in the weekly allocation of home and market work by men and women over that four-year period. Among people ages 25 to 44, men decreased their market work by one hour and increased their home work by three hours. Women, on the other hand, increased their market work by four hours and decreased their home work by almost 1.5 hours. Juster also found that between the mid-1960s and the early 1980s, the ratio of the average amount of time that women spent on home work compared to the average amount of time that men spent on home work declined from four to one to a little over

Table 3.7 • TIME USAGE BY SEX, MARITAL STATUS, AND LABOR FORCE STATUS, 1975–76 (in hours)

	Female			*Male*		
		Married			*Married*	
Time Usage	*Unmarried*	*Full-time Paid Worker*	*Not in Labor Force*	*Unmarried*	*Full-time Paid Worker*	*Not in Labor Force*
Labor market-related work[1]	22.2	39.1	3.2	32.8	48.6	6.6
Home-oriented work[2]	23.5	24.6	40.9	12.0	12.7	20.0
Total work time	45.7	63.7	44.1	44.8	61.3	26.6

[1]Includes market work and education.

[2]Includes house/yard work, child care, and services/shopping.

Source: Martha Hill, *Patterns of Time Use,* 1984, Table 7.3.

two to one. Women still typically bear more of the responsibility for household tasks than men, but the disparity is less dramatic than it was.

Of all home responsibilities, the most critical for many households is the care of children. As noted above, the fact that women today are having fewer children is in part the result of women's increased labor force participation. The large increase in paid employment among mothers—particularly mothers of preschool children—raises serious questions about how women are managing to cope with their dual responsibilities to their jobs and to their children.

There is no question that children greatly add to the home work burden of women, and the younger the children, the more time required. Hill and Stafford (1984) found that the presence of preschoolers (ages 2 to 5) in a household typically increased the child care time of a college-educated woman by more than four hours per week, increased her other household work by 7.5 hours a week, decreased her labor market work by eight hours a week, and decreased her personal time by two hours a week. Husbands also spent time in caring for their children, but, unlike their wives, did not increase the time they spent on other household tasks. The priority that women gave to their children was also clear. Among employed college-educated women, time spent on the paid job had almost no effect on the time they spent caring for their children. Hill and Stafford found that when a woman increased her hours on the paid job, she typically decreased time spent on leisure activities or other household tasks so that she could maintain the same amount of time with her children. (See also Leibowitz, 1975.)

Working mothers not only spend a great deal of their time at home caring for their children, they must also devote considerable time and effort to making sure that their children are cared for while they are at work. The type of child care working mothers use depends on their income and on the opportunities available where they live (Stolzenberg and Waite, 1984). Table 3.8 shows, for 1965 and 1984–85, the types of child care used for preschool children whose mothers worked full time. It demonstrates how markedly the patterns of child care for working mothers have changed. Children were only about half as likely to be cared for in their own homes in 1984–85 as they had been two decades earlier. Reliance on relatives for child care had become much less common, while the use of group child care facilities had increased. Fully 19 percent of the women in the 1984–85 study reported using more than one form of child care, a state of affairs that could require coordination and scheduling of different arrangements on different days. Many have suggested that the availability of good child care arrangements is a determinant of women's work efforts. One survey, for example, found that one-fourth of the mothers not currently in the labor force said they would look for work if they could find adequate child care (Bureau of the Census, 1983).

Increased market work by wives not only changes time demands and time allocation in a household, it also changes the household's income needs and consumption patterns. Increased work often increases the demands on household income. A woman who wants to enter, or return to, paid employment may find herself in the anomalous situation of trying to decide whether she can afford to work, taking into consideration both what she will have to pay for child care and the increased expense the family is likely to incur for such things as more meals eaten out, assistance in the home, or yard maintenance.

Table 3.8 • PRIMARY CHILD CARE ARRANGEMENTS FOR PRESCHOOL CHILDREN WITH FULL-TIME WORKING MOTHERS,[1] 1965 AND WINTER 1984–85 (in percentages)

Type of Child Care Arrangement	*1965*	*Winter 1984–85*
Care in child's home	47.2	24.4
By relative	28.7	19.4
By nonrelative	18.5	5.0
Care in another home	37.3	42.2
By relative	17.6	14.7
By nonrelative	19.6	27.5
Group-care facility	8.2	28.0
Mother cares for child while working	6.7	5.0
Other	0.7	0.4

[1]1965 data are for ever-married women with children under age six. 1984–85 data are for mothers between the ages of 18 and 44 with children under age five. (Because the 1984–85 figures refer solely to the children of mothers who are employed full time for pay, they will differ from the figures presented in the Statistical Appendix to this volume, which are for the children of both full- and part-time workers.)

Source: Bureau of the Census, Current Population Reports, Series P-23, No. 117, 1982, Table A; and Series P-70, No. 9, 1987, Table 1.

In the long run, changes in household income and composition may not be the most important effects of women's increased labor force participation. Of far greater significance may be changes in the nature and division of household work, in fertility patterns, in the ways in which children are cared for, and in household expenditure and consumption patterns.

Overall Individual and Household Well-being

Both positive and negative aspects of women's increased labor force participation have been discussed above. On the one hand, increased paid work by women has provided additional income to their households. On the other hand, it has created additional demands on women's time and may have necessitated expenditures for goods and services their families would not otherwise have needed. How do these factors stack up in determining whether increased labor force participation has made women better off or worse off? At some level this is an impossible question to answer, if only because science has devised no good measure of "satisfaction" or "welloffness." There are, however, at least a few ways in which the question can be approached.

The Effects of Paid Employment on Women's Health

For many people, work is more than just a way of providing income; it is a source of self-definition and self-affirmation. One of the first questions in a conversation between strangers is often "What do you do?" Knowing that society is willing to pay for one's talents is clearly a psychological boost as well as a source of economic security. And many people enjoy their work.

On the other hand, to the extent that paid employment increases the demands on women, forcing them to "work two jobs," it may be physically and emotionally exhausting. Especially among low-income single mothers who must not only work as much as possible to make ends meet (often at low-wage and psychologically unrewarding jobs), but also must bear all the responsibility for child care and household management, it would not be surprising to find that the stress of juggling paid and nonpaid work responsibilities have a negative effect on women's health.

In general, evidence seems to show that paid employment has a positive effect on women's health. But when there are small children in the household demanding more home work time, the combination of this demand with market work has a negative effect on women's health status (Wolfe and Haveman, 1983). Surveys among single working women who head households, especially divorced and separated women, indicate that they are less satisfied with their lives than any other group of men or women (Cain, 1985). These women in particular must cope often with the daunting combination of marginal economic status and full responsibility for child care. Alternatively, having fewer children and having them later has been found to result in greater family well-being in the long run (Hofferth, 1984), and, as noted above, increased labor force participation delays childbearing and decreases fertility rates.

Thus, the general effect on women's health of increased participation in the labor force is somewhat mixed. While many women have found independence and affirmation in their jobs, as well as economic rewards, there are clearly some for whom the pressure of work and home demands creates health problems.

Does the Increased Income Justify the Costs of Work?

Women who earn income are obviously raising the total economic resources of their households. But they are also typically sacrificing both leisure time and home work time—time with their children, time to prepare home-cooked meals—as well as increasing the income demands on their families. Two studies have tried to measure both of these effects. Lazear and Michael (1980), using information on relative expenditure levels among different types of households, and making some assumptions about what constitutes satisfaction, estimate that a household with two full-time labor market participants needs to earn at least 30 percent more income in order to purchase the goods and services that make their dual-earner household as well off as a one-earner household with a wife working full time in the home. Since two-earner households averaged only 20 percent higher income in Lazear and Michael's data, these researchers were led to conclude that despite their seemingly higher incomes, two-earner couples, on average, may actually be worse off economically than single-earner couples.

A comparison of data cited earlier in this chapter (see especially Table 3.5) with the results from Lazear and Michael's research is tricky because the latter compare one-earner couples in which the husband is the earner with two-earner couples. Table 3.5, however, includes *all* nonelderly black and white married-couple households, in some of which there are no earners while in others only the wife works. Unlike those in Lazear and Michael's data, the working wives included in Table 3.5 comprise part-time and part-year workers as well as full-time workers. However, applying Lazear and Michael's standard (that a full-time working wife needs to add at least 30 percent to household income for her work to be economically worthwhile) to the data in Table 3.5, one would conclude that among black married-couple families it unquestionably pays for wives to work. The total income of those families was nearly 80 percent higher than it was for black married couples without working wives. The situation is less clear with respect to white married couples with working wives, who averaged only 26 percent more income than those in which the wife did not work for pay. This smaller percentage may reflect, at least in part, the fact that white working wives are less likely than black working wives to work full time.

In an effort similar to Lazear and Michael's, Fuchs (1986) looked at the satisfaction levels of men and women ages 25 to 64 by trying to measure their "full income"—total money income, plus the value of home production, plus the value of their leisure hours. Using several alternative assumptions about how to measure the value of both leisure hours and home work, Fuchs computed the combined effects of the increases in household income and the decreases in home goods and personal time. Under each of his assumptions, Fuchs found that women's full income (access to goods, services, and leisure) relative to men's was lower in 1979 than it had been in 1959.

These two studies are very technical, and the results substantially depend on the assumptions used to measure well-being and satisfaction. However, the findings do suggest the possibility that the revolution that brought more women into the paid workforce may have had mixed effects.

In any case, these studies underscore the need to be aware of both the positive and negative aspects of women's increased labor force participation. On the one hand, the entrance of women into a variety of careers and occupations that were once closed to them has transformed the aspirations of many young girls, made the lives of many women more interesting, and given many women a level of personal confidence and economic security with regard to their own future that can only be counted as positive, to say nothing of the important economic contribution that many working women do make to family well-being. On the negative side is the stress that may result from the demands—particularly on the mothers of young children—of handling both a paid job and family responsibilities. Combining the role of breadwinner with that of parent is particularly burdensome for the growing number of working single mothers who have no one with whom to share these responsibilities.

Some Final Issues

This chapter has avoided referring to "the increase in working women," for the truth is that women have always worked. In fact, throughout much of history, women have produced both home goods and market goods. In agrarian societies where most of the production takes place at or near home, the division between home work and market work is not a clear one, and women frequently do a great deal of the production and marketing of crops. It was only with the industrial revolution, when market work moved away from the home and home work became defined as the exclusive realm of women, that a clear line was drawn between the two (Brown, 1982; Davis, 1984). Thus, the involvement of contemporary women in the paid labor force is in some sense the reemergence of the pattern in the preindustrial past, when women contributed routinely to both the market and the home production of their households. However, as much of the above discussion suggests, there are some areas deserving serious attention by policymakers and society at large.

First, the relatively low wages that many women earn in the labor market means that the economic situation of many households supported by women is particularly precarious. The low wages of female household heads supporting children are particularly appalling. Much has been written about this issue (see, for instance, Smith and Ward, 1984, or Barrett, 1987), and discussion continues regarding the relative roles played by lack of training, sex and race discrimination, occupational segregation, and other causes of low female earnings. The encouraging data in this area indicate that, in recent years, women's wages have been rising relative to men's, and that occupational segregation is decreasing (see "American Women Today: A Statistical Portrait" in the Appendices). However, far too many women still find themselves in poorly paid jobs with few opportunities for advancement.

The issue of low wages is intimately connected to the second policy concern, the growth in the number of female-headed households. Recent estimates are that the average adult will spend one-third of his or her years between the ages of 20 and 55 in a single-adult household (Cain, 1985). This means that women need to be better equipped with the skills and opportunities that will let them survive when they are the household's primary earner. By 1985, when almost 30 percent of all households were female-headed, labor force participation by women had gone far beyond the category of an "optional lifestyle choice"—it had become an absolute economic necessity. The poverty rates among female household heads with children in the 1980s is evidence of the need to prepare people better for the world of work and to provide opportunities for work that pays a decent wage.

Third, too many households face serious difficulties in arranging for all of the household goods and services that were once provided by women who worked only in the home. Most crucial is the need for businesses and communities to ensure that adequate child care facilities are available, especially to women who must work to support themselves and their children. This may involve subsidizing the creation and cost of child care facilities, or it may involve more generous and perhaps refundable tax credits to low-income women with small children to increase their ability to afford child care. Typically, it is the women who have the least choice about whether to work—female household heads or women in low-income two-adult families—who have the greatest difficulty in finding and affording adequate child care.

Beyond the child care issue, the ready provision of food and household maintenance is often a continuing problem for women who find themselves permanently short of time for all the things that need doing. Clair Brown (1982) suggests that the nuclear family has become a very inefficient provider of household services in modern times. Increasingly smaller families mean that individual households no longer can achieve economies of scale; as a result, many women spend precious time on work that could be more efficiently provided on a larger scale.

Finally, closely related to the issue of home production is the need to recognize fully that the revolution in women's work requires an equivalent revolution in men's behavior as well. As women put more hours into work outside the home, men must increase their contribution to household and child care tasks. Moreover, when families with children divorce, the fathers must be responsible for sharing child support and child care until their children reach adulthood.

It is also important to recognize that there are advantages for men as more women go to work. Having two earners allows many married-couple families a measure of economic security they would not otherwise have known. This may allow husbands more leisure time. It can also mean opportunities for either partner to change jobs, go back to school, or take a career risk that would not otherwise be possible.

And dual-earner couples are also in a better position than single earners to cope with one spouse's unemployment.

Many two-earner households have not yet become completely accustomed to the changed circumstances of their lives. Both women and men are still adjusting to the new opportunities, as well as to the responsibilities and expectations, that arise in a world where both women and men make significant contributions to household income. As women continue to increase their participation in the paid labor force, changes in the economic status, the behavior, and the structure of households will continue to occur.

FOUR **Women and Health Care**[1]

KAREN DAVIS

Highlights

WOMEN TODAY are living longer, healthier lives. Their mortality rates continue to decline, and—just as men are—they are improving their health habits. When anyone needs medical care, America can provide high-quality services, but in this country's uniquely market-oriented health care system, major segments of the population do not have ready access to medical attention because they lack health insurance. Lack of access affects a disproportionate share of women because women are more likely than men to be poor, older and/or out of the labor force and thus not covered by an employer's insurance plan, and in low-paying jobs that do not provide health insurance at all. The following figures highlight the status of women's health and access to health care today.

- A female born in 1985 has a life expectancy of 78 years, which is seven years longer than the life expectancy of a male born that year and five years longer than that of a female born in 1960.

- Black women are less healthy than white women. Their life expectancy at birth is five years less, and their death rates tend to be higher.

- Infant mortality rates declined from 25 deaths per 1,000 live births in 1960 to 11 deaths per 1,000 births in 1985, though black infant mortality remains double that of white infants. Deaths of mothers in childbirth or from complications of pregnancy dropped from 32 to seven per 100,000 live births between 1960 and 1984.

- Death rates for women and men from most major diseases—heart disease, stroke, pneumonia, influenza, diabetes—have dropped markedly over the last 25 years.
- Death rates from lung cancer, however, quadrupled for women and doubled for men between 1960 and 1984.
- Women tend to suffer more than men from infections and respiratory diseases and from such chronic conditions as arthritis, gallbladder conditions, and diseases of the urinary system.
- While younger men are more likely to be injured than younger women, women over age 65 are more likely than men that age to be injured in falls and to suffer from osteoporosis.
- Women are less likely than men to have life-threatening health problems, such as heart disease and emphysema.
- Smoking among women declined slightly from 1965 to 1985, but not as much as it did among men. Women and men between the ages of 20 and 24 smoke at the same rate.
- In 1985, 18 percent of all women were moderate to heavy drinkers, well below the figure of 43 percent for men. But among adolescents, the rates of drinking, at least as of 1982, were the same for boys and girls.
- Women see physicians more than men—an average of 5.8 times a year compared to 4.5 times in 1985. This difference

is largely due to the medical care requirements of childbirth.

- Women are also more likely than men to receive regular care from a physician. In 1985, 10 percent of women, but 17 percent of men, had not seen a physician for two or more years.

- Men are hospitalized more frequently than women, but women outnumber men in nursing homes by nearly a 3-to-1 ratio.

- The rate of private health insurance coverage among women and men between the ages of 18 and 64 is virtually identical—78 and 79 percent, respectively, in 1984.

- Approximately half of all unemployed persons—both women and men—lacked health insurance protection.

- About 80 percent of divorced or separated women who are out of the labor force had no health insurance in 1984. Uninsured divorced or separated women outnumbered uninsured divorced or separated men by 40 percent (1.7 million versus 1.2 million).

- Although Medicaid is an important source of health insurance for many poor women and their children, it covers less than 40 percent of all poor children.

- Over 30 percent of all poor women with incomes below the poverty level were without health insurance in 1984.

- Even though Medicare covers nearly all persons age 65 and over, plus some disabled persons, it provides little coverage for two services that women use more than men—nursing home care and long-term care.

Introduction

It is difficult these days to watch television, flip through magazines and newspapers, or wander through our nation's cities and suburbs, and not be impressed by women's avid interest in health.

The senses are assaulted by ads for health clubs, exercise equipment and clothes, and for nutritious foods and drinks. Public service messages urge regular checkups to detect breast cancer early or assure well-baby care. One can read stories almost every day about medical advances that are reducing the threat of killer diseases, or about grandmothers running marathons. And in this Olympic year, the entire country will become vividly aware of the ultimate models of physical fitness and health.

Indeed, American women are healthier. A baby girl born in 1985 can expect to live an average of 78 years (Table 4.1). That is an impressive five years longer than a baby girl born a quarter-century earlier. And although the well-publicized male-female gap in life expectancy is narrower today than it was in 1970, girls born in 1985 can expect to live an average of seven years longer than boys born that year.

Many of the major causes of mortality have decreased in both sexes since 1960, with particularly strong declines in deaths from strokes and heart disease. Significant declines have also been registered in pneumonia and influenza, diabetes, and accidents.

When it comes to seeking, or needing, the high-quality medical attention that the American health care system can provide, women visit physicians more than men, although this difference is largely related to childbirth. When it comes

Table 4.1 • LIFE EXPECTANCY AT BIRTH, 1960, 1970, 1980, AND 1985

	All Races			*White*			*Black*		
Year	*Both Sexes*	*Female*	*Male*	*Both Sexes*	*Female*	*Male*	*Both Sexes*	*Female*	*Male*
1960	69.7	73.1	66.6	70.6	74.1	67.4	63.2	65.9	60.7
1970	70.9	74.8	67.1	71.7	75.6	68.0	64.1	68.3	60.0
1980	73.7	77.4	70.0	74.4	78.1	70.7	68.1	72.5	63.8
1985	74.7	78.2	71.2	75.3	78.7	71.8	69.5	73.7	65.3

Source: National Center for Health Statistics, *Health United States 1986*, 1986, Table 12.

to inpatient care, women are not hospitalized as often as men—partly because of men's increased exposure to accidents and job-related diseases. However, mostly because of their greater longevity, women are far more likely than men to be institutionalized in old age; they are some three-fourths of the population in nursing homes.

So, overall, women (and men) are living longer and enjoying healthier lives along the way. Given the current emphasis on proper diet, exercise, and safer conditions in the workplace, as well as the constant stream of "breakthroughs" that America's medical researchers keep registering, there seems to be no major reason why this trend will not continue.

Yet there are some dark clouds hovering over this portrayal of women and health care. For while women are healthier and can get quality care when needed, if they can afford it, financial access to America's health care system is a problem for millions of people.

Unlike most industrialized nations, the United States does not have a universal health care system that guarantees financial access to medical services. Instead, in the U.S., entry into the health care marketplace depends upon health insurance coverage or sufficient income to afford needed care out of one's own pocket. The U.S. has a patchwork system of health insurance coverage through a combination of public programs and employer-provided health insurance that leaves 37 million Americans without *any* health insurance and millions more with inadequate coverage. Of those 37 million Americans, women are especially vulnerable to the market-oriented system. The most obvious reason for this is that poverty is higher among women, particularly among older women and women who head single-parent families. Women who are poor must depend on inadequate public programs, such as Medicaid and Medicare, to give them access to health care services. However, even nonpoor women are at risk. They are less likely than men to be in the labor force and thus less likely to be covered by an employer's health insurance benefits. Even a woman who is included in her husband's employee health insurance plan may find that coverage ends with divorce or separation.

Because they live longer than men, older women are at much greater risk of needing long-term care in nursing homes as their health deteriorates and they become unable to care for themselves. Those who are married tend to outlive their husbands, and, just as women who have always lived alone, widows may wind up lacking the social supports to receive care and attention at home when they lose functional capacity.

As disturbing as this picture is for women in general, it becomes more so for minority women. Black women, for example, typically have lower incomes and during their lives face even greater financial obstacles to health care services. They may have to deal with other hurdles as well, such as lack of access to medical facilities because of the neighborhoods they live in or because of cultural or discriminatory barriers.

Statistics show that black women have poorer health than white women and are less likely to receive health care on a regular and timely basis. Even so, black women's life expectancy has risen sharply since 1960, and black women outlive black men by a longer period than white women outlive white men; in 1985, the difference in life expectancies at birth between the sexes was 8.4 years for blacks, but 6.9 years for whites (Table 4.1). Data on Hispanic women are even more scarce than those for black women; however, the numbers suggest that this growing minority segment of the U.S. population is especially disadvantaged with respect to health care.

Because of all these barriers to adequate medical services, which have been demonstrated to contribute to poor health outcomes (Lurie et al., 1984; Hadley, 1982), this chapter focuses first on what is known about women's health status, their use of medical services, and their health insurance coverage. It then discusses the obstacles that deny many women access to needed health care throughout their lives; emphasis is placed on lower-income women, minority women, and older women. This chapter does not attempt to analyze some of the much broader issues that also affect the health of women, such as the training and orientation of physicians, the adequacy of biomedical and social science research on health problems of women, the availability of specialized treatment for mental health problems, alcohol and drug abuse, or nonfinancial barriers to health care.

Health Status of Women

Life Expectancy and Mortality Rates

As discussed above, both the life expectancy of women and the advantage in life expectancy that women have historically enjoyed over men continue. The difference in male-female life expectancy, while still significant, began to narrow after 1970. Will this gap shrink further as more women enter the workplace and face increased exposure to on-the-job accidents, job-related stress, and more rationalizations to smoke and drink? There is speculation that it will; however, to date, about the only suggestion of this is that women's mortality rates from lung cancer quadrupled from 1960 to 1984, a period during which the rate for men doubled.

An analysis of the causes of death show that men's death rates exceed women's rates for every major cause.[2] In fact, men's death rates for heart disease, pulmonary disease, liver disease and cirrhosis, accidents, and suicide and homicide are more than double the rates for women.

The differences are not so marked for diabetes and strokes, though men still die at a greater rate than women from those two causes. High blood pressure, which is an important factor in strokes if left untreated, is more common in men under age 65 than in women, but women over age 65 are more likely to have high blood pressure than older men. The similarities in stroke death rates may reflect that function of age.

The other major killer is violence—accidents, homicides, suicides. Rates for men are again more than double those for women, reflecting social pressures to behave recklessly, higher alcohol consumption, and more hazardous jobs and leisure activities.

Both sexes and all races have experienced general improvement in mortality rates in recent decades. From 1960 to 1984, the most notable improvements were recorded for strokes and heart disease, while significant declines were also recorded in deaths from pneumonia, diabetes, and accidents. Cited as important contributors to these developments were improved access to health care, better monitoring and treatment of high blood pressure, and advances in medical technology and treatment (Davis and Schoen, 1978).

It is disturbing, though, that little progress has been made in reducing deaths from cancer. Breast cancer and prostate cancer death rates have remained relatively stable, and only a slight decline in colorectal cancer has been realized since 1960.

One of the most important improvements in the mortality figures deal with infant mortality. Although a good number of other countries continue to record better rates than the United States, this country did cut its infant mortality rate in half between 1965 and 1985. Furthermore, maternal mortality rates from complications of pregnancy and childbirth have declined markedly in the last 25 years, probably as a result of better and earlier prenatal care.

The mortality outlook is not as bright for black women. They have higher overall death rates than white women, and, in fact, their death rates from diabetes and homicide are more than double those of white women. The diabetes discrepancy may be partially due to the tendency of more black women to become overweight, and partially to the lower likelihood of receiving regular care from a private physician. The greater likelihood that black women live in high-crime neighborhoods may account for the difference by race in homicide rates.

Differences in prenatal care probably explain two other large discrepancies between black and white women. The black infant mortality rate is double the rate for whites, and black maternal mortality continues to be more than four times the rate for whites.

In three areas, white women have the dubious distinction

of recording higher mortality rates than black women, reflecting different lifestyles and economic status. White women die at a higher rate from lung cancer; the explanation is apparently that, while current smoking rates are similar for black women and white women, white women are much more likely to be heavy smokers (25 or more cigarettes a day). White women also die more frequently in accidents and from suicide. Because white women have generally higher incomes than black women, they are more apt to have their own automobiles and to consume alcohol, which may contribute to their higher motor vehicle death rate.

Health Conditions and Behavior

Differences in daily behavior and obligations imposed by work or family may explain a great deal of the variation between the sexes in health conditions and status. For example, men are more likely to have visual or hearing impairments, and to suffer loss of limbs or paralysis—largely because of their increased exposure to work hazards and increased time spent on the nation's highways.

Men up to age 45 are more likely than women to be injured in accidents; overall, men lead riskier lives because they smoke and drink more, use illicit drugs more, drive more, and pursue hobbies or sports with high injury rates (Verbrugge, 1985). They have more exposure to occupational health and safety risks and place greater stress on their bodies through time pressures, the drive to achieve, impatience, and other tensions.

On the other hand, older women suffer more from falls and injuries than older men, probably because their smaller bone mass makes them more prone to osteoporosis. Women have higher rates than men of varicose veins, constipation, gallbladder conditions, chronic enteritis, arthritis, diseases of the urinary system, thyroid problems, anemia, migraines, corns, and bunions. The reasons for these higher rates are not fully understood, although childbearing, blood loss from menstruation, stress, diet, and styles of dress may contribute to these conditions.

Women also have more contact with young children, who may expose them to infectious diseases, and they may face added emotional distress from juggling multiple roles and responsibilities.

The sexes also show notably different patterns in personal living habits that can affect their health. One study suggests that a substantial portion of the difference in male and female mortality rates may be related to smoking (U.S. Congress, 1985). Men are more likely to be smokers. The difference by sex is not as marked, though, as it was in 1965, when 52 percent of men and 34 percent of women smoked. Since then, the smoking rate for men has dropped to 33 percent, while women have shown a modest decline to 28 percent. Smoking rates for men exceed those for women in all age groups, except among 20- to 24-year-olds where the rates are similar.

Men also tend to drink more. In 1985, 43 percent of men were listed as moderate or heavy drinkers, compared with 18 percent of women. Again, a disturbing note is found among the young: in 1982, among adolescents between the ages of 12 and 17, boys were more likely to smoke and use marijuana than girls, but girls and boys had similar rates of alcohol consumption.

Women, however, are a bit more likely to be overweight (30 percent versus 27 percent for men)—a condition that is considered an important risk factor in diabetes and heart disease. The problem of overweight varies markedly by age and race. Among those 65 and older, 26 percent of both white and black men, 37 percent of white women, and 61 percent of black women are overweight.

Health of Mothers and Children

The United States has made significant strides in one area that is of particular concern to women—infant and maternal mortality (Davis, 1986). Much of the improvement can be attributed to better nutrition, improvements in sanitation and general living conditions, and increased access to effective medical care.

Infant mortality rates, which are one of the most easily measured indicators of health status, have been decreasing steadily for several decades. In 1955, 26 infants died in the first year of life for every 1,000 babies born. By 1965, the year Medicaid became law, the infant mortality rate stood at 25 deaths per 1,000 live births. By the early 1980s, that rate had been cut in half, to 11 deaths per 1,000 births. Much of that progress parallels efforts to expand access to health care under Medicaid and to improve care under maternal and child health programs.

Despite these gains, this nation continues to display some unfortunate contrasts. As the life span of the average American increases, infants continue to die within the first year of life at inordinately high rates. Even as we develop more sophisticated medical technologies, many children fail to receive the most basic preventive care. As we debate ways to contain health care costs, millions of children and pregnant women lack adequate financial resources to purchase care.

In 1980, one birth in 20 was to a mother who received

prenatal care only after the seventh month of pregnancy—or, in some cases, no prenatal care at all. Women in low-income families are 50 percent more likely to receive late or no prenatal care than their more affluent peers. Adding to the problem is the rate of adolescent pregnancy among low-income women, because teenage mothers are less likely to get care early in pregnancy than older mothers. Also, black women are more likely to delay obtaining prenatal care than whites: in 1980, 77 percent of pregnant white women received prenatal care in their first trimester, compared to 59 percent of black women.

The result of this lack of prenatal care is a much higher proportion of low-weight babies, who in turn are at much higher risk of dying or being physically or mentally handicapped. Nearly seven percent of all babies—and 22 percent of the babies born to women who have not received prenatal care—are low birth-weight babies (less than 2,500 grams). Black mothers are twice as likely as white mothers to have low birth-weight babies. In addition to obvious health advantages of prenatal care, an Institute of Medicine (1985) report found that for every $1 invested in prenatal care for poor women, $3.40 was saved in the first year of the infant's life from reduced hospitalization costs.

These figures on lack of prenatal care are especially troubling because health care received during pregnancy and early childhood influences a child's health throughout life. Early prenatal care is essential so that such conditions as hypertension, diabetes, and iron deficiency anemia can be diagnosed early and brought under control. Without such care, premature births with physical and mental handicaps will occur frequently. Adequate medical care in the first year of an infant's life is also important to provide prompt attention for gastrointestinal, respiratory, or other disorders that can be life-threatening for a vulnerable infant, and to ensure that appropriate immunizations and other preventive services are obtained.

Throughout their childhoods, children from low-income families tend to face health problems, some of which stem from inadequate prenatal and infant care. They are more likely than nonpoor children to suffer from low weight at birth, congenital infection, iron deficiency anemia, lead poisoning, hearing and vision problems, and other conditions amenable to medical care. Poor children are also more apt to become ill, suffer adverse consequences from an illness, and die.

According to a National Health and Nutrition Examination Survey, the proportion of children found with significant abnormal conditions increases as family income decreases. Children who are poor are 75 percent more likely to be admitted to a hospital in a given year and, when admitted, stay twice as long as nonpoor children. These medical problems affect other aspects of the children's lives too. Poor children lose 40 percent more days from school, and the costs to society from greater health problems and consequent reduced productivity are significant, or, in some cases, unmeasurable. (Starfield, 1982.)

Use of Health Care Services

Because of their greater rate of health problems, particularly those related to reproduction, women see physicians more often than men do. As shown in Table 4.2, women saw physicians about 30 percent more often than men did in 1985. While such extra use of physicians is expected, it is difficult to conclude, on the basis of such physician visit data, whether women or men were more disadvantaged in access to physician services.

Table 4.2 • SELECTED HEALTH SERVICES UTILIZATION BY SEX, 1985

	Total	*Female*	*Male*
Physician Services			
Visits per capita	5.2	5.8	4.5
Source of care (percent)			
Doctor's office	57.1	57.4	56.5
Hospital outpatient dept.	14.6	12.7	17.4
Telephone	13.8	15.5	11.4
Interval since last physician visit			
Less than 1 year	74.3	79.2	70.1
1 to 2 years	10.7	9.8	11.6
2 years or more	13.1	9.7	16.7
Hospital services			
Discharge (no. per 1,000)	104.3	103.2	107.0
Days of care (no. per 1,000)	745.5	703.8	793.3
Average length of stay (days)	7.1	6.8	7.4

Source: National Center for Health Statistics, *Health United States 1986,* 1986, Tables 52, 53, 57, and 65.

Women are also less likely than men to go extensive periods of time without seeing a physician. In 1985, 10 percent of women had not seen a physician in two years or more, a much lower figure than the 17 percent for men. Since regular physician care is important to detect health problems in the early stages when they can be more effectively treated, it might be suggested that women make better use of physician services.

Men, however, spend more time in the hospital (Table 4.2). They use about 13 percent more days of care than women per 1,000 persons, and their average length of stay is longer, 7.4 days versus 6.8 days. This greater use of inpatient care in part reflects their propensity to more life-threatening diseases and their exposure to work-related accidents and other riskier events.

As the population gets older, women surpass men in needing more intensive care. Nursing home patients also tend to be women; in 1977, the latest year for which data are available, 800,000 out of a total of 1.1 million nursing home patients age 65 or older were women (73 percent). Six percent of all women age 65 and older were in nursing homes; this was twice the rate for men that age. Because nursing home patients also use hospital services, women in this age group are higher users of hospital care than men of this age.

Differences in Health Status by Sex

As is evident, a variety of factors—some over which individuals have control, and many over which they do not—contribute to the differences seen between men and women in the mortality and morbidity rates. Biological differences play a part, particularly women's role in childbearing, and the attendant use of, or lack of, prenatal and infant care. There are the differences in "good" and "bad" health behavior. And one of the most significant factors is the lack of access to health care services, especially among poor and many minority women. Verbrugge (1985) has summarized the research findings on the causes of male-female differences in mortality and morbidity:

- Biological risks

  Women's sex hormones provide a buffer against cardiovascular disease.

Men are at less risk of osteoporosis, in part because of their greater bone mass.

Reproductive conditions account for a substantial portion of women's excess morbidity at ages 17 to 44.

- Acquired risks

  Women are at higher risk of common respiratory infections because of their closer contact with children.

  Men's higher lifetime intake of tobacco and alcohol are major factors in excess mortality and morbidity from cardiovascular diseases and cirrhosis of the liver.

  Women tend to have better social supports than men, which may lead them to cope better with stress and major illness.

- Psychosocial aspects of symptoms and care

  Women and men with comparable health problems and work roles seek out medical care and restrict their activities at the same pace. Men do not delay more than women in seeking care.

  Women are more likely to have a regular source of medical care; however, women face greater financial barriers to obtaining that medical attention.

- Health reporting behavior

  Research is inconclusive about whether women are more willing to report health problems or to remember them when asked.

- Prior health care and caretakers as causes

  No evidence exists on whether women's greater use of health care services for less serious, acute, and chronic health conditions helps reduce longer-term illness and serious disability.

Limited evidence suggests that physicians have different images of men and women patients, but the implications of this for health are not clear.

Insurance Coverage

One of the primary reasons for the general improvement in the health status of American women, in addition to increased efforts by women themselves to improve their physical well-being, is this country's strong medical research community and health delivery system that can provide first-rate care when it is sought or needed. America's health care professionals have great capacity not only to treat and cure existing health conditions, but also to prevent the development of other serious problems—for most people, much of the time. But, as noted, this is not true for all. And, for many, care is not obtained nearly as often as it is needed.

Unlike the situation in most industrialized countries, the United States has a market-oriented health care system, and access to it is based on insurance coverage. Traditionally, private payments and plans have provided the insurance coverage, and the growth in protection has been fueled in recent decades by increases in employer-provided coverage of workers. Since the 1960s, private plans have been supplemented by some government programs, mainly Medicare and Medicaid, that have been developed to meet obvious needs for better access to health care. The principal beneficiaries of these government programs have been (1) older Americans, whose declining incomes and loss of employer-provided insurance make them vulnerable to the major health care costs associated with growing old, and (2) the poor, who simply cannot pay the health care costs which are rising faster than the cost of living.

Clearly, the major deterrent to needed medical services for many Americans, both men and women, is lack of health insurance coverage (Davis and Rowland, 1983). As pointed out earlier in this chapter, it is estimated that at least 37 million persons, or approximately one in six Americans, lack any health insurance, and millions more have inadequate coverage. In one recent study, 13 million Americans reported that they did not obtain needed medical care because they could not afford it, and one million reported being turned away for financial reasons when they attempted to obtain treatment (Freeman et al., 1987). It is the women of this country who suffer disproportionately from this lack of access to medical care. Why is this so?

Private Health Insurance

In the United States, health insurance coverage is tied to the workplace. Most workers obtain group health insurance coverage through their employers. Typically, employers pay all or a substantial portion of the premiums for employees' health insurance, and most employer plans also cover dependents. While the employer is less likely to pick up the cost of coverage for dependents (Taylor and Lawson, 1981), many workers at least have a reasonable option of providing protection for their families.

The extent of employer-provided health plans, though, varies by size and type of business. Health insurance coverage is more common in larger firms and in certain industries such as manufacturing. Coverage is less typical in smaller firms and in industries such as agriculture, service, or retail trade (Davis, 1987).

All these patterns of private medical protection have major implications for women, for example:

- Women are less likely than men to be in the workforce and, therefore, less likely to have health insurance coverage paid for by an employer. In 1985, only 65 percent of women ages 18 to 64 were in the labor force, compared to 88 percent of men in that age range (Bureau of the Labor Statistics, 1986).
- Women who are married are more likely than single women to be covered, since dependents are typically, though not consistently, protected under employer plans. (If employed, married women may also have their own employer-sponsored coverage.) This means that divorced or separated women may not be insured unless they are working (Berk and Taylor, 1984).
- Women tend to be in less well-paying jobs with lower rates of insurance coverage than in higher-paying ones. Employment in part-time or temporary jobs where coverage rates are low is also more common among women than among men. Offsetting these factors is the continued high concentration of women in nursing, teaching, and secretarial positions that are more likely to provide health insurance coverage, while such male-dominated jobs as agriculture and construction are less likely to have it.

Table 4.3 illustrates how important a woman's work and marital status are in determining her health insurance coverage. Overall, there was virtually no difference in the percentage of 18- to 64-year-old women and men who were covered by private medical plans in 1984—78 and 79 percent respectively. Among the unemployed, however, where coverage rates are lowest, 52 percent of women and 44 percent of men had private health insurance plans; the higher rate for women was largely a consequence of marriage. Among those not in the labor force, 68 percent of women and 54 percent of men had some medical coverage; these persons may have been included in a spouse's plan, a parent's plan if they were still in school, or a plan they purchased themselves.

Table 4.3 • HEALTH INSURANCE COVERAGE OF PERSONS BY AGE, SEX, LABOR FORCE PARTICIPATION, AND MARITAL STATUS, 1984 (in percentages)

	Marital Status				
Labor Force Participation	*Total*	*Married*	*Widowed*	*Divorced/ Separated*	*Never Married*
Total	78.9	85.0	68.8	62.0	68.5
Employed	85.9	89.8	84.8	77.1	77.7
Unemployed	47.8	59.6	49.8	23.6	39.9
Not in labor force	64.4	74.8	52.5	19.6	49.2
Females, total	78.4	85.1	63.8	59.7	68.7
Employed	86.7	90.8	85.5	77.0	81.0
Unemployed	51.7	69.3	46.5	24.1	38.2
Not in labor force	67.9	78.4	53.3	17.5	45.0
Males, total	79.4	83.1	69.0	66.2	68.3
Employed	85.3	89.2	81.8	77.3	75.2
Unemployed	44.2	50.4	63.8	22.8	41.1
Not in labor force	53.5	57.8	45.6	26.0	53.8

Source: Estimates based on the National Center for Health Statistics Health Interview Survey, 1984.

At first glance, these figures may not seem to place women at that much of a disadvantage in health insurance coverage, as the rates are fairly similar for several categories of men and women, and in some cases favor women. But there are major discrepancies in coverage. For example, the lowest rate of private health insurance protection was found among divorced or separated women not in the labor force (18 percent). In absolute numbers, this translated into 40 percent more divorced or separated women than men (1.7 million versus 1.2 million) without health insurance coverage (estimates from the National Center for Health Statistics [NCHS] Health Interview Survey, 1984).

These rates may improve because of the enactment of the Consolidated Omnibus Budget Reconciliation Act of 1985, which permits divorced or separated women to continue their coverage by paying the health insurance premium plus a two percent administrative charge.

Insurance Coverage, Income, and Race

As expected, the absence of health insurance coverage is concentrated among persons least able to afford medical care. Table 4.4 shows that among those ages 18 to 64, 31 percent of women and 39 percent of men with incomes below the federal poverty level in 1984 were uninsured by any program, private or public.

Private health insurance covers only a fraction of low-income persons. Only 41 percent of all people between the ages of 18 and 64 with incomes below the federal poverty level had some private health insurance in 1984; women were less apt than men to be covered (only 38 percent versus 44 percent, respectively). If Medicare and Medicaid are included, another 31 percent of women and 17 percent of men below the poverty line had some insurance coverage. But since poor women outnumber poor men, in absolute terms there were more uninsured poor women: 3.5 million versus 3.2 million

Table 4.4 • HEALTH INSURANCE COVERAGE OF PERSONS BY SEX AND INCOME LEVEL, 1984 (in percentages)

	Type of Insurance				
Income Level	*Total Insured*	*Medicare*	*Medicaid*	*Private Others*	*Uninsured*
Total	85.1	1.7	4.5	78.9	14.9
Below poverty level	66.0	3.3	22.0	40.6	34.0
100 to 149% of poverty level	72.1	3.6	6.8	61.7	27.9
150 to 199% of poverty level	79.8	2.3	2.6	74.8	20.2
200% or more of poverty level	91.8	1.0	0.9	89.9	8.2
Female					
Below poverty level	69.3	2.4	28.9	38.0	30.7
100 to 149% of poverty level	74.8	2.6	9.4	62.9	25.2
150 to 199% of poverty level	82.1	1.4	3.7	77.0	17.9
200% or more of poverty level	92.7	0.8	1.2	90.8	7.3
Male					
Below poverty level	61.4	4.6	12.7	44.2	38.6
100 to 149% of poverty level	69.0	4.8	3.8	60.4	31.0
150 to 199% of poverty level	77.2	3.4	1.4	72.4	22.8
200% or more of poverty level	90.8	1.1	0.6	89.1	9.2

Source: Estimates based on the National Center for Health Statistics Health Interview Survey, 1984.

(estimates from the NCHS Health Interview Survey, 1984).

These gaps in health insurance are a particular problem for blacks. As can be seen in Table 4.5, 19 percent of black women and 26 percent of black men ages 18 to 64 had no

Table 4.5 • HEALTH INSURANCE COVERAGE OF PERSONS BY AGE, SEX, AND RACE, 1984 (in percentages)

	Type of Insurance				
Race and Sex	*Total Insured*	*Medicare*	*Medicaid*	*Private Others*	*Uninsured*
White					
Females, 18 to 64	87.1	1.2	4.5	81.4	12.9
18 to 29	81.4	0.2	6.9	74.3	18.6
30 to 44	89.4	0.5	4.0	84.8	10.6
45 to 64	90.6	3.0	2.7	85.0	9.4
Males, 18 to 64	85.3	2.0	1.8	81.5	14.7
18 to 29	76.7	0.4	2.5	73.9	23.3
30 to 44	87.9	0.9	1.6	85.4	12.1
45 to 64	91.7	4.9	1.3	85.4	8.3
Black					
Females, 18 to 64	80.8	2.0	19.4	59.4	19.2
18 to 29	77.1	0.6	25.2	51.3	22.9
30 to 44	85.3	0.6	18.5	66.1	14.7
45 to 64	80.6	5.6	12.3	62.7	19.4
Males, 18 to 64	73.8	3.2	5.9	64.7	26.2
18 to 29	64.5	1.1	7.6	55.8	35.5
30 to 44	78.0	2.4	4.0	71.6	22.0
45 to 64	83.5	7.8	5.7	70.0	16.5

Source: Estimates based on the National Center for Health Statistics Health Interview Survey, 1984.

health insurance coverage at all in 1984 (the comparable figures for whites were 13 percent for women and 15 percent for men). These uninsured women tend to be low income, and not employed in full-time jobs. An even greater disparity is seen among women 45 to 64 years old, where black women were twice as likely to be uninsured as white women (19 percent versus nine percent). These lower rates of insurance coverage among blacks in general are primarily a reflection of their lower incomes, but they are also partially attributable to the fact that blacks work in jobs less likely to offer health insurance coverage.

Black women between the ages of 18 and 64 are far less likely than white women to have private health insurance plans—59 versus 81 percent in 1984. (The coverage of black men is also low relative to that of white men.) As one result, 19 percent of black women were eligible for Medicaid, compared with just under five percent of white women. Differences in coverage between black and white women are a direct reflection of the poverty rates among women; 31 percent of black women ages 18 to 64 were poor in 1984, compared to 11 percent of white women (Bureau of the Census, August 1985).

Medicaid

A major effort to help close some of the gaps in health insurance coverage for Americans with low incomes has been made by Medicaid, the federal-state program that finances health care services for certain low-income individuals and families.

Medicaid has been particularly vital to women because the program is oriented toward single-parent families, and women are more likely than men to be poor heads of families. Indeed, 75 percent of all adult Medicaid beneficiaries are women. Medicaid covers individuals receiving cash assistance from the Aid to Families with Dependent Children (AFDC) program. AFDC is largely restricted to single-parent households headed by women, although some states provide coverage to families with an unemployed father in the home. Children in a poor two-parent family may be included under special provisions, but parents would not be eligible for Medicaid (Health Care Financing Administration, 1986).

Medicaid's coverage for women varies with age. Table 4.6 reveals that in 1984, 10 percent of younger women (ages 18 to 29) were covered by Medicaid. In midlife, however, Medicaid does not provide as much assistance to women (Swartz and Moon, 1986; ICF, Inc., 1986). Poor women no longer qualify for Medicaid when their children are grown, and even destitute single persons or couples without children would not receive health benefits under Medicaid unless they were disabled. As a result, just four percent of women between the ages of 45 and 64 were covered by Medicaid in 1984, which was still twice the figure for men in that age range.

Table 4.6 • HEALTH INSURANCE COVERAGE OF PERSONS BY AGE AND SEX, 1984 (in percentages)

	Type of Insurance				
Age and Sex	*Total Insured*	*Medicare*	*Medicaid*	*Private Others*	*Uninsured*
Total, 18 to 64	85.1	1.7	4.5	78.9	14.9
18 to 29	77.9	0.4	6.5	71.1	22.1
30 to 44	87.7	0.8	4.0	82.9	12.3
45 to 64	90.1	4.1	2.8	83.1	9.9
Female, 18 to 64	86.2	1.3	6.5	78.4	13.8
18 to 29	80.7	0.3	9.6	70.8	19.3
30 to 44	88.7	0.5	5.9	82.3	11.3
45 to 64	89.4	3.2	3.8	82.4	10.6
Male, 18 to 64	83.9	2.1	2.4	79.4	16.1
18 to 29	75.1	0.5	3.3	71.3	24.9
30 to 44	86.7	1.1	2.0	83.6	13.3
45 to 64	90.8	5.2	1.8	83.8	9.2

Source: Estimates based on the National Center for Health Statistics Health Interview Survey, 1984.

Among the disabled covered by Medicaid, men are more likely to be the recipients; but among Medicaid-covered elderly, women predominate because they are more likely to be poor and they live longer.

But perhaps Medicaid's main accomplishment has been in improving access to care for millions of poor and near-poor mothers and children. In 1982, 800,000 pregnant women and eight million children received health care under Medicaid. The program has also given the poor access to early prenatal care. In 1963, before Medicaid was enacted, only 58 percent of poor women obtained such care; by 1970, 71 percent were receiving it. Despite these improvements, Medicaid still covers less than 40 percent of children in poverty, leaving nearly six million children in families with incomes below the poverty level without Medicaid protection. Two million of these poor children live in families with incomes below 50 percent of the poverty level.

These gaps in coverage occur largely because states are not required to provide Medicaid to children living in two-parent families, and because state income standards for program eligibility are generally far below the federal poverty level. Currently, only 12 states have AFDC income eligibility cutoff limits for Medicaid greater than 60 percent of the federal poverty level; 20 states have income requirement levels between 40 and 60 percent of poverty; the remainder of the states have income eligibility cutoffs below 40 percent of the federal poverty level (Health Care Financing Adminstration, 1986).

Furthermore, several policy changes in the 1980s have served to widen the gaps in health care coverage, rather than close them. Nearly a million poor children and pregnant women have lost Medicaid through cutbacks in federal financing for Medicaid in 1981 and through reduced coverage of the poor under AFDC (Rowland et al., 1988). These cutbacks in federal support were particularly ill-timed because of the rapid rise in poverty among children during the early 1980s.

Congress has moved to reverse this trend by expanding Medicaid coverage for poor children and pregnant women. A key step consisted of provisions in the Deficit Reduction Act of 1984 and the Consolidated Omnibus Budget Reconciliation Act of 1985 to mandate coverage of pregnant women, infants, and children up to the age of five in families with incomes below state income standards. Under these provisions, no longer will pregnant women or young children with incomes below state income eligibility levels be denied coverage because both parents are in the home or because the family does not receive welfare.

Another step was taken in the 1986 budget reconciliation law, which (1) permits states to expand Medicaid coverage to all children under age five, pregnant women, and the elderly and disabled with incomes up to the federal poverty level but (2) does not require expanding coverage for welfare income assistance. By the end of 1987, more than 20 states had taken advantage of this option to cover at least certain groups of low-income pregnant women and children.

As the battles continue over what Medicaid will cover, it might be instructive to look at what may be the best single measure of the extent to which Medicaid has improved the poor's access to medical care—utilization of physician services. How much has Medicaid improved the probability that the poor will see physicians as frequently as the average American with similar health problems? As a matter of record, dramatic gains have been registered over the past 20 years.

In 1964, the nonpoor saw physicians an average of 4.8 times per year, while the poor visited physicians only 3.9 times, in spite of the fact that they were sicker and needed more health care. But by 1977 this situation had been radically altered. The poor who had insurance, notably Medicaid, were seeing physicians 4.2 times per year, compared to 3.8 visits per year for the nonpoor (Davis and Rowland, 1983). However, the uninsured poor still lagged considerably behind, at 2.3 visits per year. Uninsured minorities, who made only 1.5 visits per year, clearly fared even worse.

Medicare

The other major government program to fill in the gaps in health insurance, and thus access to health care, is Medicare, enacted in 1965 to provide health insurance to the aged. Medicare covers all those age 65 and older who are eligible for Social Security or railroad retirement insurance, plus persons with end-stage renal disease and persons permanently and totally disabled for two years or more. Coverage for hospital benefits is automatic for eligible persons, but that for physician and ambulatory benefits is voluntary, with recipients who elect such coverage under Medicare Part B paying a premium amounting to 25 percent of the estimated program costs for older enrollees.

In practice, 95 percent of both men and women age 65 and over are covered by Medicare, leaving very few elderly without health insurance. Because they do not encounter as many life-threatening situations, women between the ages of 45 and 64 are less likely than men in the same age group to be covered under Medicare's disability provisions (three percent of women versus five percent of men). However, since more than half of Medicare's 30 million beneficiaries are women (17 million), the program clearly is important in helping older women pay their medical bills.

Health Care for Older Women

Despite the attempts to narrow the gaps in health insurance coverage, serious problems remain, as we have seen, concerning poor women and many minority women. An even larger set of problems faces many of America's women who are elderly, particularly those who are now alone, whose incomes cannot cover any major, unexpected bills, and who might need long-term care in nursing homes. (Because Medicare covers virtually no nursing home care, and Medicaid is available to people only after they have become impoverished, elderly women are very vulnerable to the problems of getting access to needed health care.)

Health Care Expenses of the Elderly

In 1984, a total of $120 billion was spent in the United States on personal health care services to the elderly. About two-thirds of that, $81 billion, was picked up by Medicare, Medicaid, and other public programs, while the remainder were private expenditures, including $30 billion in direct, out-of-pocket payments and $9 billion in private insurance payments (U.S. Congress, 1987).

On a per capita basis, that amounted to $4,200 per elderly person in 1984. Medicare paid just under half of this amount ($2,050); Medicaid contributed 13 percent ($540); the elderly paid one-fourth of the total through out-of-pocket expenditures ($1,060); and the remaining $550 was absorbed by other public and private programs. Obviously, these sums represent large portions both of the incomes of many elderly persons and the budgets of federal and state governments. On average, elderly persons devoted 15 percent of their incomes to health care expenses in 1984, up from 12 percent in 1977.

The source of financing depends on the type of health care delivered. Public programs pay 89 percent of the hospital expenses of the elderly and 60 percent of physician expenses, but only 48 percent of nursing home expenses. Private health insurance pays for eight percent of the elderly's hospital expenses and 14 percent of physician expenses, but only one percent of nursing home expenses.

About half of the elderly persons in nursing homes in 1985 were covered by Medicaid, and still others will exhaust their financial resources and eventually become eligible for Medicaid. Such figures are certainly not encouraging, but those in the half not covered by Medicaid may face another devastating possibility. Their private, out-of-pocket expenses came to about $20,000 per person in 1984—a figure that can easily impoverish spouses, usually wives, living at home. For the frail elderly who will require years of nursing home care at the end of their lives, the financial hardship can be catastrophic for both the sick while they live and for those they leave behind.

Of course, the elderly not in nursing homes can incur substantial private expenses too. The hospital deductible for Medicare increased from $204 in 1981 to $540 in 1988. If their hospital stays are lengthy, the elderly can exhaust their Medicare benefits. As of 1988, the elderly are required to pay one-fourth of the deductible, or $135, for each day between the 61st and 90th day of care in a given episode of illness, and $270 for each day of care in a 90-day lifetime reserve. Once these days of hospital care are exhausted, the elderly must pay all of their hospital expenses.

Even if the elderly do not have inpatient expenses, they may have to pay expensive physician charges. The elderly pay the first $75 of physician bills during the year, 20 percent of Medicare-allowed physician fees above that deductible amount, and the excess of all charges that physicians make above the Medicare allowable fee. These charges can quickly become a major burden. For physician coverage, the elderly must pay a premium of $24.80 per month in 1988, up from $11 in 1981.

Finally, excluded from Medicare coverage are many items that the elderly frequently need—prescription drugs, dental care, eyeglasses, hearing aids, and many other services. Here again the costs can quickly become formidable.

Facing such potentially ruinous financial situations, some elderly persons purchase private health insurance to supplement Medicare. However, few so-called "Medigap" insurance policies pick up physician charges in excess of Medicare's allowable fees. In addition, such supplementary policies can be extremely expensive, providing few benefits in exchange for hefty premiums.

As currently constructed, Medicare payments concentrate on the sickest elderly. About six percent of Medicare's aged beneficiaries account for 61 percent of all Medicare reimbursements for the aged. At the other end of the spectrum, about 40 percent of those eligible for Medicare do not receive any reimbursement from Medicare, and another 36 percent incur less than $500 in Medicare-reimbursed services.

Poverty and the Elderly

Although the poverty rates among the elderly have declined in recent years through improved Social Security benefits, the popular image of the elderly as uniformly prosperous and able to meet most of these types of medical expenses is false. In 1984, Social Security benefits lifted approximately 9.5 million older persons out of poverty, reducing the poverty rate among the aged from 47.6 percent to 12.4 percent (U.S. Congress, 1987). But many of those elderly were barely lifted out of poverty and hovered in the near-poor ranks, where noncovered health expenses remained a major problem.

Poverty among the elderly varies considerably by race and living arrangement. Nearly 36 percent of all black elderly women were poor in 1986, compared to 13 percent of elderly white women (Bureau of the Census, July 1987). Of elderly persons living alone, most of whom are women, 19 percent are poor, compared to just four percent of elderly couples (Commonwealth Fund Commission, 1987a).

Medicaid and the Poor Elderly

Although many view Medicaid as designed for low-income mothers with children, it is essential to the well-being of older poor Americans. It is, in fact, largely a program for the old and disabled, with more than 40 percent of Medicaid expenditures going for acute and long-term care services provided to the elderly, and another 30 percent going to assist disabled persons.

Medicaid supplies important supplementary coverage to Medicare for 3.2 million older persons. For the elderly poor on Medicare, Medicaid pays the cost-sharing requirements and premiums and provides coverage for additional services, most notably prescription drugs, dental care, and nursing home services. For the elderly poor not entitled to Social Security, Medicaid provides full health care coverage.

Most states cover all elderly poor persons receiving federal income assistance from the Supplemental Security Income

(SSI) program. However, eligibility for Medicaid is determined in part by state rules, and states differ greatly in their coverage of the poor and near-poor elderly. Eleven states cover virtually all of the aged poor and some near poor.

Out-of-pocket medical expenses are a particular burden for the elderly who do not have supplemental coverage to Medicare, either from Medicaid or private health insurance. Although 66 percent of the elderly have private health insurance in addition to Medicare, this coverage varies widely by income: 78 percent of the high-income elderly, but only 47 percent of the poor and near-poor aged, have such private protection. Even persons with supplemental plans can encounter burdensome medical expenses if they are seriously ill. Of the elderly of all income levels who ran up health care bills exceeding $2,500 in 1977, those with Medicare coverage alone spent 37 percent of their income on health care, those with both Medicare and Medicaid spent nine percent, and those with Medicare and private insurance spent 18 percent.

As burdensome as the situation was for the elderly in general, things were much worse for poor and near-poor elderly households. Of the households that spent $2,500 or more on health care in 1977, those with Medicare coverage alone spent more than half (53 percent) of their total incomes on out-of-pocket health care expenses; those with Medicare and Medicaid spent 10 percent, and those with Medicare and private health insurance spent 30 percent. Since these figures are based on persons living at home, even greater hardships would be seen for any households that also have the financial burden of nursing home care for elderly persons not eligible for Medicaid.

Access to Health Care

Even when covered by Medicare, some of the elderly poor and near poor are deterred from obtaining health care by the significant deductible and coinsurance provisions of the program (Commonwealth Fund Commission, 1987b). A study by the National Center for Health Services Research reported that the poor and near-poor elderly who have only Medicare coverage average but 4.2 physician visits per year, well under the seven visits per year by the elderly with both Medicare and Medicaid protection and the 6.5 visits annually by those with Medicare and private health insurance (Wilensky and Berk, 1983).

The study also found similar differences in the use of prescription drugs and hospital care. Those poor and near-poor elderly with Medicare alone averaged 8.7 prescriptions per year, those with both Medicare and Medicaid coverage averaged 15 prescriptions annually, and those with Medicare and private health insurance averaged 12 prescriptions. When it came to hospitalization, 18 percent of those with Medicare alone were hospitalized, while the figure was 22 percent among those who had either Medicaid or private health insurance to supplement Medicare.

These marked differences in utilization of health care services cannot be attributed to better health status. Indeed, the poor and near-poor elderly are much sicker than other elderly. Death rates are 50 percent higher for persons covered by both Medicare and Medicaid than for other Medicare beneficiaries. Even excluding the medically needy who may qualify for Medicaid because of a serious illness, death rates are 20 percent higher for cash assistance recipients than for other Medicare beneficiaries.

Elderly Persons Living Alone

Aside from any obstacles they confront in gaining access to the health care system, the elderly face a problem even if they only need some help and support in their home or community instead of inpatient or physician care. The absence of adequate home and community-based long-term care services is a major problem for such elderly persons. Although Medicaid has expanded coverage for some poor elderly in recent years, most aged Americans do not have public or private health insurance coverage to finance such support services—even if they could cope with the confusion and frustration that often accompanies efforts to discover, and buy, them. These barriers to long-term care services are obviously greater for the growing number of elderly living alone. In 1984, 30 percent of all elderly, about eight million persons, lived alone, up from 27 percent in 1970 (Harris, 1987). Members of this population are more likely to be women, very old, and poor.

Without any support services, the only alternative for many elderly living alone is institutionalization once their physical or mental decline limits their ability to shop, prepare their own meals, dress, bathe, remember to take their medications, pay their bills, or perform such basic, but vital, functions as turning off the stove. This specter of institutionalization presents a much higher risk to women—not because they are more limited than their male counterparts in taking care of themselves, but because they have no one at hand to help them cope with basic household tasks. Twenty-five percent of elderly persons living alone have no surviving children, while another 20 percent do not have a child within an hour's driving distance (Harris, 1987). The families who do have elderly parents may worry about them and may phone or check on them regularly, but they may also live too far away to provide physical assistance.

The recent changes in Medicare that encourage hospitals to discharge patients earlier may adversely affect elderly persons living alone. Walking up a flight of stairs or preparing a meal can be painful or virtually impossible for a frail person who has recently undergone surgery.

Somehow, somewhere, policymakers must develop more humane solutions for the needs of elderly persons living alone.

Health Policy Agenda

The gaps and inadequacies in access to health services and long-term care cry out for change and reform. The nation could well take a number of steps to assure that men and women of all ages have the health care needed to lead enjoyable, long lives. These steps could include:

- Mandating health insurance coverage of workers and their families under employer plans. Comprehensive coverage of prenatal, delivery, and infant care should be included in employer health insurance plans.

- Raising eligibility for Medicaid to the poverty level for anyone not in the workplace, and permitting uninsured persons above the poverty level to purchase Medicaid coverage on a sliding scale basis.

- Expanding Medicare's acute care benefits to include catastrophic expenses and prescription drugs.

- Adding long-term care coverage as a Medicare benefit.

Improvements for the Working Population

Nearly all of the 37 million Americans without any health insurance coverage are age 65 or younger. A majority of them are in families with a working member, but they do not receive health insurance coverage through that employer. Another 10 million do not receive adequate protection against catastrophic expenses.

The most important step that could be taken to assure minimum protection for these uninsured workers would be to require employers to provide minimum health insurance coverage to all workers and their dependents. Senator Edward M. Kennedy (D-Massachusetts) and others in Congress have introduced a bill calling for such mandatory coverage. The bill (which was approved by the Senate Labor and Human Resources Committee in February 1988) includes provisions for:

- Coverage of workers employed 17.5 hours or more per week and their dependents, with employers paying at least 80 percent of the premiums.
- Extension of protection for a period of time after a worker terminates employment, with employers continuing to pay their share of the premium. A benefits package that covers, at a minimum, inpatient hospital services, physician and other ambulatory services, and preventive care (including complete prenatal, delivery, and total infant care without cost-sharing), home health care, and limited mental health care.
- Maximum cost-sharing of $2,500 per family or $1,250 for an individual, plus maximum deductibles of $500 and coinsurance of 25 percent.

- Choice of federally qualified health maintenance organizations (HMOs) and preferred provider organizations (PPOs), where available.

While the specifics of this plan could be altered, the basic approach of building an employer-based private health insurance coverage is a sound option. It would go a long way toward reducing the ranks of the uninsured. It would provide health insurance to an estimated 22 million persons, dropping the number of uninsured from 37 million to 15 million. Given the current large federal deficit, it is highly unlikely that Congress will enact a totally public plan of health insurance coverage that would require transferring to the public sector the current $120 billion spent by employers on health insurance for their workers.

Expanding Medicaid Coverage

Enactment of such a mandatory employer-provided health insurance program would still leave many low-income people uninsured. One tactic to reduce those numbers would be to include more of the poor under Medicaid. Actually, Congress has slowly been expanding coverage under Medicaid, beginning with poor children, pregnant women, the elderly, and the disabled. The following still needs to be done:

- Provide automatic coverage of all individuals living under the poverty level.

- Provide optional purchase of Medicaid on a sliding-scale premium to all low-income persons not protected under an employer plan.

- Expand Medicaid to cover (in addition to the current mandatory benefits) prescription drugs without arbitrary limits on amount, duration, or scope of benefits. Include modest cost-sharing provisions for individuals who are purchasing coverage with a sliding-scale premium.

These expansions in Medicaid would cover seven million of the approximately 15 million persons with incomes below the federal poverty level who are uninsured. Another three million persons with incomes between the poverty level and twice the poverty level would become eligible to purchase Medicaid coverage. The approximately five million remaining uninsured persons, with incomes twice the poverty level, could purchase Medicaid by paying the full actuarial fair premium.

Catastrophic Health Insurance

As of early 1988, the most immediate change needed in Medicare is adding adequate catastrophic protection, because the elderly and disabled lack sufficient protection from the financial hardship that serious illnesses can bring. Of the $4,200 spent in 1984 on health care for the average person age 65 or older, Medicare paid less than half. Persons who encounter multiple hospital stays and ongoing chronic health problems face very serious financial burdens stemming from Medicare's cost-sharing requirements and noncovered services.

A catastrophic-coverage provision in Medicare would include a ceiling on out-of-pocket expenses for the elderly and disabled, and improvements in the acute care benefits covered by the program. Such a proposal has been put forth by President Reagan, and expanded versions passed both the Senate and House in 1987. As this chapter is being written, enactment by Congress in 1988 seems likely but by no means certain. [The bill was passed in June.-*Ed.*]

The catastrophic provisions in the proposed legislation would be financed from premiums paid by the elderly, according to their income. Unlike the current Medicare structure, general tax financing would not be used to pay for the expanded benefits. As a result, none of the cost would fall on the working population. In addition, for the first time the elderly with higher incomes would be asked to contribute a larger premium. This has the advantage of expanding the revenue base of Medicare while avoiding the burdens that an increased premium could pose for many poor, near-poor, and modest-income older persons.

Long-term Care

Perhaps the most difficult issue facing health policy officials—an issue of particular concern to women—is how to finance long-term care. The current system is clearly inadequate and undesirable.

In order to qualify for assistance with nursing home bills, a person must become impoverished and then qualify for Medicaid. This robs many elderly of their dignity and sense of accomplishment achieved over their lifetimes. Yet there are few alternatives available for people who can no longer care for themselves, particularly if they lack family to help them. Formal support services in the home or community usually do not exist, and, even if they are available, the finances to obtain them usually are not there.

Home health care will become a pressing long-term care need. In the absence of home health services, a nursing home may be the only alternative for many elderly people, particularly those who live alone. Home health care can allow an elderly person to remain at home through the provision of skilled nursing, therapy, and personal care and homemaker services.

Medicare is not currently meeting this pressing need. While Medicare provides post-acute care services, there is a gap in the provision of long-term care services under Medicare to the chronically ill and functionally impaired. Even the adequacy of Medicare's post-acute care is under scrutiny as hospitals restrict lengths of stay and Medicare's nursing home use is tightened. In the light of these cutbacks and an increasing need for home health care, reforms to the Medicare post-acute home care benefit are necessary to provide a broader array of comprehensive and coordinated services. Further, home health services need to be considered as an integral part of long-term care. The addition of a long-term care benefit to Medicare would enable many elderly people to avoid institutionalization and to remain in their own homes.

The lack of revenue to finance expanded long-term care coverage under Medicare is a serious obstacle. But whatever the financial mechanism is, an adequate long-term care plan that covers home, community, and institutional services should be an important component of future health and long-term care policy.

Conclusion

The men and women of this country are continuing to see improvements in their life expectancy, and are enjoying better health while doing so, but there is clearly room—and opportunity—for improvement. A country as prosperous and ingenious as this one is should not tolerate the great disparities that exist between men and women, between the poor and the nonpoor, and between whites and minorities in something so vital and basic as health care.

Of course, efforts to improve individuals' health should start with the individuals. More citizens need to become aware of ways to prevent illnesses, to lead healthier lifestyles, to maintain and improve their health. The nation must get more serious about combating abuses of harmful substances, including tobacco, alcohol, and illegal drugs. More attention must be placed on workplace safety and mental health and stress, caused in part by a faster-paced, more complex economy that puts multiple and competing demands on women as well as on men.

In addition to what people can do for themselves, major efforts must be mounted to close the gaps in health care insurance coverage that block, or limit, access to needed health services for millions of Americans, a majority of whom are women. Such efforts would also lift the financial burdens that our market-driven health care system can impose on millions more who suffer from a serious illness or injury, or the deterioration that accompanies the aging process.

Starting with adequate health care for pregnant women, to assure that babies get a healthy beginning, and continuing through the long-term care needs of millions of elderly, access to quality health care must be a cornerstone of national policy. This nation can do no less if it really wants to provide all citizens with the opportunity to fulfill their potential and live their lives in dignity.

Women in Brief

The Critical Moment: The Educational Status of Black Women

MARGARET B. WILKERSON

"LIFTING AS WE CLIMB." "Up from slavery." "A mind is a terrible thing to waste." These statements reflect the faith that black Americans have placed historically in education. Education has been a traditional value in black communities and has been viewed as the major means of attainment and mobility in this society. For much of the twentieth century, steady (though often slow) progress has been made in broadening educational opportunity. But the 1980s have brought a severe erosion and, in some instances, a reversal of the gains made in recent decades, and the educational status of black women should be viewed within this context. The deadly combination of high poverty levels, unemployment, and cutbacks in social programs—including reduced funding for education—during the Reagan years has devastated the progress of blacks in education. The educational status of the black woman cannot be discussed apart from these contextual issues that affect her community as well as her own opportunities and aspirations.

This article is based on available data, resources that have become more scarce in recent years because states are no longer keeping records on minorities as comprehensively as they did at the beginning of this decade. The American Council on Education's Office of Minority Concerns recently reported that only 26 states responded to its questionnaire surveying the status of minorities. Due to cuts in staffing, federal agencies which collect data are no longer as responsive as they were even five or six years ago. The National Research Council's Survey of Earned Doctorates form omitted race and ethnicity data for 1985, making it impossible to compare that year with other years for doctorates conferred on minorities. The disaggregation of data according to racial/ethnic and sex characteristics seems a luxury of a bygone era, as the status of women of color gets buried within the limited data available on racial and ethnic groups. Thus, where specific data on black women are not available, statistics on blacks in general are used.

A review of the data reveals that the educational trends for black women are quite similar to those for black men, although in most instances, the trends for black men are even more distressing. For purposes of illustration, this article will occasionally compare the two groups. However, the most important comparisons are between black women and men and their white counterparts. These comparisons, especially with white males who experience the least amount of discrimination, are more significant in the drive toward educational equity.

Despite general improvement in high school completion and dropout rates among the total population of persons between the ages of 14 and 34, blacks still graduate from high school at significantly lower rates than whites. Higher dropout rates greatly reduce the numbers prepared to enter colleges and universities. However, a March 1985 study by the American Association of State Colleges and Universities revealed that between 1975 and 1982 the *number* of blacks completing high school increased by 29 percent. This increase

"Traditionally black institutions continue to provide fertile ground for nurturing black women at all levels . . ." © *Marvin T. Jones*

was attributed to the larger numbers of blacks in the 18 to 24 age cohort in that period. Despite this "improvement," whites still completed high school at a higher rate than did blacks (84 percent compared to 80 percent in 1985) (American Council on Education, 1986). And while dropout rates have decreased substantially since 1970, as of 1985 the dropout rate for black women between the ages of 14 and 34 (15.4 percent) remained significantly higher than for white women in that age group (11.1 percent) and white men (11.8 percent). Moreover, the difference between black and white women's dropout rates tends to increase with age: a two percentage point deficit for black women at ages 16 to 17 has increased to a nearly nine percentage point deficit for women between the ages of 30 and 34. (U.S. Department of Education, 1987). Given the fact that a high school education is the barest minimum of preparation for citizenship and employment in today's world, these dropout rates for black women—even though they are lower than in 1975—are cause for alarm. (It should be noted here that the dropout rates for black men remain higher than for black women as well as for white men and women.)

Although teenage pregnancy and employment are cited as major causes for the attrition rates among black high school girls, researchers must look for deeper causes and perhaps ask more probing questions. Are our schools and our social institutions failing these young women? Would more stimulating course work, inspired teachers, and safer school environments, coupled with better education in human sexuality and better access to birth control, make a difference in the lives of these girls? Why are more and more girls searching for meaning in early motherhood or in work outside of formal schooling? Poverty and its grinding effects have a heavy impact on the decisions of these girls. The Bureau of the Census reported that 42.7 percent of the children under age 18 in black families were living below the poverty level in 1986—a poverty rate nearly three times that for children in white families. For children in black female-headed families, the poverty rate was 67.1 percent (Bureau of the Census, July 1987). The persistently high unemployment rate for blacks in all categories (adult women and men, and teenagers), which has remained at double the rate of whites for more than two decades, continues to take its toll on the aspirations of, and opportunities for, black women and children.

The statistics for blacks in higher education are even more disturbing than for those in high school. A number of recent reports document the fact that blacks are losing ground at most levels in higher education. The larger number of blacks graduating from high school is not reflected in college enrollments. On the contrary, in 1984, some 8,500 fewer black women were enrolled in undergraduate and graduate schools combined than had been enrolled in 1980, although black women still outnumbered black men at the undergraduate level, since black male enrollment declined as well. Retention once enrolled remains a critical problem: black students often cite financial problems as the reason for leaving college before completing a degree.

Enrollment of blacks of both sexes at the graduate level has also decreased (by 11.9 percent between 1980 and 1984). In professional schools, however, the number of blacks seeking a first professional degree increased, but by only 419 or 3.3 percent, with 767 *more* black women and 348 *fewer* black men enrolled (American Council on Education, 1986). In February 1988, the National Research Council reported that doctorates earned by blacks during the past 10 years declined by 26.5 percent (Hirschorn, 1988). The fact that black women earned more than 60 percent of the 820 doctoral degrees awarded to blacks in 1986 is small comfort in view of the overall declining numbers of black women and men enrolled, and completing degrees, at the undergraduate and graduate levels. Unless more blacks complete doctoral programs, college and university faculties in the foreseeable future will be as white as they now are: in predominantly white institutions, blacks account for only 2.3 percent of the full-time faculty, and black women are a very small fraction of that group.

Statistical data do not yield much information about the quality of education for black women, especially in colleges and universities. However, the news stories of increased racial and sexual incidents and violence on college campuses, and the calls by college students for a curriculum that reflects this nation's history and demography in racial/ethnic, class, and gender aspects, are indicative of the severe problems yet to be addressed. The fact that, with very few exceptions, black women are absent from major educational policymaking, administrative, and faculty positions leaves students with few role models and robs institutions of sensitive leadership from this group.

Despite the bleak picture painted by this statistical summary, the belief persists among many educators that the individual can make a difference, and that each black female (and male) student is a precious resource to be treasured. Traditionally black institutions (TBIs) continue to provide fertile ground for nurturing black women at all levels, accounting for a significant proportion of bachelors', masters', and doctoral degrees awarded to blacks, despite the increased racial diversity of their student populations. In 1987, three TBIs (Bennett College in North Carolina, Lincoln University in Pennsylvania, and Spelman College in Georgia) selected black women as their presidents, the latter two naming the first black women presidents in their histories. The scholarship and brilliant literary work produced by black women continues to enrich the humanities and social sciences, creating greater pressure on curricula and disciplines for redefinition of their priorities.

These last years of the twentieth century are a critical time for educational institutions in this country. The potential, the resources, and the urgency exist to bring the fullness of equity and opportunity to all citizens. It is, however, primarily a question of will. Because blacks (and Hispanics) constitute a significant percentage of youth who must be prepared to work, to support a Social Security system that relies on their productivity, and to contribute to the economic growth and social health of the United States in a highly competitive world, the education of black women and men must be addressed immediately and effectively. Otherwise, the twenty-first century bodes ill for all, and the United States remains a nation at great risk.

High School and Beyond: The Young Hispanic Woman

RAFAEL VALDIVIESO

WHILE MANY OF TODAY'S young women are experiencing a society more open to their full participation, young Hispanic females (referred to as Latinas hereafter) are too often caught in a web of adult responsibilities and traditional female attitudes that limit their ability to take advantage of new opportunities. These circumstances are often engendered by others' low expectations for these women, as well as by their socialization into traditional female roles, and are frequently compounded by poverty and its attendant ills.

The extent to which the socialization of Latinas differs from that of black and white women, and the impact of that socialization on career goals, can be examined in a major longitudinal study of young Americans, High School and Beyond (HSB), which is being sponsored by the U.S. Center for Education Statistics. Hispanic, black, white, and other high school sophomores of both sexes were first interviewed in 1980. Follow-up interviews in 1982, 1984, and 1986 enabled researchers to obtain information on trends for young Americans regarding education, work, family formation, and other activities.

This article focuses on what the Latinas who had been high school sophomores in 1980 were doing with their lives when surveyed in 1984, by which time they should have graduated from high school. The analysis is based on a division of young women into three groups: those who had graduated with average grades in high school of C+ or higher (referred to herein as graduates); those who graduated with average grades of C or lower (at-risk graduates); and those who had not graduated from high school (nongraduates). The term "at-risk" describes graduates whose poor academic preparation in high school jeopardizes the possibility of living a fulfilling and productive adult life.

Several HSB survey questions dealt with what respondents were doing at the time of the interview. When asked, "What were you doing the first week of February 1984?" the respondents could mark *all* activities that applied to them from a list summarized as follows: working for pay; taking vocational or technical courses; enrolled in academic, graduate, or professional school courses; participating in an apprenticeship or training program; serving in the Armed Forces; keeping house (without other job); on temporary layoff; looking for work; taking a break from school; and "other."

Among the Latina graduates, the activity most frequently cited—by six out of 10—was working for pay. In second place was academic coursework, cited by one-third of the Latina graduates; this proportion is smaller than for both black and white female graduates (43 percent and 49 percent, respectively). Even more disturbing is the fact that two-thirds of the Latinas with good high school grades had apparently not attempted to continue their education and enhance their prospects for a more productive adult life.

The desire of many Latina graduates to maintain strong family ties probably contributes to the decision—more frequent among Latinas than among any other group—to live at home and commute to local community colleges, or to go to work full time rather than attend college at all. When surveyed in high school, Latinas who went on to graduate with good grades were 35 percent more likely than their white counterparts, and twice as likely as their black counterparts, to regard living close to their parents "very important." Overall, more than four-fifths of the Latina graduates considered living close to their parents important to some degree: 28 percent said "very important," 54 percent said "somewhat important." (Undoubtedly, the need to provide financial support for themselves and/or their families—which is common among Latinas—also contributes to the decision not to leave home.)

The three groups of Latinas showed sharp differences when asked whether they were keeping house (and not otherwise employed) in 1984: only 14 percent of the graduates answered yes, compared to 22 percent of the at-risk graduates, and nearly half—48 percent—of the nongraduates. In fact, keeping house was the activity cited most often by the nongraduates, only 36 percent of whom were working for pay.

Looking at the incidence of motherhood among the three groups of Latinas, one can understand the differences in their rates for keeping house. Latina nongraduates were just over four times as likely as Latina graduates to have children. The progression is clear: graduates who were parents, 14 percent; at-risk graduates who were parents, 25 percent; nongraduates who were parents, a staggering 58 percent.

The public is generally not aware of the high childbearing rates among young Latinas because the rates are masked by their marriage rates, which are considerably higher than those for either their black or white counterparts. According to the Bureau of the Census (November 1986a), for example,

20 percent of Hispanic women age 18 to 19 were married in 1985, compared to three percent and 13 percent, respectively, of their black and white counterparts. The overlap between married Latinas and Latina mothers is, to be sure, not nearly complete. Of Latina mothers in both the graduate and nongraduate categories, roughly one in three was not married. Of those in the at-risk category, the proportion was about one in two.

In 1984—just two years after they should have graduated from high school—the Latina nongraduates were more than twice as likely to be married (48 percent) as graduates (21 percent) and at-risk graduates (23 percent).

When they were high school sophomores in 1980, half of the Latina at-risk graduates and nongraduates had thought that having children was "very important." This proportion exceeded the proportions for both their black and white counterparts. The difference was especially marked in comparison with black at-risk graduates and nongraduates, of whom 26 percent and 31 percent, respectively, had said as sophomores that they considered having children very important. The Latinas who would go on to graduate with good grades had also thought having children was very important (42 percent). The difference between the three groups of Latinas is that four years later, most of the graduates had deferred having children, as had somewhat fewer (but still a majority) of the at-risk graduates, while a majority of the nongraduates had become mothers.

Early parenthood almost always limits a young woman's opportunities for further education and the development of solid job skills. In the short term, it is likely to force a young woman into a state of dependence on others or on the government. In fact, one-fifth of the Latina nongraduates received welfare benefits in 1983—just a year after they should have graduated from high school. (The comparable percentages for black and white nongraduates were 28 percent and 14 percent, respectively.) Among Latina graduates, on the other hand, the proportion dependent on welfare in 1983 was only two percent.

The presence of a husband does not necessarily mean economic security for the young family. If the young man also lacks an adequate education, the family is likely to be among the working poor—those who work for their incomes but are still below the official poverty level. In 1986, the median income of Hispanic married-couple families was the lowest and their poverty rate the highest of any major group of married couples—16.6 percent, compared to 10.8 percent for black married-couple families and 6.1 percent for white married-couple families (Bureau of the Census, July 1987).

Given the wide presence of the working poor and the welfare-dependent among young Hispanic families, it is not difficult to see why, in 1986, one-fourth of all Hispanic families were in poverty, compared to about 11 percent of families overall, and why nearly 40 percent of all Hispanic children lived in poverty. Of the nearly 1.1 million poor Hispanic families, about half (48.7 percent) were maintained by women with no husband present. Families with householders who had completed less than four years of high school constituted 62 percent of the Hispanic families below the poverty level in 1986 (Bureau of the Census, August 1987).

It would be idle talk to say that the present situation of low educational attainment and the early assumption of adult responsibilities such as parenthood can be easily turned around for many young Latinas. A combination of factors is necessary to make a difference in their lives. These young women must perceive real opportunities in their environments, and they need the confidence and capabilities to take advantage of any opportunities.

By the time students, especially those who are disadvantaged, reach the secondary school years, they need to have encountered a variety of incentives and supports that actively encourage them to stay and do well in school. In exchange for doing well, students must see that they will have increased opportunities in employment and higher education. Perhaps more difficult to deal with are the subtle ways in which females generally are not encouraged and supported in school to do their best.

Finally, Latinas and their families must be helped by school personnel and others to understand that preparing for a career is not being disloyal to the family, and that being educated will allow them to contribute to the betterment of their families—both financially and psychologically.

Women in Music

JUDITH TICK

WHEN WALTER DAMROSCH said: "I do not think that there has ever been a country whose musical development has been fostered so exclusively by women as America" (Beard and Beard, 1927, II: 457), the famous conductor surely referred to the role of women as promoters of culture in America, not as performers or composers. For in music, as in other fields, women have had to struggle for creative and professional opportunities, and they have by no means yet achieved equality with men. There has, however, been slow but steady progress over the course of this century, and in the last 15 years things have improved significantly, even though the gains have been uneven.

Women are still far from proportionately represented among professional musicians overall. In 1986, women accounted for 32 percent of the 164,000 people employed in the occupational category "musicians and composers" (Bureau of Labor Statistics, January 1987). While the numbers of both women and men in this category have increased significantly since 1970, the female proportion has not increased—in fact, it has decreased slightly in recent years.

The majority of those in the Census's musician/composer category are not employed full time—only 25 percent were considered full time in 1980 (National Endowment for the Arts, 1985). Among the part-timers, men were more likely to be freelancers playing popular music for social occasions, and women were more likely to be music teachers. The membership of the Music Teachers National Association, about three-quarters female, reflects the predominance of women among private and often part-time music teachers.

The ratio is very different among teachers in conservatories and music departments in colleges and universities, where most classical musicians work. Less than one-quarter (22 percent) of full-time college music faculty was female as of 1985–86, and, while that proportion represents an increase over what it was 20 years ago, there has not been much change in the past decade. In nontenure-track positions the proportion of women is much higher—about 40 percent (Block, forthcoming).

Women are now earning a proportionate share of undergraduate music degrees, more than half of which went to women in 1984–85, and are gaining significantly in advanced degrees. Most important, the percentage of women among recipients of doctoral degrees in music more than doubled between 1971 and 1986: from 16 percent to 37 percent (U.S. Department of Education, forthcoming). Perhaps in the long run, these developments will boost the representation of women among music professionals. No one seems to have definitive answers as to why that representation is as small as it is now; some possible answers are that the job market for music faculty as a whole is stagnant, that academic discrimination is still a factor, and that women outside of academia who might once have settled for part-time work as musicians are choosing more lucrative professions.

In music, as in many other fields, there are (to use a still relevant nineteenth century concept) a few special "spheres" in which women have always been well represented and successful. Gender is obviously no hindrance to success for female opera singers; prima donnas attain the pinnacle of their profession.

But it is only fairly recently that women instrumentalists have been found in appreciable numbers in the opera's orchestra pit or on stage at the symphony. American symphony orchestras were virtually all-male preserves until World War II, and discrimination against women players has been persistent. It wasn't until 1966 that the New York Philharmonic Orchestra accepted its first female player (Tick, 1987). Since then, with the help of antidiscrimination laws and the widespread use of "blind" auditions, in which performers play behind a screen so that listeners have no clue as to their race or gender, women have made considerable progress in becoming members of "major" and "metropolitan" orchestras across the country. Among the major U.S. orchestras, the 30 or so internationally known ensembles, the female proportion increased from about 18 percent, a proportion that had prevailed from 1955 through the late 1960s, to 28 percent in 1985. Women players are approaching parity in the metropolitan orchestras, where, according to the American Symphony Orchestra League, they accounted for 47 percent in 1985. (A metropolitan orchestra is one that serves a city and its suburban areas. Its seasons are usually shorter than those of major orchestras, and its members tend to earn less.)

Since it has taken so long for women to be accepted as players in American symphony orchestras, it is not surprising that women very rarely have the opportunity to conduct one. The stereotypical orchestral conductor of American tradition was male, white, and preferably European born. Although today's "maestro" may be nonwhite and/or Asian or American born, he is a male. Small wonder that we are still witnessing firsts for "maestras," who are few and far between. Two such firsts occurred in 1976. Margaret Hillis, the founder of the Chicago Symphony Chorus, made the front page of the *New York Times* when she became the first women ever to conduct a regular subscription concert of the Chicago Symphony Orchestra. Sarah Caldwell, founder of the Opera Company of Boston, became the first woman to conduct a performance at the Metropolitan Opera. These were highly symbolic events that occurred in a period of cultural activism. More than a decade later, although there seem to be more opportunities for women to conduct vocal music, orchestral conducting is still overwhelmingly dominated by men. To counteract this, the Exxon/Arts Endowment Conductors Program has provided special support for women conductors. There was another "first" last year: when Catherine Comet was appointed Music Director of the Grand Rapids Symphony for the 1986–87 season, she became the first woman conductor to direct a regional symphony orchestra in the United States ("Equal Opportunity . . . ," 1987).

With respect to musical composition, the picture is equally mixed. In terms of pure numbers, composition is still an occupation identified with males. The principal source of employment for classical composers is the university, and surveys by the College Music Society indicate that only eight percent of the college faculty teaching composition in 1985–86 were female. In the catalogue *Composers Recordings Inc.*, a principal label for twentieth century American music, works by women account for only about five percent of the entries for the period 1954–82.

Fortunately, not everything in art can be measured by numbers. Although women composers are still few in number, there has been progress. American Women Composers,

JoAnn Faletta, Music Director of the Bay Area Women's Philharmonic, Denver Chamber Orchestra, and Queens Philharmonic. *Courtesy Steve Sherman*

Inc., an organization celebrating its tenth anniversary in 1986, was founded, according to its president, "to break a vicious cycle: women's works were not performed because they were not recognized, and they were not recognized because they had not been published . . . Ten years ago, an ensemble or conductor who was interested in a woman's piece may have given up trying to find the score, which was probably unpublished. Today our library of over 3,000 scores, available to everyone . . . is one of the most rapidly growing aspects of our organization" (American Women Composers, 1986).

The cultural feminism of the 1970s changed the way music by women was received, and in the last 20 years many of the stereotypes about women composers have been laid to rest. Critics seem more sensitive to the pitfalls of sexual aesthetics, less likely to describe music written by women in such terms as "delicate" and "intuitive." Women composers have achieved much greater recognition in the last 10 years than ever before. More than twice as many Guggenheim Fellowships in composition were awarded to women in the 1970s than had gone to women in the preceding 40 years, to take but one example. About 11 percent of the National Endowment for the Arts awards in composition go to women. In 1983, Ellen Taafe Zwillich became the first female composer to win the Pulitzer Prize in music.

In addition, there is a growing body of literature about women and music, accompanied by revivals of the music of women composers of the past because of recordings and the publication of scores (Block and Neuls-Bates, 1981; Bowers and Tick, 1986).

There is also a special political-artistic offshoot of the women's movement in music that coalesced in the 1970s and is still alive today. As defined in *The Ladyslipper Catalog,* a guide to records and tapes by women, the term "women's music" signifies "music springing from a feminist consciousness, utilizing women's talent . . . with production, presentation, and finances controlled by women." With annual festivals in Ann Arbor, Michigan, "women's music" has retained a stable following over the last 10 years.

There is no one conclusion to be drawn from the statistics or from informal observation on women in music. Our musical life, particularly with respect to classical music, is fragmented; the performing arts economy is vulnerable. Female musicians are aware of their ascent from marginal status, the overall positive developments of the last 15 years or so, and, at the same time, the continued need for improvement.

Women in Nursing

DONNA F. VER STEEG

THE NEARLY 1.5 MILLION registered nurses (RNs) employed in the U.S. in 1986 represented a record, both in number and in proportion to the population as a whole. In 1986, 600 RNs (over 94 percent of them women) were employed for every 100,000 people in the U.S. population, an increase from slightly under 500 per 100,000 in 1977 and only 319 per 100,000 in 1966 (Bureau of Labor Statistics [BLS], January 1987; American Nurses' Association [ANA], 1977; 1985). Yet, according to the ANA, more than four-fifths of the nation's hospitals reported vacancies on their nursing staffs in 1986. What accounts for this anomaly?

Rapidly developing medical technology, changes in health policy, and the aging of the U.S. population are several of the interrelated factors contributing to the nursing shortage. But at its heart are the demands on, the rewards for, and the perceived status of nursing as a profession at a time when American women have a wide range of professions and careers to choose from.

These issues are intimately related to the fact that nursing is a profession for which women have largely developed the standards, and which has primarily been practiced by women. Long one of the very few professional occupations regarded as appropriate for women, nursing was considered to be a "natural" extension of "women's domestic impulses" (Evans, 1987: 41). Even though the male proportion of RNs has crept up in recent years, from around 3.3 percent in 1977 to 5.7 percent in 1986, women accounted for 88 percent of the increase in the number of nurses over that period (Bureau of Labor Statistics, January 1978; January 1987).

In the nineteenth century, nursing's position subordinate to medicine was an artifact of women's subordinate role in society, and old attitudes linger. Even the recognition of nursing—and therefore "women's"—knowledge as a legitimate field of scientific study in its own right has been slowed by continued opposition on the part of a male-dominated medical profession (Freidson, 1970; Starr, 1982).

The last 25 years have seen ever greater demands and reliance on nurses' skills, expertise, and judgment. Historically, nurses were forbidden by state nurse practice acts to "practice medicine," defined as including the right to diagnose and treat all human illness. This was reserved for physicians and surgeons (Starr, 1982). But in the real world, there were growing discrepancies between what the law said and the roles nurses were actually being called upon to play in providing care. These discrepancies were initially handled by informal (and illegal) agreements between medical, nursing, and hospital associations that it was all right under defined conditions for nurses to exceed the limitations of their practice acts (Ver Steeg and Croog, 1979). In the mid-1960s, when the inauguration of Medicare and Medicaid brought concerns about how to handle an increased demand for care in the face of a presumed shortage of physicians, programs were designed to prepare nurse practitioners, physician assistants, and others to help meet the demand. The extra-legal responsibilities that nurses had been successfully but invisibly assuming for years became visible in connection with the need to give legal status to physician assistants. Ultimately it became necessary to rewrite state nurse practice acts to reflect current nursing practice. These laws now provide for nurses to make nursing diagnoses (which describe clusters of signs and symptoms for which there are nursing interventions) and nursing interventions. The nature of nursing is such that there is inevitable overlap with medicine, but nurses ask different questions and deal with different outcomes. And in settings ranging from slums, schools, and workplaces to high technology hospital intensive care units (and in every war beginning with the British war in the Crimea in 1854), nursing knowledge *added* to that of medicine has produced far better results than medicine practiced alone (Benner, 1984; Kalisch and Kalisch, 1986).

Increasingly complex medical technology and cost-saving programs have resulted in a generally sicker patient population both in hospitals and at home (American Hospital Association [AHA], 1987; U.S. Department of Health and Human Services, 1986). Caring for these patients typically requires much more staff and the scientific knowledge and analytical skills provided by, at a minimum, a bachelor's degree in nursing (BSN) (Benner, 1984). While the number of hospital beds declined from 1.7 million in 1960 to 1.3 million in 1986, the number of hospital personnel (full-time equivalent) more than doubled over the same period, from 1.6 million to 3.6 million (AHA, 1987). Still, although hospitals employ roughly two-thirds of all RNs—or did as recently as 1983—the vast majority of hospitals across the country report nursing vacancies, many of them in the specialized units requiring expert nurses.

A major reason for vacancies is that among the nearly 1.5 million RNs, there are too few with at least BSNs to fill all the jobs—in and out of hospitals—that require such training.

These days, hospitals do not control job market options for RNs. They must compete with new systems of health care delivery, such as health maintenance organizations, ambulatory surgical centers, and community clinics, that often offer nurses opportunities with better and more satisfying working conditions (better hours and more control over their own practice, for example). Some hospitals do compete successfully (both for nurses and for patients) by improving the status of nurses in various ways. One study found that hospitals where nurses felt that they had more control over their practices and more opportunity to provide good nursing care also had far less turnover (American Academy of Nursing, 1983).

But even if all hospitals took the steps that seem to attract and retain skilled nurses, shortages would continue, at least in the near term. Projections show a 48 percent undersupply of BSNs by 1990 (U.S. Department of Health and Human Services, 1986). College-bound women, especially, who might be potential recruits to nursing have many other options available to them now, and they are electing those options in droves. In 1986–87, more freshman women reported planning to enter medical school than to enter nursing. A combination of factors, including relative prestige, control over practice, and income, makes it possible that in 1990, more MDs than generic BSNs may be awarded (Green, 1987).

As may be inferred from the brief discussion above of hospitals that are successful in retaining skilled nurses, job satisfaction is strongly related to such factors as a sense of autonomy and a supportive work environment. But financial rewards, or the lack thereof, are also significant to both nurses already practicing and young women considering a career in nursing.

Like other traditionally female professions, nursing does not typically pay as well as traditionally male professions. Nursing salaries still seem to reflect an assumption that nursing is an interim job between school and marriage, although this has never been the case for the majority of the profession (Kalisch and Kalisch, 1986). In 1979 (the most recent year for which there are statistical breakdowns of earnings by detailed occupation and sex), female RNs working year round, full time annually earned, on average, 24 percent less than male electricians and only three percent more than male automobile mechanics. In a list of 421 occupations ranked by how well women in them were paid, nursing ranked 80th in 1979 (Bureau of the Census, November 1986b). (However, unpublished BLS statistics showing median weekly earnings of usually full-time workers by detailed occupation and sex hint that nurses' earnings may have made relative gains between 1979 and 1986. At $458, female RNs' 1986 median weekly earnings were up 70 percent from 1979. This gain compares favorably to those of both female workers in general, and workers of both sexes, up 59 and 49 percent, respectively.) For nurses engaged in clinical practice (that is, direct patient care), an unusually narrow spread between entry level and highest salary means not only that there is relatively little monetary reward for competence gained on the job, but also that there is little economic impetus for undertaking additional education. To advance financially, nurses have usually had to leave the bedside to become nursing educators and administrators (Benner, 1984). (It should be mentioned that in some respects this situation produced positive results for nursing as a profession because it encouraged preparation in management and education—logical extensions of the management and education skills inherent in bedside nursing. In 1962, federally funded nurse-scientist graduate training grants in anthropology, psychology, sociology, anatomy, physiology, and microbiology significantly broadened the doctoral education opportunities for nurses [Kalisch and Kalisch, 1986]. Nurses thus prepared helped develop the scientific basis for the clinical practice unique to nursing.)

Public perceptions of the status of nursing compared to other professions no doubt partly reflect the less than full autonomy of nurses implicit in how nurses are compensated for their services under third-party (government and private insurance) payers. Organized nursing is in agreement that an autonomous and directly reimbursable role for nurses across settings and organizational boundaries is needed to make health care more effective and affordable in the future. In other words, professional nurses ought to have a direct, autonomous relationship with patients in which the nurse determines and provides appropriate nursing care, if needed, and bills the patient or insurer directly. This arrangement would reduce red tape and improve cost effectiveness (U.S. Congress, 1986). Yet organized medicine has succeeded in limiting third-party reimbursement for nurses' services to indirect payments, available only if a physician orders the service (Pinsky, 1988). Some services that nurses provide that are essential to health (Benner, 1984) are not reimbursable at all under current fee schedules. In some states, nurses now may receive direct reimbursement for some services, but much remains to be done.

Any discussion of the serious shortage of BSNs and the need to attract new recruits to baccalaureate nursing programs should also stress the need to encourage and assist RNs without baccalaureates to continue their education. Many RNs are graduates of so-called diploma programs (providing training of a technical, nonacademic nature) or two-year associate degree nursing programs. Diploma programs have been steadily decreasing in number (as baccalaureate programs have been increasing) since the 1920s. However, in some parts of the country diploma programs still account for a significant proportion of initial nursing programs (over one-quarter—27 percent—in the North Atlantic states) (National League for Nursing [NLN], 1987; American Nurses' Association, 1985). Diploma programs are rare in the West, where associate degree programs account for three-quarters of the initial nursing programs. Cost considerations may often underlie the decision to elect an associate degree program rather than a baccalaureate program in nursing: 89 percent of associate degree programs are publicly funded (NLN, 1986), compared to about half of baccalaureate programs. Tuition for privately funded diploma programs, probably reflecting Medicare education subsidies to the sponsoring hospitals, is less than that for either associate degree or BSN programs (ibid.; U.S. Department of Health and Human Services, 1986).

The role of the RN prepared to a technical level (that is, with less than a baccalaureate) should not be undervalued. According to a statement adopted in 1987 by the ANA's House of Delegates, technically prepared RNs provide direct care to clients and families in organized health care settings. They are equipped to deal with well-defined problems with predictable outcomes using policies, procedures, and protocols developed by professional nurses (that is, nurses with a baccalaureate or more). But at least a baccalaureate is necessary to equip nurses for practice in any setting, caring for individuals, families, or groups of individuals such as students in a school, employees in a work setting, or members of a community. Professional nurses are prepared to provide not only direct care but case management of care. Professional nurses engage in nursing administration, education, and research, as well (American Nurses' Association, 1987).

Thus, to advance in nursing, both associate degree and diploma nurses face extra years of education. Nevertheless, many of these RNs do go back to school to earn baccalaureate degrees—the number who did so increased by 17 percent in the last decade, and in 1985 nearly one-third of baccalaureate students in nursing were already RNs (National League for Nursing, 1986). Some hospitals are using tuition support in nurse recruitment and retention strategies. But the ultimate costs to the student and to the state of installment-plan nursing education have yet to be calculated.

Preparation for advanced nursing practice has increasingly moved to the master's level. Moreover, the shift from diploma to academically based nursing education, and the pressure to develop a unique body of nursing science, led to a dramatic increase in doctoral programs in nursing—up from only five in 1966 to 33 in 1985 (ibid.). The development of a critical mass of doctorally prepared nurse researchers was recognized in 1986 by the establishment of the National Center for Nursing Research within the National Institutes of Health. The center will further nursing as a unique discipline with its own contribution to the health and welfare of the public.

Women in the Clergy

BARBARA BROWN ZIKMUND

THE MOVEMENT OF WOMEN into the ordained leadership of churches and synagogues in America began over 100 years ago. It started when women parishioners sought the right to speak up in mixed church meetings, and soon women wanted to vote on local congregational matters. This led to the question of whether women could "represent" a local congregation at regional, diocesan, or national meetings. Eventually women evangelists and musicians led church worship, albeit on a less than equal basis with men. Recently, the case has been made that churches and synagogues have no good reason not to ordain women (Zikmund, 1986: 337–348).

The first woman ordained in a major American denomination was Antoinette Brown, a Congregationalist. The ordination took place in the small town of South Butler, New York in 1853. It did not require national approval, only local congregational vote. During the later years of the nineteenth century, other women were officially recognized as authorized clergy among the Unitarians, Northern Baptists, and Disciples of Christ (Zikmund, 1981: 193–241). Groups like the Society of Friends (Quakers) and the Salvation Army (which functioned like a Protestant denomination in the nineteenth century) never denied women equal leadership roles. Mary Baker Eddy, founder of Christian Science, and Ellen Gould White, Seventh Day Adventist, were important religious leaders. During the Holiness revivals in the nineteenth century, and within the Pentecostal movement of the early twentieth century, female leadership was prominent.

Gradually, however, as new religious groups organized into denominations and fundamentalism matured, limitations upon women's ministries developed. In Christian and Jewish history, there is reference to three sources of authority: scripture, tradition, and personal experience. At every period in history when religious groups have legitimatized religious authority predominantly through the Holy Spirit, women's leadership has been honored. When the primary understanding of authority was linked to the Bible, however, or tied to ecclesiastical tradition, women have had a much more difficult time (Ruether and McLaughlin, 1979: 16–28).

In those denominations where the local congregation plays the dominant role in selecting and authorizing clergy, the cycle from lay membership to full-clergy status for women took place in the late nineteenth century. According to a handwritten list found in a file at the library of the Harvard Divinity School, there were 67 ordained and eight licensed women in Congregationalism in 1913. However, it was not until between 1957 and 1977 that five of the largest Protestant denominations (Methodists, Presbyterians, National Baptists, Lutherans, and Episcopalians), most of which have more centralized authorization procedures, formally approved the ordination of women. Southern Baptists and Missouri Synod Lutherans officially still refuse to ordain women, although individual congregations sometimes override these policies (*The American Baptist*, 1987: 31).

Today, 26 percent of all theological students are women. In 1972, the first year for which figures on women seminarians are available, the comparable figure was just over 10 percent. The change is even more dramatic when a compari-

The Reverend Canon Carol A. Crumley, Canon Pastor, Washington Cathedral. © *Morton Broffman*

son is made of students in preordination programs: in 1972, just under five percent of the students in seminaries preparing for ordained ministry were women; by 1986, that figure had increased to 19 percent. Since 1976, the number of female seminary graduates receiving the basic degree leading to ordination has increased by 219 percent, while the number of male graduates has risen by less than eight percent (*Fact Book on Theological Education, 1986–87*: 8–12). Because many churches still cannot imagine a woman as their pastor, placement of women in parish settings is difficult. Women completing seminary often serve in education, counseling, and ecumenical work. This is true in spite of the fact that as many as 80 percent of the Protestant denominations in the United States now ordain women (*The American Baptist*, 1987: 31).

For Roman Catholic women the movement from active lay leadership to clergy status is far from over. Many Roman Catholic women acknowledge that it may not come in their lifetime, but they are preparing for the priesthood anyway. The story is further complicated by Roman Catholic religious orders, whose numbers of professed sisters, or nuns, have decreased by 29 percent since 1956 (Jacquet, 1987: 268). Since the Second Vatican Council, these women in religious communities have democratized their orders and challenged clerical authority. At the same time, the official stance of the Roman Catholic Church has grown more rigid in its insistence that women cannot be ordained clergy. Women lack the male "image of Christ" needed to carry out the sacramental roles. Many American Roman Catholics, however, do not agree with the ruling of the Vatican.

Since 1975, an ongoing Women's Ordination Conference has brought Roman Catholic women who believe that women should be ordained together at regular intervals. Because of the shortage of priests, many trained women are serving parishes in team ministries. They do not consecrate the Eucharist or hear confession, but they do almost everything else without being officially "clergy." Other Roman Catholic women have moved to create alternative church structures. They have developed a network of women-church communities where feminist values are nourished and old distinctions between clergy and laity are abolished. The Women's Alliance for Theology, Ethics, and Ritual (WATER) is an ecumenical center and think tank that provides resources and leadership for this network.

For Jewish women the story is much the same. Nineteenth century reform efforts began in Germany and moved to the United States. Changes were made in worship practices and women were counted in the quorum necessary for worship. A few women attended Hebrew Union College during the late nineteenth century. In the 1920s Martha Neumark tried to get the Central Conference of American (Reform) Rabbis (CCAR) to approve her ordination. Although she did not succeed, the CCAR finally endorsed the ordination of women in 1956. It took until 1972, however, before the first woman rabbi in America, Sally Priesand, was admitted to the rabbinate by Hebrew Union College and the Jewish Institute of Religion.

The Jewish Reconstructionist movement also grants women rabbinic ordination. Building upon its understanding of Judaism as a "religious civilization," its educational institutions have accepted and encouraged the ordination of women. Sandy Eisenberg Sasso became the first female Reconstructionist rabbi in 1974. Conservative and Orthodox Jewish groups still do not ordain women to the rabbinate (Umansky, 1979: 338–350).

All women who seek ordination today are confronted with a dilemma. On the one hand they feel that they deserve equal access to the powers and privileges of the clergy. If God created men and women equal, the gifts of ministry must be honored equally. At the same time many women are challenging the very assumptions and patterns that divide religious communities into "clergy" and "laity." Women want to help churches and synagogues cultivate new patterns of liberation and equality before God. Women want to be ordained and receive all of the rights and privileges previously enjoyed by men, and women want to serve in ways that will destroy the destructive assumptions of hierarchy that support clericalism (Carroll, 1983: 1–19).

The number of women clergy has increased dramatically in the last two decades. Still, a National Council of Churches study of clerical salaries shows that women clergy earn less than male clergy in an already underpaid profession. Although some of the discrepancy can be explained because, on average, women clergy are younger than men, patterns of remuneration remain unequal. Clerical salaries have not kept pace with inflation, especially for women. Many women seminary graduates cannot find opportunities to serve in parish ministries, therefore, the percentage of ordained women in part-time, specialized, and underpaid ministries is especially pronounced (Jacquet, 1984).

Job satisfaction, however, remains high among women clergy. Women clergy measure success in terms of the functions of ministry, rather than dwelling upon the size and status of the churches they are serving. A career counseling center serving church workers reports that the typical female minister has greater ego strength and less dependency than the typical male minister. Women clergy are in the system to stay (*The American Baptist*, 1987: 31).

Yet, for the most part, members of local churches still remain unaware of these changes. Only churches looking for new pastors among recent seminary graduates know anything about the dramatic increase in the number of women entering the ministry. Denominational pronouncements about these developments make little difference in local churches. For most people church life is a very local matter. Only when they need a new pastor and become aware of the shortage of priests and the work of female parish associates (Roman Catholic), or the increasing number of qualified women candidates seeking a call to parish ministry in local congregations (Protestant and Jewish), does the real situation become evident (Lehman, 1985: 17–18).

The pressure is on churches and synagogues to change. There is an embarrassing inconsistency when religious communities uphold religious values of spiritual freedom while continuing to deny women full participation in ecclesiastical ministries. On this issue one writer has suggested that the churches have been "caught with their platitudes down" (ibid.: 296). There is little question that women are capable of doing the job. It is a matter of whether they will be allowed to do it. If churches refuse to recognize the legitimacy of women's call to serve in places heretofore reserved for men, history will find the churches wanting (ibid.: 296–297).

Farm Women

WAVA GILLESPIE HANEY

WOMEN AND FOOD PRODUCTION have been linked throughout human history. Nevertheless, even though most writers about U.S. agriculture in the twentieth century made the point that farming was a unique sector of the economy where *family-centered* production predominated, they went on to talk about the men on farms as the farmers. Women's roles in agriculture were ignored; they were the "invisible farmers" (Sachs, 1983). So strong was the masculine connotation of "farmer" that not until 1978 did the census of agriculture first ask the sex of the farm operator. Even then, however, the assumption remained that a farm had only one operator; the census did not allow for the possibility that it might be jointly operated.

By the late 1970s, historians and sociologists began to document both the household form of production in farming and the overlap in farm women's work and family roles. In the early 1980s, the farm financial crisis drew the attention of the media and the film industry to farming and the farm family. Sally Field, Jane Fonda, Jessica Lange, and Sissy Spacek played the roles of farm women in films released between 1983 and 1986. The same period brought books on women and farming from Carolyn Sachs (1983), Jacqueline Jones (1985), Rachel Rosenfeld (1985), and Joan Jensen (1986). Collectively, these works highlighted farm women's involvement in agricultural production, off-farm income generation, farm organizations and farm movements, building social institutions in rural communities, and nurturing and training farm families.

Both the academic and popular works focused mainly on women married to farm men, and, indeed, most farm families include a husband and a wife. Eighty-six percent of the 1.8 million U.S. farm households in 1984 were married-couple families (Bureau of the Census, December 1985). Married women not only provide labor for the farm, but many also jointly own the farm with their husbands, and they see themselves as partners in the daily operation and management of the farm. In 1978, nearly 45 percent of the farms in the United States were owned jointly by husband and wife (Rosenfeld, 1985). In the first national survey of farm and ranch women, conducted in 1980, 55 percent of the women said that they considered themselves a major operator of the farm. Sixty percent of the married farm women felt capable of running the farm without their husbands (ibid.).

Few of the farm women surveyed in 1980 reported that they did no farm work at all. Most were involved at least occasionally in a range of farm tasks. The range and frequency of women's farm work depended at least in part on the need for their labor, tending to be related to farm and family characteristics such as the size and type of the operation and whether the husband worked off the farm. Women on livestock farms were more active in farm work than those on farms that specialized in crops. Women did some field work, although not on a regular basis, but were more likely to care for farm animals. On larger farms, women did a smaller range of tasks; smaller farms demanded more of women in terms of the amount of their labor and the variety of their tasks. Women who had legal control over the land farmed, and those whose husbands were employed off the farm tended to do the broadest range of farm tasks. Even when actively involved in farm work, almost all of these farm women did all of the housework and child care.

Married women are not the only women who farm (Tigges and Rosenfeld, 1987). In 1982, just over five percent of the nation's farms were solely or principally operated by women (Kalbacher, 1985). Because women are more likely to acquire their farms by inheritance than by purchase, they typically become owners at a later age than men. Most independent women farmers operate small farms which they own. Their farms averaged 285 acres in 1982, compared to 423 acres on average for farms operated solely or primarily by men. A 1980 study showed independent farm women to be economically worse off than other farm women (Tigges and Rosenfeld, 1987).

There are more independent women farmers in the South than in any other single region of the U.S. To some extent this is a reflection of the fact that independent women farmers are more commonly found among blacks and other minorities than among whites.

Farm women's economic contributions are not limited to their farm and family roles. Off-farm employment of women and men in farming continues to increase and plays a major role in the economic well-being of many farm families. Nearly two-fifths of the farm women surveyed in late 1980 and early 1981 were employed off the farm at that time (Rosenfeld, 1985). In one-fourth of the families surveyed, both spouses reported off-farm employment. Farm women earned about 40 percent of what farm men earned; they were less likely than farm men to work full time but more likely to have professional jobs (ibid.). The male-female gap in earnings reflects differences in the total hours worked, as well as differences in wages.

Rural communities as well as farm families owe much to women. It was farm women who created the networks of sharing and exchange called upon for survival and a sense of belonging and solidarity, and who created the traditions that give meaning to life. Evident to observers of the current farm crisis is that today's farm women continue to mend, extend, and transform these networks, and to revitalize and continue traditions. In so doing, they play a major role in providing the immediate emotional support, as well as the long-term organizational and political leadership, needed to help farm families and communities endure and move to alternative sources of livelihood.

A vital part of this political and organizational work has been done by farm women willing to defy laws and customs that excluded women from the political process. Farm women were involved in the populist reform movements of the late nineteenth century and in the early farm organizations that grew out of these movements (Miller and Neth, 1988). Using speeches, songs, poems, and newspaper articles, farm women mobilized coalitions of farmers and town and city supporters to oppose economic policies that they perceived not to be in their best interest.

At the beginning of the twentieth century, two streams of protest and reform engaged farm women. Women from prosperous farms pressed for more scientific information to increase production and make farming more businesslike. Other farm women pressed for improvements in the condi-

Until recently "women's roles in agriculture were ignored; they were the 'invisible farmers'." *Courtesy USDA photo*

tions of farm and rural life (Knowles, 1988). In the 1970s, farm women again began to organize pressure groups and policy-oriented study groups. While continuing to push male-dominated farm organizations to recognize females' leadership capabilities, farm women have also formed independent organizations whose principal goals are focused on both family welfare and farm economic issues (Miller and Neth, 1988).

The recent scholarship on farm women continues to develop a more accurate historical record of their contributions to farm, family, and community. New studies also allow us to see more clearly how the changing structure of agriculture is shaping both women's relationship to agricultural production, as well as their family and community roles. This understanding is essential, both in helping women define their options in agricultural production and rural community life, and in enabling policymakers to develop food and agricultural policies, as well as rural community development policies, that recognize farm women's roles and give them more control over their lives.

Women in Road Construction

WENDY JOHNSON

I know I can do the work required; I have previously worked for Ford Motor Company which called for some very hard labor under very hot conditions. This, of course, was before my layoff.

My previous job . . . was farming. I worked in the field with machinery, trucks, tractors and milked and cared for a herd of 60 cattle six days a week. I am very much interested in outdoor work and dependable.

Office work and waitressing do not pay enough for me to pay bills and feed and clothe my kids . . . I know that construction pays well and is hard and dirty work and I know with proper training I can do good work.

I want a good paying job and I don't care how hard the work is.

—Excerpts of responses from women to a notice for road construction jobs advertised by the Southeast Women's Employment Coalition in the *Louisville Courier-Journal* and the *Lexington Herald-Leader*, 1981.

WOMEN BUILDING ROADS? Twenty years ago, it would have been hard to imagine that many people would look to highway construction as an appropriate occupation for women. Yet federally aided road building should and could offer tremendous employment opportunities in nontraditional, well-paying jobs for women in both the public and private sectors at local and state levels.

To begin with, road construction jobs pay well. According to the Bureau of Labor Statistics (January 1987), highway and street construction workers had average weekly earnings of $470 in December 1986. Moreover, it is likely that highway construction will continue to produce well-paying jobs in the future. The Surface Transportation and Uniform Relocation Assistance Act of 1987 (P.L. 100–17) allocates $87.5 billion for highway construction over the next five years.

The key to opportunities for women in this field is that the costs of road construction and reconstruction are substantially financed by federal contributions to state highway fund allotments. There are strings attached to these federal funds. Under federal law, state departments of transportation receiving federal aid dollars and the private companies to which they contract road work are obligated to implement the fair employment policies and equal employment opportunity laws required by Executive Order 11246 and Section 162(a) of the Federal Highway Act of 1973 (23 U.S.C. 324), as well as by Title VII of the Civil Rights Act of 1964. In addition, private contractors doing public work are required by the office of Federal Contract Compliance to employ women at a minimum level of 6.9 percent of all hours worked in each job category. (Unless otherwise noted, the statistics in this article are taken from unpublished data from the Federal Highway Administration.)

While there are still relatively few women working in road construction, their numbers have increased since 1976 when only 2,573 women—accounting for two percent of the workers—were so employed. Ten years later (as of July 1986), the number of women employed in road construction was 11,688, or six percent of the road construction workforce. About one in six of these women was a woman of color.

It should be stressed, however, that the proportion of

women is not only still smaller than the targeted minimum level of 6.9 percent but also includes many women in clerical jobs. In fact, clerical workers account for nearly one-third of the females employed. As in so many fields, occupational segregation is the rule rather than the exception. Very few women in road construction are actually on site digging ditches, grading or paving roads, operating heavy machinery, or even waving flags.

In nearly all of the traditionally male-dominated job categories, women accounted for far less than 6.9 percent of the workforce: supervisors (two percent), forepersons (two percent), equipment operators (three percent), mechanics (less than half of one percent), truck drivers (four percent), ironworkers (two percent), carpenters (three percent), cement masons (one percent), electricians (two percent), pipefitters/plumbers (one percent), painters (six percent), semiskilled laborers (six percent), and unskilled laborers (eight percent). Women were better represented (16 percent) among officials/managers. On the other hand, they were heavily overrepresented (78 percent) in clerical jobs.

Job development for women in federally aided road construction may constitute an important weapon against the occupational and economic segregation of women. The Federal Highway Administration is required by law to have special training programs and supportive services aimed at increasing the number of women in road construction. In fact, women's presence in these positions exceeds the targeted minimum. As more women are trained for well-paying, skilled road construction jobs, their proportion in these job categories should increase.

In 1986, according to Federal Highway Administration records, 26 percent of the 2,600 job trainees were women; of these women, over one-third were women of color. Women were 17 percent of the 2,000 apprentices; 28 percent of these women were women of color. This is a considerable increase from 1976, when only four percent of the 2,300 job trainees and one percent of the 2,000 apprentices were women.

Among job trainees in specific craft categories, about one in three managers, forepersons, equipment operators, and truck drivers was a woman. Of trainees in ironwork and carpentry, approximately one in five was a woman. In only three of 15 job categories were female trainees less than 10 percent of the workforce.

Women have made fewer inroads in apprenticeships. Among apprentices in five of the same 15 job categories, including unskilled laborers and iron-workers, women accounted for 10 percent or less of the total. No women were apprenticed as managers, supervisors, or forepersons, although nine men were. However, nearly 30 percent of the apprentice equipment operators, 20 percent of apprentice painters, and 20 percent of apprentice carpenters, were women.

Some organizations have campaigned for greater participation of women in road construction. In 1979, for example, 17 organizations, among them the Southeast Women's Employment Coalition, the Coal Employment Project, and the American Civil Liberties Union, filed an administrative complaint against the Federal Highway Administration alleging its failure to enforce antidiscrimination laws and affirmative action policies. The complaint was based on an examination of employment and hiring practices of state departments of transportation and selected private contractors. The complaint is still in the process of being resolved.

The issue of women seeking job equity and economic

"Job development for women in federally aided road construction may constitute an important weapon against the occupational and economic segregation of women." *Courtesy Southeast Women's Employment Coalition/Joseph Viesti, photographer*

opportunity in the road construction industry calls for the full attention and participation of women leaders, policymakers, public officials, and job developers. Hope for continued change lies in the ability to stimulate a renewed commitment to creating equal access for women in highway road work. That commitment must be sustained by the belief that expanding women's employment opportunities to higher-paying job sectors, such as road construction, is one of the many ways to move women forward.

Women in Law Enforcement

KATE MCGUINNESS *and*
TRISH DONAHUE

THE FACE OF AMERICAN law enforcement is changing. The traditional image of police officers as the "men in blue" is no longer accurate as women join the ranks of state and local police departments and federal law enforcement agencies. In 1986, women accounted for 11 percent of the nearly 666,000 nonsupervisory police and detectives nationwide (Bureau of Labor Statistics [BLS], January 1987). As recently as 1971, women's share of these occupations was only 1.5 percent (BLS, unpublished data).

In the early 1970s, equal opportunity legislation opened doors for women to enter fields that had long been overwhelmingly, if not exclusively, male. The 1972 amendments to Title VII of the Civil Rights Act of 1964 were of particular importance to women in gaining equal access to law enforcement jobs. These amendments extended job discrimination prohibitions to public employers, creating several mechanisms for the Department of Justice and Equal Employment Opportunity Commission to enforce bans on sex discrimination and for individuals and groups to file complaints and discrimination suits against their agencies.

One breakthrough involved successfully challenging the relevance of certain physical criteria required for police work. It had long been assumed that women lacked the physical strength needed to perform effectively as law enforcement officers. Encouraged by federal legislation mandating equal opportunity, many individuals and groups filed suits against law enforcement agencies, charging that height and weight requirements used to screen applicants were not bona fide occupational qualifications and effectively discriminated on the basis of sex. Two significant legal victories for women were *Officers for Justice v. Civil Service Commission, City of San Francisco* (1975) and the 1977 Supreme Court case *Dothard v. Rawlinson* (Sulton and Townsey, 1981). The result of this litigation has been a move toward replacing irrelevant job requirements that served largely to keep women out of law enforcement, with legitimate job requirements that do not discriminate on the basis of sex.

At least partly as a result of these developments and affirmative action plans in some jurisdictions, nearly 73,000 women were employed in the BLS classification "police officers and detectives" in 1986. However, women's distribution in the various subcategories of that classification differed markedly from that of the 593,000 male police officers and detectives (Bureau of Labor Statistics, January 1987). Nearly half of the women, but only one-fourth of the men, were officers in correctional institutions; slightly more than one-third of the women, but nearly two-thirds of the men, were municipal, state, or federal law enforcement officers. One in seven of the women, compared to one in eight of the men, was a sheriff, bailiff, or "other" law enforcement officer. In short, women in law enforcement are overrepresented in the least prestigious jobs and underrepresented in the most prestigious.

As might be surmised from the distribution statistics, the female percentage is far from consistent across the various types and levels of law enforcement jobs. The statistics vary

Private first class Marylou Barkman of the University of Maryland Police Department. *Courtesy University of Maryland, College Park Police Department/Andy Shupe, photographer.*

widely from state to state and from city to city, and comprehensive, comparable data are very difficult to come by. In 1986, women accounted for seven percent of municipal, state, and federal law enforcement officers overall, but for less than four percent of all state police officers (Federal Bureau of Investigation, 1987). Women seem to have made greater gains on municipal police forces. In 60 cities with populations of 250,000 or more, women were nearly 10 percent of all police officers (ibid.).

Precise 1987 data are available for federal law enforcement agencies, where women are a growing proportion of the agent workforce. Eight percent of the Federal Bureau of Investigation (FBI) special agents were female in 1987, and of the 769 females, 13 percent were minority women. (In 1978, there were only 94 female FBI agents.) As of September 1987, the Drug Enforcement Administration (DEA) employed 199 women special agents (accounting for seven percent of all); 22 percent of these women were minority women. (Just five years earlier, women were only three percent of DEA's total agent workforce.)

The Secret Service, regarded by many as the most elite of federal law enforcement agencies, had the smallest proportion of women agents in 1987. Its 75 female special agents represented only four percent of all Secret Service special agents. The 62 women in the Secret Service uniformed division accounted for six percent of the division's workforce. Nevertheless, this represents progress; before 1971, the Secret Service employed no women in these capacities.

Women classified as police officers and detectives typically have lower earnings than their male counterparts. In 1986, according to unpublished BLS data, women police officers and detectives had median weekly earnings of $350, compared to $443 for men. This variance may be due to differences in seniority, job tenure, work assignments, and the concentration of women in the lowest paying of law enforcement jobs, correctional institution officers. Still, women officers' wages were substantially above women's overall median weekly earnings of $290 in 1986 (Bureau of Labor Statistics, January 1987). Moreover, the earnings of women in these law enforcement jobs have increased by 17 percent since 1983, slightly more than the 13 percent increase men have experienced (Mellor, 1985; BLS, unpublished data).

Women have also made gains in penetrating supervisory and command positions in law enforcement. In 1983, 2,400 female police and detectives were in supervisory positions. By 1986, their number was 4,200, an increase of some 75 percent. Still, women accounted for only five percent of the 88,000 police and detective supervisors (Bureau of Labor Statistics, January 1984; January 1987). According to 1987 membership information from the International Association of Police Chiefs, no major cities—such as New York City, Cleveland, Washington, D.C., Chicago, or Miami—had women police chiefs, although at least 11 smaller cities did.

A factor preventing greater gains for women in promotion to supervisory positions may be that law enforcement women are less likely than men to be given the opportunity for jobs that are official or unofficial prerequisites for promotion. Women are not assigned in proportionate numbers to higher-level law enforcement jobs, including violent crime investigations and special task forces. Policewomen and observers agree that a disproportionate number of women are assigned to administrative or public relations positions, and to work with juveniles and families. Furthermore, women officers note that their assignments are changed less frequently than those of male officers. As a result, women may not acquire the diverse operational knowledge of their law enforcement agencies that is considered necessary for promotion.

Law enforcement agencies are not only recognizing the importance of addressing these and other issues of particular concern to women—such as sexual harassment and pregnancy leave—but are also beginning to take better advantage of women's skills by encouraging defensive tactics that rely more on agility and conflict resolution than on physical strength during training sessions, and using women officers as trainers, for example. A Los Angeles Police Department report noted that its attrition rate for women police academy students dropped dramatically—from 50 percent to seven percent—when women began to facilitate training sessions, and programs included special sessions for the concerns of women students. Women law enforcement officers themselves are also creating formal and informal networks to address issues of concern. Many state police organizations now have women's caucuses, and the National Black Police Association has an informal women's caucus. The Committee on Women in Federal Law Enforcement in Washington, D.C. was created to study the reasons for the low participation of women in federal law enforcement and to deal constructively with the problems faced by women who are federal law enforcement agents. The International Association of Women Police is devoted to furthering the education and training of law enforcement personnel, and encouraging the general improvement of police services. Progress toward equal opportunity in the traditionally male field of law enforcement is slow and hard won. Women law enforcement officers deal with problems ranging from citizens doubting their abilities to perform their duties, to uniforms and equipment that fit improperly, to the common stress of balancing families and careers every day. Police women continue to experience discrimination, isolation, and harassment from their coworkers. However, women officers are working hard to overcome these obstacles, and it is likely that their numbers will continue to increase.

Occupational Resegregation

BARBARA F. RESKIN

MOST OCCUPATIONS are segregated by sex. Women are concentrated in the small number of jobs that society has labeled "female," e.g., teacher, secretary, waitress, dietitian. Men dominate most others, e.g., construction worker, truck driver, engineer, architect, dentist, clergy. (See "American Women Today: A Statistical Portrait" in the Appendices for tables on occupational distribution and concentration by sex.) The more female an occupation's workforce, the less the average pay for workers of both sexes. In fact, occupational segregation accounts for an estimated 30 to 45 percent of the wage gap between the sexes. Advocates of equality have therefore seen integrating women into predominantly male occupations as a key strategy to shrink the wage gap.

Between 1970 and 1980, women did make inroads in several traditionally male occupations, posting moderate gains in such diverse occupations as systems analyst, insurance agent, and baker, and even larger gains in a few occupations, including manager, insurance adjuster, and typesetter (Reskin and Hartmann, 1986). As a result, occupational segregation declined by about 10 percent—the largest decline in this century. Even so, most working women remained in segregated occupations in 1980: over 60 percent of them would have had to change occupations for women to be distributed across occupations in the same proportions as men.

However, integrating occupations will reduce the wage gap permanently only if the occupations remain integrated, but not if integration is a temporary stage in a process of resegregation in which occupations ultimately become predominantly female. There is reason for concern that women's recent integration into some male occupations is part of a process of resegregation.

The sex composition of most occupations has changed very little over time. Nonetheless, relatively large numbers of women have occasionally entered an occupation that men dominated. Within a decade or two, most such occupations have become predominantly female.

Male-to-female resegregation involves two factors: (1) a decline in the number of male workers because the occupation no longer attracts or retains men and (2) a large influx of female workers. The number of men declines when the work or its rewards become less attractive compared with other options available. For example, working conditions or job content may deteriorate; wages may fail to keep pace with those in other occupations requiring the same qualifications; advancement opportunities may disappear; more desirable jobs that demand similar qualifications may become available. Schoolteaching, for instance, became increasingly a female occupation around the turn of the century after school boards demanded more education for teachers and restricted teachers' autonomy in the classroom during a period when many other opportunities were available to educated men (Strober, 1984).

Of course, when they can, women move into occupations that appear to offer better rewards than do the available alternatives. Traditionally male occupations are attractive to women because they almost always pay better and are more likely to offer advancement opportunities than female occupations. Most traditionally male occupations, however, remain inaccessible to most women (Reskin and Hartmann, 1986). Various barriers that continue to discourage or bar women's entry range from overt discrimination, exclusion, or discouragement from necessary prior training (for instance, apprenticeship programs) to institutionalized barriers, such as rotating shifts that make child care almost impossible, or required credentials that many women lack—and that are not necessary for job performance. As a result, the few male occupations that do become open draw large numbers of women. But the same factors that open an occupation to women are apt to discourage men from entering. In turn, an occupation's failure to attract men creates additional openings for women, so the pioneering women are usually followed by larger cohorts of women.

Neighborhood racial/ethnic resegregation provides a useful model for understanding occupational resegregation. Neighborhood resegregation occurs when majority-group members abandon an integrating neighborhood, either because it was already becoming less desirable, because the majority-group fears that the minority-group presence will make it so, or simply out of prejudice. Similarly, as an occupation's sex composition begins to shift, some men see a threat to the occupation's prestige or its economic standing. If they cannot keep women out, men who have alternatives are likely to leave the occupation.

Declines in any of the rewards an occupation offers workers—wages, benefits, prestige, opportunities, autonomy, challenge—relative to those offered by comparable occupations open to equally qualified workers can prompt men to abandon an occupation to women. A technological change that makes the work more routine or clerical is often the precipitating factor. A century ago, for example, women replaced men as cigarmakers after the work was mechanized (Hartmann, 1976). Contemporary examples include typesetter/compositor and insurance adjuster/examiner. With the perfection of electronic typesetting and composing, newspapers substituted video display terminals for hot-metal linotype machines, and, while the total number of typesetter/compositors decreased, the proportion of women in the occupation skyrocketed from 17 percent in 1970 to 56 percent in 1980 (Roos, 1986). After insurance companies computerized claims processing in the 1970s, adjusters' real wages dropped sharply; they lost much of the discretion they had had in settling claims, and women became the majority (Phipps, 1986).

Reduced prestige and fewer opportunities to advance contributed to bank telling becoming female. Before World War II, when bank telling was predominantly male, it paid well relative to similar occupations. But the prestige of the job declined after the war, making it harder for banks to attract men. Women accounted for nearly half (45 percent) of all bank tellers by 1950, and by 1981 the occupation had become 94 percent female (Strober and Arnold, 1987).

Declining income and fringe benefits spurred the transformation of residential real estate sales from a male to a female occupation. Although other factors made residential sales attractive to women, openings for women were created when income declines in residential sales during the 1970s encouraged men to shift into other real estate specialties (Thomas and Reskin, 1987).

As noted earlier, the higher the proportion of women in an occupation, the less the average pay for both female and male workers in that occupation. After women replaced men as the majority among cigarmakers, teachers, insurance adjusters/examiners, and residential real estate salespersons, earnings either declined or failed to keep pace with inflation. There are signs of a similar trend in occupations that are becoming more female but in which women do not yet make up the majority. For example, among pharmacists, men's earnings dropped between 1969 and 1979 by almost $1,300 as women's representation doubled from 12 to 24 percent.

Determining which is the chicken and which the egg in the relationship between wages and sex composition is difficult, since declining wages contributed to the feminization of some of these occupations. The fact that women, having relatively few occupational choices, tend to flood into a newly opened male occupation may further reduce wages (Bergmann, 1974), but the depressing effect of feminization on an occupation's wages is not simply the result of an oversupply of women. The feminization of bank telling spurred the decline in tellers' relative wages (Strober and Arnold, 1987).

More information is needed in order to understand thoroughly how changing sex composition affects occupations' wages. Nevertheless, preliminary data indicate that wage levels in male occupations that became female in the 1970s are moving closer to the levels in traditionally female occupations. These include insurance adjusters, bank tellers, residential real estate sales people, editors, and reporters. As a result, the integration of significant numbers of women into several largely male occupations in the 1970s has not substantially reduced the wage gap between the sexes.

Concern that women's entry might reduce an occupation's prestige and earnings has provoked male workers' resistance to women in the past (Hartmann, 1976), and similar concerns have surfaced recently in some occupations that are rapidly becoming more female. Public relations, for example, which was 27 percent female in 1970 and 51 percent female in 1986, has been described as a "velvet ghetto." Illustrative of the fears evoked by the feminizing of an occupation is the debate over the effect that women's numerical dominance among journalism students may have on the status of journalists. Women are already the slight majority—50.5—of reporters and editors.

Is resegregation the inevitable outcome of occupational integration? The answer is probably yes as long as only a small number of traditionally male occupations become open to the large number of women who want and need better paying jobs. There is no way to keep the sex ratio within any particular occupation at some level that represents true integration. The only effective way to prevent resegregation is to ensure that the full range of occupations is open to women so that they will not need to crowd into just a few, and men will not need to fear that the entry of women presages feminization and, consequently, loss of wages and status.

Women and Pension Coverage

MARGARET W. NEWTON

EMPLOYER-SPONSORED PENSIONS are an important source of retirement income for millions of Americans. In 1985, an estimated 18 million beneficiaries received pension benefits as retired workers, survivors of retired workers, or disabled workers. (Some individuals are beneficiaries of more than one pension.) Twenty years earlier, the comparable figure was 3.8 million (McArdle, 1987). Almost half (48 percent) of all current retirees have income from pensions, with annual benefits averaging $5,300 for single individuals and $7,100 for married couples. Future retirees should fare considerably better: not only the percentage receiving pensions but also the average amounts received are expected to increase significantly (Chollet, 1987). But even today, income from pensions along with Social Security and individual savings has given many retirees a standard of living equal to, or often exceeding, that of most other age groups (Employee Benefit Research Institute [EBRI], 1985).

The ultimate receipt of a pension is directly tied to employment and the provision of a pension plan by an employer. Women's presence in the paid labor force and, consequently, pension receipt have been more limited than men's. Whereas 38 percent of retired pension recipients age 65 and older in 1984 were women, they constituted some 60 percent of the aged population that year.

This should not be considered extremely unusual, however. Female retirees of 1984, in many cases, were not working in the 1940s and 1950s when they would have been accumulating pension credits. Women's increased participation in the workforce will help bolster their receipt of pensions in the future. In fact, there are already signs of increased pension protection for women.

The percent of women in full-time private sector jobs who were included in an employer's pension plan (participation rate) jumped from 36 in 1972 to 41 in 1983. (Unless otherwise noted, all data in this article are from a 1983 EBRI/Department of Health and Human Services survey reported in more detail in Andrews, 1985. An EBRI update is planned for 1988.)

Nevertheless, working women are still less likely to participate in pension plans than working men, whose participation rate is 50 percent. The increased rate at which women workers are participating in pension plans thus lags behind their increased labor force participation rate. A number of factors may account for this situation.

Recent analyses suggest that differences between women and men with respect to pension coverage may be the result of certain workplace and individual work characteristics that apply to working women to a much greater extent than to working men. These factors can be broadly grouped in two categories: those that apply to the workplace, such as firm size, unionization, and industry; and those that apply to the worker, such as job tenure (number of years on the job), hours worked, earnings, and age.

Firm size and unionization are probably the two major factors determining pension coverage. In fact, one analysis suggests that these two factors in combination account for more than one-half of the variation in rates of coverage. The remaining 49 percent is attributed in roughly equal proportions to differences among industries; the combination of age, hours worked, and job tenure; and differences in wage rates (Andrews, 1985).

In general, large firms and unionized companies are more likely than other employers to have pension plans. For example, in 1983, more than four-fifths of the workers in private sector firms with 500 or more employees were covered by a pension plan, as opposed to less than one-fourth of the workers in firms with fewer than 100 workers. Mid-sized firms with 100 to 499 workers fell between these two extremes. Union firms were nearly twice as likely as nonunion firms to have workers covered by pension plans—82 versus 44 percent, respectively. Although large firms are more likely to be unionized than small firms, the effect of unionization is strong even in small firms. Three out of four workers under union contract in firms with fewer than 100 employees were covered by pension plans. This compares to less than one in four nonunion workers in such small firms. The most likely explanation for the effects of unionization, say Mitchell and Andrews (1981), is the ability of multiemployer pension plans to bring economies of scale into pension investment and administration. (Multiemployer plans cover workers, usually represented by a union, in a group of related companies.) Furthermore, pension plans are typically negotiated as part of a union collective bargaining agreement.

The extent of pension coverage among workers is also related to the industry in which they are employed. Historically, pension coverage has been widespread in manufacturing but less common in construction, retail trade, apparel, and business and professional services (aside from hospitals). The differences in pension coverage among industries is probably attributable to the characteristics of a particular industry group. Typically, lower-coverage industries are characterized by small, nonunionized companies. High-coverage industries are represented by large firms with workforces that are largely under union contract.

Pension coverage also varies by characteristics of the employee. Workers under the age of 25 are less likely to be covered than workers between the ages of 25 and 44 (35 percent versus 60 percent). Part-time workers who work fewer than 1,000 hours a year have a coverage rate of 28 percent, far less than the rate (more than 50 percent) for those working 1,000 hours or more per year.

Job tenure is also a factor: the longer the time on the job, the higher the coverage rate. Of workers with less than one year on the job in 1983, 29 percent were covered, as opposed to 56 percent of those with between one and nine years on the job. The pension coverage rates related to age, hours worked, and job tenure can be explained by the fact that employers may require employees to meet certain age and service criteria before becoming eligible for participation in a pension plan. However, under the federal law known as the Employee Retirement Income Security Act of 1974 (ERISA, as amended in 1984 and 1986), employers must meet certain minimum standards. Generally, employees who are age 21 or older, have one year of service with an employer, and work at least 1,000 hours per year with the same employer, must be included in a pension plan if the employer has one.

Pension coverage also varies by earnings. Thirty-two percent of workers earning less than $10,000 were covered by an employer-sponsored pension plan, compared to 82 percent of those earning $25,000 or more. Earnings per se, however, are probably not the determining factor here; other characteristics of low-wage earners help identify why this group has a lower pension coverage rate. For example, many workers who earn less than $10,000 are on part-time schedules or work in firms with fewer than 100 employees, where pension plans are less common. Such low-wage workers may also be young workers.

Those familiar with the employment circumstances typical of women workers will no doubt have recognized the characteristics associated with low pension coverage as much more common among women workers than among their male counterparts. In 1983, for instance, women were less likely than men to work in large firms (50 percent versus 55 percent), less likely to be in unionized firms (26 percent versus 35 percent), and less likely to work in the industries where pension plans are most common (34 percent versus 46 percent). Women were also more than twice as likely as men (27 percent versus 11 percent) to be part-time workers (Bureau of Labor Statistics, October 1987). However, taken alone, part-time employment among women is not necessarily a crucial factor, because many women working part time actually work 1,000 hours per year (or 20 hours per week)—that is, enough hours to meet the minimum required for pension participation under ERISA. EBRI reports that women tend to work more hours than the ERISA minimum standard (Employee Benefit Research Institute, 1985). But many part-time workers (male as well as female) who work enough hours to satisfy the minimum hours rule may not meet other ERISA standards. For example, they may be under age 21 or have been with their current employer less than one year.

Women are also more likely than men to be in low-paying jobs: 81 percent of all full-time working women earned less than $20,000 in 1983, as compared to 43 percent of men. As of 1987, full-time working women earned 70 percent of what full-time working men earned (Bureau of Labor Statistics, 1988).

Several federal laws have been enacted in the last five years to help expand pension coverage among the population in general and, more specifically in some cases, among women. One of the more significant is the 1984 Retirement Equity Act (REA) which, among other provisions, lowered the age requirement for participation in a pension plan from 25 to 21 and liberalized the rules for crediting years of service prior to what is known as breaks in service. The latter provision allows individuals who leave a job and return within five years to count the years before the break as service for the purposes of accruing pension credits. Both of these provisions were designed with the special needs of women and families in mind. The 1986 Tax Reform Act made an important change in vesting rules of pension plans. Until this legislation was enacted, an employer could require an employee to work 10 years before he or she vested in the plan—that is, gained nonforfeitable rights to pension benefits from the plan. Because many workers change jobs frequently during their working life and do not remain with a single employer 10 years or more, they risk accumulating no pension benefits under such a provision. Beginning in 1989, the maximum number of years an employee in the private sector must work before becoming vested is reduced to five. This new law could be particularly helpful to those who leave the labor force early in their careers—to raise a family, for example.

These reforms are designed to improve the economic prospects of women and men at retirement by increasing the likelihood that an individual who works with an employer providing a pension plan eventually receives pension benefits.

The law is now more responsive to an increasingly mobile workforce and to workers who have childbearing and child-rearing responsibilities. The reforms, however, do not reach all workers, specifically those whose employer does not sponsor a pension plan. Recognizing the limitations of today's pension system and adjusting individual savings decisions accordingly are vital to a financially secure and happy retirement.

Women and Marriage: Choice or Chance?

MARY BARBERIS

"TOO LATE for Prince Charming?" For those who feared they had tripped into a 1950s time warp, a second glance at the *Newsweek* article revealed a June 2, 1986, dateline. "A new study reports that college-educated women who are still single at the age of 35 have only a five percent chance of ever getting married." The chance disclosure of an obscure academic study to a small Connecticut newspaper for its Valentine's Day feature had triggered a press and broadcasting extravaganza that was still playing in the national media over a year later.

Pop demographics splashed over the wires, were featured by "Donahue," *People, Us, Ms., USA Today,* and, among others, such divergent columnists as Ellen Goodman and Ben Wattenberg. "For those who wait to get married, 'not now' probably means 'never,' " *Newsweek* warned. Lines like, "They're men, their chances are better!" appeared. Mixed in with the free-flowing (and often incorrect) demographics were heavy doses of pop sociology and pop psychology, demonstrated by such lines as "Survivors of the 'Me Decade' " and "Baby boomers . . . most populous segment of American society . . . arguably the most spoiled." Women were told that marriage is "central" to their "basic identities."

Behind all this was an unpublished research paper by Neil

G. Bennett, an assistant professor of sociology at Yale; David E. Bloom, an associate professor of economics at Harvard, and Patricia H. Craig, a graduate student in sociology at Yale (Bennett, Bloom, and Craig, 1986). Using a statistical technique called parametric modeling, they extrapolated from their marriage histories the marriage prospects of women college graduates between the ages of 25 and 29 in 1982. These researchers projected that just 78 percent of the white women in this group would marry, a much lower proportion than the over 90 percent of college graduates now in their mid-forties who, according to U.S. Census Bureau figures, have been married at least once. Bennett, Bloom, and Craig went on to project the probability of marriage for the women in their study who remained single at specific ages. If a woman hadn't married by age 30 the study said, the probability of her ever marrying was reduced to 20 percent. By age 35, the probability was only five percent, and at 40, it had dropped to one percent. Black women in the group had an even smaller probability of marrying, according to the researchers.

While the media sought pronouncements from "experts" all around the country, Jeanne E. Moorman, a demographer working on marriage and family statistics at the Census Bureau, decided to run her own calculations (Moorman, undated). Using a different set of data and different demographic assumptions from those used by Bennett, Bloom, and Craig, Moorman calculated high- and low-range marriage probabilities for women at various ages. According to Moorman's unpublished projections, a 15-year-old female who goes on to complete college before she marries has a 94 to 96 percent probability of eventually marrying. The probability of marriage for a college graduate not married by 30 is between 58 and 66 percent. At age 35, it drops to 32 to 41 percent, and at age 40, it is between 17 and 23 percent. Moorman's results were more in line with the marriage patterns of the previous generation and obviously quite at variance with the Bennett, Bloom, and Craig projections.

It is not disputed that college graduate women typically marry later than women with less education. The 1980 census found that 23 was the median age of marriage for women college graduates, compared to 20 for women with only a high school education. The heart of the controversy between the two studies is whether there is a new trend among today's college-educated women not only to delay marriage, but to forego it altogether.

The long and complex mathematical equation used in the Harvard-Yale study defines the shape of a curve that represents an age pattern of marriage based on three parameters: (1) the proportion in an age group who marry; (2) the average age at marriage; and (3) the time frame around the average age of marriage. It was from these marriage history parameters that the researchers derived the probability of marriage at different ages for women in the study group. Their model, which is essentially a mathematical picture of a pattern of dating, meeting a future spouse, getting engaged, and getting married, can be applied to different age groups and to populations as disparate as Taiwan, Sweden, and the United States, according to Ansley Coale, one of the equation's original creators and a former teacher of Bennett and Bloom.

However, Bennett, Bloom, and Craig may have applied Coale's model incorrectly to the subgroup of the U.S. population represented by college graduates. "The model should be used cautiously," says Coale (in telephone conversation with the author, June 25, 1987). It is not logical, he warns, to apply the model in a retrospective study using marriage histories, when the subjects of the study are defined by their current status, i.e., college graduates. Looking at the marriage histories of women college graduates since they first began dating in high school is akin to looking at the lifetime earnings of lawyers since they began delivering newspapers at age 12. It doesn't say much about the lawyers' prospective salaries after they pass the bar. Being a college graduate in 1982 is not a determinant of "marriageability," as Coale puts it, because marriageability begins when a woman starts dating, well before she ever reaches, much less graduates from, college.

Moorman and several of her colleagues at the Census Bureau have written another paper spotlighting another technical criticism of the Bennett, Bloom, and Craig study: it uses the same marriage time frame from all educational groups (Moorman, Gibson, and Fay, 1987). In other words, the Harvard-Yale team didn't allow college graduate women, who presumably have longer-range career goals than less well-educated women, any more time to get married than someone who didn't complete high school. Their equation specified that a constant percentage of women, regardless of educational attainment, would be married within four years on either side of the average age of marriage estimated for that subgroup. This puts too much of a rush on college graduates, reasons Moorman.

Moorman's analysis used a standard life-table model, the same type used by actuaries to determine life expectancies for insurance purposes. Using this technique, Moorman found that a single woman with four years of college has a *larger* probability of marrying than a woman with some high school or college, at least until age 35. But Moorman's approach, too, has been criticized. Some demographers call it "simplistic," even "primitive," since it does not allow for the possibility that people might change their views about marriage; her approach assumes that 1978–79 age-specific marriage rates will remain static over the next 50 years.

Neither study differentiated between women who want to get married, those who don't, those who favor living together without marriage, those who have had plenty of opportunities to marry, those who haven't, and those who haven't given it a thought. The statistical technique of determining probabilities simply reflects the outcome of people's behavior, but says nothing about their motivation. The question of individual choice—the fact that women in all age groups are *choosing* not to marry—was almost universally ignored in the media blitz that surrounded the Harvard-Yale team's study.

The media's reaction was to view the prospect that a greater proportion of women might remain unwed as a national and, especially, a personal calamity. In reality, whether it turns out that women are only delaying marriage or that they are foregoing it altogether, the patterns can be seen as evidence that women's choices are improving. The probability of marriage, after all, reflects the *decisions* women are making, not a giant game of chance. With increased education and opportunities in the workplace, women no longer must derive their economic or social status from a husband. Possibilities other than marriage are presenting themselves, and women are increasingly opting for them.

The media's treatment of this subject is but another example of why research findings—from any type of study, whether about the effects of federal spending or about a pattern of eating that might contribute to cancer—should always be presented with clear caveats and specifics about the limitations of the assumptions and statistical methods used. This particular debate over parametric versus standard life-table modeling would have been best left to the academic journals, where there is no need to remind the reader that projections are *not* predictions and certainly are not a guarantee of what the future will hold for any individual.

However the debate about statistical projection methods might be resolved, today's woman will find more relevance in the point made by Bennett and Bloom themselves in a 1986 newspaper article: "... [W]omen are increasingly empowered to contemplate and exercise their own will. Rather than condemn women for taking advantage of the freedoms that men have always enjoyed, society should seek to ... better accommodate contemporary values and behavior."

Reproductive Hazards for High-tech Workers

MICHAEL ROSE

THEY'RE CALLED "CLEAN ROOMS," those sterile halls where workers in spotless caps and coveralls manufacture silicon computer chips. But we're finding out that these workplaces, where the chips are scrupulously protected from contamination, may not be safe for the humans who work there. Evidence is mounting that the environment in clean rooms is hazardous to women's reproductive health—and women account for nearly three-quarters of the 76,000 workers on computer-chip production lines.

The resolution of the legal, social, and regulatory issues raised by this evidence will affect many more than these 55,000 women, however. The National Institute for Occupational Safety and Health (NIOSH) has estimated that six million workers are exposed to the eight substances believed to pose the most serious threats to human reproduction. An additional nine million workers are exposed to radio-frequency/microwave radiation, another suspected reproductive hazard. And if research reveals that video display terminals (VDTs) belong on the list of reproductive hazards, some 11 million female VDT workers of childbearing age may be at risk as well.

It wasn't supposed to turn out this way. The theory was that as the U.S. economy moved away from heavy manufacturing and its attendant chemical processes toward information and service industries, workers' exposure to dangerous substances would decline. "Light" high-tech industries extolled the virtues of what they called a "super clean" record.

The evidence that the manufacturing of silicon chips—the building blocks of high-tech industries—may threaten grave reproductive impairment in women represents more than a simple blemish on that record. The evidence has become a powerful reminder that reproductive hazards in the workplace are likely to endure as a serious occupational and women's health problem. Yet there is little consensus not only with respect to how to deal with a hazard once it is discovered, but also with respect to the proper methods of investigating whether a hazard exists.

Reproductive hazards in the modern workplace are a relatively new concern. In an exhaustive review of research on reproductive hazards from occupational exposures, congressional researchers found 300 such studies, but only seven were conducted before 1970 (U.S. Congress, 1985). Concern over high-tech reproductive hazards is an even more recent phenomenon. The first cluster of reproductive problems among VDT users was reported in 1980 (Elinson et al., 1980). In 1984, 150 women who worked on the semiconductor production lines at a GTE Corporation plant in Albuquerque, New Mexico sued GTE, claiming that exposure to chemicals at their jobs caused miscarriages, uncontrolled bleeding requiring hysterectomies, and children born mentally retarded or with learning disabilities. While this suit for workers' compensation has been pending, four of the plaintiffs have died from diseases associated with the chemicals found at their work site. In 1986, the workers also filed a multimillion dollar reckless endangerment suit against GTE.

But it was not until November 1986, when University of Massachusetts researchers released a study they had conducted for Digital Equipment Corporation (DEC), that the debate over reproductive hazards in the workplace began to draw renewed public attention. The researchers found a higher than normal miscarriage rate for women who worked at DEC's Hudson, Massachusetts chip production line, where workers were exposed to some of the same gases containing arsine and chlorine compounds as were the Albuquerque GTE workers (Calabrese and Tastides, unpublished).

It is no exaggeration to say that the DEC findings sent shock waves throughout the computer industry. Both DEC and IBM notified their workers of the study's findings and encouraged not only pregnant women, but all women of childbearing age, to transfer off the chip production line if they were concerned about the possibility of hazards to their reproductive health. The Semiconductor Industry Association and IBM both decided to undertake extensive studies to determine if the DEC study findings were indicative of the hazards in the industry as a whole.

AT&T took more drastic action: on December 29, 1986, it prohibited women of childbearing age from working in its clean rooms. AT&T explained that its action was a precaution to protect women until the potential dangers of the chip assembly line received further study. In general, AT&T's female employees were pleased by the company's decision because they felt that the company acted to protect their health ("Profile of a Warning," 1987: 1).

Many others see AT&T's action as insidious, however. Some labor unions and women's groups, for example, worry that a pattern is developing in which industry reacts to health hazards on the job not by making the worksite safe but rather by closing it to workers thought to be especially at risk. Management leans toward the latter approach because it wishes to avoid damage suits for workplace injuries and because transferring workers is far less expensive and troublesome than making a work area safe for the most susceptible workers. At least 15 *Fortune* 500 companies have policies excluding fertile or pregnant women from certain jobs (U.S. Congress, 1985).

There are, however, fundamental flaws in the rationale for instituting a so-called fetal protection policy, which bases job placement on the notion that women are far more susceptible to reproductive hazards than men. Many more studies have been done on the links between exposure to certain chemicals and damage to the female reproductive system and the fetus than on the effect of similar exposure on the male reproductive system. Thus, fetal protection policies are disadvantageous to females to the extent that the policies deny women employment and advancement opportunities available to men; on the other hand, the policies are disadvantageous to males if the substances to which they are exposed—and from which women are protected—turn out to be hazardous for men as well.

A fetal protection policy may constitute illegal sex discrimination under Title VII of the Civil Rights Act of 1964. This is the contention of a lawsuit filed by the United Auto Workers (UAW) against the Johnson Controls Company of Milwaukee. Since 1982, the company has excluded all women of childbearing age from those areas of its automobile battery manufacturing plant where workers' exposure to airborne lead causes them to absorb at least 30 micrograms of lead per 100 milliliters of their blood. Johnson Controls maintains that its policy is intended solely to protect the health of unborn children, who may risk permanent damage if their mothers absorb this level of lead. According to a lawyer for the UAW, the union not only contends that this policy is discriminatory, it challenges the scientific basis for the policy—that is, that lead poses more of a danger to women and fetuses than to men (author's conversation with Ralph Jones, 1986). However, the U.S. District Court for Eastern Wisconsin, finding a "considerable body" of expert opinion that the risk is "substantially confined to women," ruled for Johnson Controls on January 21, 1988. The UAW intends to appeal this decision.

Beyond the arguments presented in the Johnson Controls case, labor and women's groups maintain that even the more "progressive" fetal protection policies—those that give women workers a choice about whether to move to a different job—wrongly place on workers the burden of protecting themselves or their progeny from workplace hazards. This, according to the critics, goes against the intent of the Occupational Safety and Health Act of 1970, which requires that employers provide a "safe and healthful workplace" to all employees.

But if those who make this argument are looking for enforcement of the act in this respect, they may have a never-ending wait. The federal Occupational Safety and Health Administration (OSHA) has always moved at a snail's pace. Although NIOSH ranks reproductive hazards as one of the 10 leading causes of work-related injuries and illnesses in the United States, and although there are hundreds of suspected reproductive hazards in American workplaces today, OSHA has regulated only four on that basis: ethylene oxide, lead, ionizing radiation, and dibromochloropropane.

There are two major reasons why OSHA's regulation of

reproductive hazards has been minimal so far and seems unlikely to improve anytime soon. First, because most of its regulatory actions are contested in court, OSHA issues rules only on those substances for which there is overwhelming evidence of a threat to workers' health. Conclusive evidence with respect to reproductive hazards is hard to come by because research in this area is in its infancy. Second, throughout its 18-year history, OSHA's budgets have been minuscule, given the agency's ambitious mandate. OSHA has been able to issue health standards covering only 23 substances since it was established; it has been able to conduct safety inspections of fewer than 50,000 of the nation's six million workplaces each year. Given these circumstances, it is unrealistic to expect that OSHA will devote resources to fighting corporate fetal protection policies, which represent at least an attempt to protect workers from perceived risk. Moreover, a 1984 federal appeals court ruling upheld an administrative decision striking down OSHA's only citation against a fetal protection policy (*Oil, Chemical & Atomic Workers International Union v. American Cyanamid Co.*).

The finding of possible reproductive hazards in the manufacture of computer chips has coincided with the intensifying of a simmering controversy about the safety of video display terminal. The introduction of VDTs into the American workplace has already changed the way business is conducted—most would say for the better. But according to the National Association of Working Women, many of its members who work at a computer terminal for hour after hour every day disagree. For some years, these and other VDT workers have reported headaches, vision problems, and musculoskeletal discomfort. On the basis of such complaints, organized labor has called for extensive changes in the way workers are required to use VDTs. Safeguards for VDT users have been inserted in some labor contracts negotiated by the Service Employees International Union and the American Federation of State, County and Municipal Employees. (These safeguards include clauses allowing pregnant women to be transferred to jobs not involving VDT use.) A few state governments, including California and New York, have instituted similar protections for state employees who use VDTs. No state law, however, addresses reproductive issues in connection with VDTs.

In fact, it is only within the last decade that reproductive problems have been added to the list of workers' complaints about VDTs. Evidence has been uncovered that VDT use may be associated with pregnancy difficulties, including birth defects and miscarriages. For example, NIOSH has found clusters of miscarriages among telephone operators at the offices of Southern Bell in Atlanta, General Telephone in Alma, Michigan, and United Airlines in San Francisco (National Institute for Occupational Safety and Health, 1983; 1984a; 1984b). Researchers at the University of Michigan found a slight increase in miscarriages for women who worked at VDTs for more than 20 hours per week (Brix and Butler, unpublished). Swedish researchers found an increase in fetal deaths in mice exposed to radiation similar to that emitted by VDTs (Frolen et al., 1987).

Perhaps because incontrovertible evidence linking VDT use to reproductive hazards would have such far-reaching consequences for American industry, the design of the first major study to look at this relationship has become embroiled in politics—so much so that NIOSH and many VDT researchers say that study results will not be conclusive (Butler, 1986; Selikoff, 1986; Melius, 1986). The three-year government study, begun by NIOSH in June of 1986, is examining 4,000 female VDT users at Southern Bell to determine if they have a higher than normal rate of reproductive problems and, if so, whether this rate is related to their use of VDTs.

The NIOSH researchers had urged a more comprehensive study: they wanted to include an examination of whether the fertility of the Southern Bell women had been adversely affected by their use of VDTs. NIOSH also wanted to examine the effect of stress on these workers. This was seen as particularly important because one of the main benefits of the study was supposed to be a determination of whether any reproductive problems that may be found are associated with the VDTs themselves or whether they arise from stress caused by the way jobs requiring VDTs are currently structured. This question had been raised in a 1982 study by the National Academy of Sciences (1983) that concluded there was no persuasive evidence that VDTs themselves were to blame for the reproductive problems found in some VDT users.

The Office of Management and Budget (OMB) insisted that survey questions related to fertility and stress be dropped from the NIOSH Southern Bell study. OMB argued that these questions were inappropriate because there was "insufficient evidence" relating stress or infertility to hypotheses concerning VDT exposure and adverse reproductive outcomes. According to OMB, these questions had "no practical utility" and fell "outside the purpose of the study."

The Energy and Commerce Committee of the U.S. House of Representatives not only challenged the scientific basis for OMB's conclusions, but charged that OMB's actions on the NIOSH VDT study, and on proposed studies of chemical hazards, showed a "demonstrable bias" against occupational health research. According to the committee's report,

OMB purposely selected outside reviewers to evaluate these studies who "also fail to appreciate" the importance of occupational health. The committee report concluded that OMB "unreasonably delayed, impeded, and thwarted governmental research efforts designed to answer public demands for information on serious public health questions" (U.S. Congress, 1986).

Without anticipating the results of the ongoing studies of reproductive hazards in the workplace, what is already known points to a strong probability that, in the next few years, reproductive hazards will be found to be linked to some of the jobs spawned by the computer revolution. If convincing evidence that such hazards exist is found, OSHA, Congress, corporate management, organized labor, and the public health community will most likely stake out divergent positions on dealing with these dangers. As has been the case with respect to all jobs found to threaten workers' health, there will be a demand for changes in high-tech jobs found to be hazardous to human reproduction. Because such changes would almost certainly be costly, high-tech businesses could be tempted to move overseas to countries where government regulation with respect to workplace health and safety is far less stringent than in the United States.

Government and business leaders are already increasingly preoccupied with keeping jobs in this country and with keeping America competitive in the world marketplace. One can only hope that the attempts to maintain the economic health of America do not sacrifice the physical health of Americans.

Women and AIDS

GLORIA WEISSMAN

By the end of 1987, Acquired Immunodeficiency Syndrome (AIDS) had become a major threat to the health of women in the United States. At the present time, in order to meet the Centers for Disease Control (CDC) criteria for AIDS diagnosis, an individual must have laboratory confirmation of infection with the Human Immunodeficiency Virus (HIV) and one or more of the following symptoms: "wasting syndrome" (rapid, unexplained weight loss of 10 percent or more of body weight); AIDS dementia (memory loss, forgetfulness, confusion, delusions); secondary infections (including cytomegalovirus, toxoplasmosis, and others); rare cancers (including Kaposi's sarcoma); and interstitial pneumonia.

While women account for a small proportion (seven percent) of all AIDS cases diagnosed since the beginning of the epidemic (3,349 women, 43,258 men), women now constitute the fastest growing group of people with AIDS (Centers for Disease Control, 1987).

In the first 11 months of 1987, 1,377 women were diagnosed with AIDS, accounting for eight percent of all AIDS cases reported during this period. The CDC estimates that another 6,700 to 33,000 women have AIDS-Related Complex (ARC). (ARC is now defined by the CDC as persistent, generalized lymphadenopathy [inflammation of the lymph nodes] and a few minor infections such as oral candidiasis [thrush].) A significant proportion of these women may go on to develop full-blown AIDS.

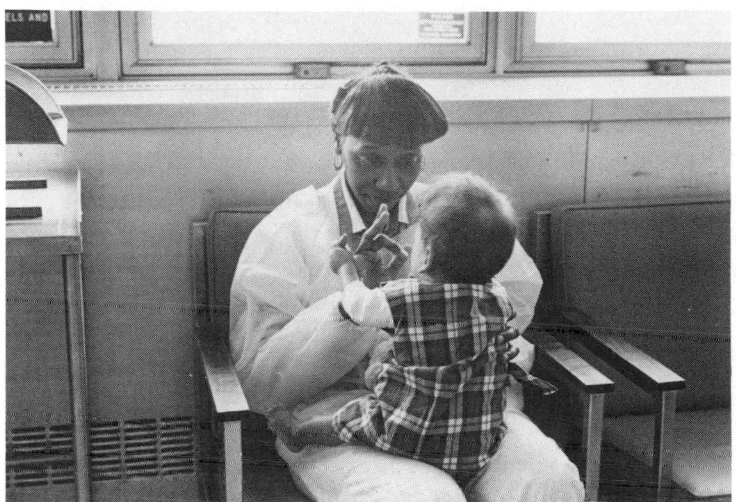

Harlem hospital volunteer with a child who has AIDS.
Jim Wilson / The New York Times

Although 43 states and the District of Columbia have reported cases of AIDS in women, over two-thirds of the female AIDS cases in the U.S. come from three states: New York (46 percent of all female cases), New Jersey (14 percent), and Florida (10 percent) (Guinan and Hardy, 1987). In New York City, AIDS is the number one killer of women age 25 to 29 (Worth and Rodriguez, 1987).

As disturbing as these numbers are, diagnosed AIDS and ARC cases are only the tip of the iceberg: the CDC estimates that there are 50 to 80 times as many women who are infected with HIV as there are women with active cases of AIDS. This translates into at least 165,000 women with HIV. Many of these women have no symptoms and are unaware that they are infected and capable of infecting others. It is not presently known how many of these asymptomatic carriers will go on to develop ARC or AIDS.

Although all sexually active women are potentially at risk for HIV infection and AIDS, the women currently at greatest risk are intravenous drug users, the sexual partners of male intravenous drug users and bisexual men, and prostitutes. Forty-six percent of female AIDS cases during 1987 occurred among intravenous drug users, with an additional 31 percent of cases attributed to sexual contact with an infected male. (Female cases attributed to sexual contact increased by 14 percent between 1982 and 1986 [Guinan and Hardy, 1987] and by four percent in 1987.) Recipients of contaminated transfusions accounted for 13 percent of all female AIDS cases in 1987, while in 10 percent of cases, the risk factor(s) could not be determined (Centers for Disease Control, 1987).

While intravenous drug users account for the largest group of women at risk for AIDS, the sexual partners of intravenous drug users are the second largest group of at-risk women. Of women infected with AIDS as the result of sexual contact, two-thirds had sexual relations with a man who was an intravenous drug user, and 16 percent with a man who was bisexual. Another 15 percent of those women who acquired AIDS through sexual contact did not know their contact's risk factor (that is, whether he was an intravenous drug user, bisexual, or the recipient of possibly contaminated blood). However, intravenous drug use on the part of the contact probably accounts for a substantial number of these cases, as well.

Women at risk mean babies at risk. Women between the ages of 13 and 39 account for four out of five (79 percent) of all female AIDS cases. One-third of all female cases involve women in their twenties. AIDS cases among children (pediatric AIDS) most commonly occur because of viral transmission, during either pregnancy or childbirth, from an HIV-infected mother. In nearly three-quarters (73 percent) of pediatric AIDS cases, the babies' mothers were either themselves intravenous drug users or had sexual partners who were. The odds that AIDS will be transferred to the unborn child are still uncertain, but preliminary studies indicate that half of the babies born to HIV-infected mothers may also be infected with the AIDS virus.

To prevent further spread of the deadly AIDS virus to women and their children, it is imperative both to educate the general public and to mount aggressive, targeted outreach efforts to women at highest risk. Many of these women are "hidden" and difficult to reach because they are unaware that their sexual partners have, or are at high risk of getting, AIDS. Preventing the spread of AIDS through sexual activity will probably be more difficult than preventing its transmission through the sharing of contaminated intravenous drug paraphernalia. For a woman to take the steps necessary to avoid sexual and perinatal transmission of AIDS may mean risking rejection, abandonment, even physical harm at the hands of her partner, and the disruption of sexual and/or family relationships. In some cases, it may mean the decision not to have children.

Educational campaigns featuring brief, clear information are a first step, but increased knowledge per se has not and probably will not reduce risky behaviors. It has been learned from other health-education campaigns that fear will not produce *sustained* change in people's behavior. Women at risk for AIDS must first be persuaded that their lives are worth saving and that it is within their power to prevent this deadly disease. Yet those women most vulnerable to infection are also economically and socially disadvantaged, poorly educated, and, typically, unemployed. Many of them feel helpless, powerless, and depressed (Mondanaro, 1987). Empowering these women must be a cornerstone of AIDS prevention; they need to learn that they can make a difference. Involving them in the development and delivery of their own programs and reinforcing whatever positive changes they can make will be crucial (Mondanaro, 1987). Once they are motivated to reduce risk, they will be receptive to learning how to prevent exposure (Mantell et al., 1988).

Denial, both by individuals and among certain groups of women, will also have to be overcome if prevention programs are to be effective. Many people in the black and Hispanic communities, for example, still believe that AIDS is a disease that only affects gay, white males, despite the fact that blacks and Hispanics have been especially hard hit by AIDS. Many women persist in the belief that they cannot contract or transmit AIDS even though their behavior places them at risk. For some women, denial may be the only defense against the fear of this fatal disease (Mondanaro, 1987; Wofsy, 1987). In developing strategies to change behavior, this denial must be taken into account.

Effective AIDS-prevention programs for women must also be designed with special sensitivity to the linguistic and cultural norms prevailing in the groups and subgroups of black and Hispanic women who are at particular risk. Minority women are vastly overrepresented among women with AIDS, accounting for 72 percent of the total (Centers for Disease Control, 1986). The cumulative incidence of AIDS in black and Hispanic women is more than 10 times that for white women.

Moreover, whatever the particular group or community to be reached, it is peers and role models from that particular group or community who will be most effective in delivering the message. Changing community norms, through the kind of organizing that has been successful in the gay male community, is an approach that may not only be effective in preventing AIDS, but in improving other aspects of women's lives.

While it is important, especially in the absence of a cure or a vaccine for the disease, to focus on *preventing* AIDS among women, the many women who have already been directly affected by the disease—as people with AIDS, as friends or relatives of people with AIDS, or as caregivers—must not be overlooked. There is some evidence that women who contract the disease may have a faster disease course from HIV and be likely to die sooner of AIDS than men (Rothenberg et al., 1987). There is a lack of specialized medical, social, and educational services for women with AIDS-Related Complex or AIDS, a lack that needs to be addressed. Attention and resources also must be directed toward the needs of women who care for people with AIDS, whether these caretakers be counselors, nurses, volunteers, mothers, sisters, or friends.

Battered Women

CYNTHIA DIEHM *and* MARGO ROSS

ANY EXAMINATION OF the status of American women cannot ignore the plight of the estimated three to four million or more women who are beaten by their intimate partners each year (Stark et al., 1981: vii; Pagelow 1984: 46). The home, once seen as a sanctuary for women, is increasingly being recognized as a place where females may be at risk of psychological and physical abuse.

Abusive and violent behavior among people who are married, living together, or have an ongoing or prior intimate relationship is referred to as spouse abuse, battering, or domestic violence. It occurs among people of all races, age groups, religions, lifestyles, and income and educational levels. Approximately 95 percent of the victims of such violence are women (U.S. Department of Justice, 1985: 21).

A battering incident is rarely an isolated occurrence. It usually recurs frequently and escalates in severity over time. It can involve threats, pushing, slapping, punching, choking, sexual assault, and assault with weapons. Each year, more than one million women seek medical assistance for injuries caused by battering. Battering may result in more injuries that require medical treatment than rape, auto accidents, and muggings combined (See Stark and Flitcraft, 1982; 1987).

A typical response to domestic violence is to question why

women remain in abusive relationships. Actually, many women do leave their abusers. In one study of 205 battered women, 53 percent had left the relationship (Browne, 1987: 109). Moreover, there is no way to know how many women have chosen not to identify abuse as the reason they ended their marriages.

Divorce proceedings can be particularly difficult for battered women, especially when child custody litigation is involved. If a battered woman has left the home without her children, she may lose custody of them because her action may be perceived as desertion. If the batterer is established in the community, the court may see him as a better custodial parent, regardless of his wife's accusations of violence, because she may appear to be in transition and unstable. If the woman is granted custody, the abuser usually is given child visitation rights—a situation that continually places the woman at risk of abuse. Some states have passed legislation that mandates consideration of spouse abuse as evidence in custody litigation.

Battered women, in general, do not passively endure physical abuse, but actively seek assistance in ending the violence from a variety of sources, including police, lawyers, family members, and the clergy. Frequently, it is the failure of these individuals and systems to provide adequate support that traps women in violent relationships. A study of more than 6,000 battered women in Texas found that, on average, the women had contacted five different sources of help prior to leaving the home and becoming residents of battered women's shelters (Gondolf and Fisher, 1988).

Certainly, many battered women suffer in silence. These women endure physical abuse for a variety of reasons:

- A woman may feel that it is her duty to keep the marriage together at all costs because of religious, cultural, or socially learned beliefs.

- A woman may endure physical and emotional abuse to keep the family together for the children's sake.

- A woman may be financially dependent on her husband and thus would probably face severe economic hardship if she chose to support herself and her children on her own.

- A battered woman frequently faces the most physical danger when she attempts to leave. She may be threatened with violence or attacked if she tries to flee. She fears for her safety, her children's safety, and the safety of those who help her.

The Legacy of Indifference

Despite the severity of domestic violence, it is a problem that, until quite recently, has been cloaked in secrecy. Up to the early 1970s, battered women had few options but to suffer in silence or to attempt single-handedly to leave controlling and violent men. To understand why society is just beginning to confront domestic violence, it is essential to view the problem within its historical context.

Domestic violence is not a new phenomenon; historically, husbands had the legal right to chastise their wives to maintain authority. In the United States, wife beating was legal until the end of the nineteenth century. Alabama and Massachusetts were on record as rescinding the "ancient privilege" of wife beating in 1871, but most states merely ignored old laws (Davidson, 1977: 19).

While battering was no longer legally sanctioned by the early part of the twentieth century, the spirit of the law remained and abuse was still common. Social and justice systems have viewed domestic violence as a private family matter and have been reluctant to intervene.

Change Through Grassroots Activism

The legacy of society's indifference to violence in the home fueled a grassroots "battered women's movement," which gained nationwide momentum in the mid-1970s. Inspired by the feminist anti-rape movement's analysis of male violence against women as a social and political issue, battered women began to speak out about the physical abuse they were suffering in their marriages and intimate relationships.

At first, battered women helped one another individually by setting up informal safe homes and apartments. In such an environment—free from intimidation by their abusers—battered women could speak openly and thus soon discovered the commonality of their experiences. As the issue was publicized, women of all races, cultures, ages, abilities, and walks of life began to expose the violence they suffered. It quickly became clear that woman battering was a pervasive problem, and a nationwide movement started to take shape.

The early experience of the movement revealed the acute need of safe shelter for battered women and their children. Unless a woman could feel truly safe, she could not effectively evaluate her situation and make clear decisions about her future. Operating on shoestring budgets, battered women's advocates began to establish formal programs around the country. Only a handful of such programs existed in the mid-1970s; today, there are more than 1,200 shelters, hotlines, and safe-home networks nationwide. Grassroots lobbying efforts at the federal level led to congressional passage of the 1984 Family Violence Prevention and Services Act, which earmarked federal funding for programs serving victims of domestic violence.

Creating and expanding a network of shelters and services for battered women and their children, while essential, was not the only goal of the grassroots movement. Equally important was the task of promoting changes in the criminal justice system that would hold abusers accountable for their violence and uphold the rights of battered women.

In 1984, the report of the Attorney General's Task Force on Family Violence reaffirmed the need for an improved criminal justice response to domestic violence, stating: "The legal response to family violence must be guided primarily by the nature of the abusive act, not the relationship between the victim and the abuser" (U.S. Department of Justice, 1984: 34). The report focused on the role of the criminal justice system and recommended actions for each of its components that would increase the effectiveness of its response and better ensure the victim's safety. Across the country advocates continue to work with law enforcement personnel, prosecutors, judges, and legislators to implement new policies and enact legislation.

The Criminal Justice Response

Domestic violence is now a crime in all 50 states and the District of Columbia, either under existing assault and battery laws or under special legislation. However, the true extent of crimes involving domestic violence remains largely unknown, since no accurate statistics on the number of battered women exist. Neither of the two sources of national crime statistics—the Federal Bureau of Investigation's Uniform Crime Report (UCR) and the federal Bureau of Justice Statistics' National Crime Survey (NCS)—is specifically designed to measure the incidence of crime in the domestic setting.

The UCR, which is based on police department reports, only collects information on the victim-offender relationship in the homicide category. Despite the UCR's limitations, it does provide a chilling picture of the potential lethality of domestic violence. According to the latest report, 30 percent of female homicide victims were killed by their husbands or boyfriends (Federal Bureau of Investigation, 1985: 11).

To supplement the UCR, the Bureau of Justice Statistics conducts an ongoing national telephone survey of some 60,000 American households to glean information on crimes not reported to police. Originally designed to collect data on such crimes as burglary and aggravated assault, the NCS also asks respondents about their relationships to offenders and thus inadvertently obtains information on domestic violence. Results of the 1978–82 NCS led analysts to estimate that 2.1 million women were victims of domestic violence at least once during an average 12-month period. This estimate is not intended to portray the true extent of the problem; rather, it is an indication of the number of women who believed domestic violence to be criminal and who felt free to disclose such information over the telephone to an unknown interviewer (Langan and Innes, 1986).

National crime statistics are based primarily on local police department reports, which traditionally have not included a discrete category for domestic violence. Police departments in a number of jurisdictions are just beginning to develop methods to report domestic violence crimes separately. It will be many years before this practice becomes universal and a more accurate picture of the nature and incidence of domestic crimes is available.

Law enforcement has traditionally operated from a philosophy of nonintervention in cases of domestic violence. Unless severe injury or death was involved, police rarely arrested offenders. Expert police opinion was that there was little law enforcement could do to prevent such crimes. Moreover, it was believed that even if an offender were arrested, cases would never go to trial because of the victim's fear of testifying against her abuser.

The police response to domestic violence has been altered significantly in the last few years. In 1982, a study in Minneapolis found that arrest was more effective than two nonarrest alternatives in reducing the likelihood of repeat violence over a six-month follow-up period. Interestingly, only two percent of abusers who were arrested in the study went before a judge to receive court punishment. Thus, the Minneapolis study showed that arrest appears to reduce recidivism, even if it does not lead to conviction (Sherman and Berk, 1984). The results of the study were widely publicized and have contributed to a more aggressive law enforcement response to domestic violence.

Research results, however, have been only partially responsible for changes in police policies. Class action lawsuits brought by victims against police departments for lack of protection also have effected policy change. In 1985, for example, a battered woman in Torrington, Connecticut won a multimillion dollar settlement from the city for the failure of the police department to protect her from her husband's violence. *Thurman v. Torrington* was a catalyst for the state's passage of the 1986 Family Violence and Response Act, which mandates arrest in domestic violence cases when probable cause exists (Epstein, 1987).

For the past several years, the Crime Control Institute has conducted a telephone survey of police departments serving jurisdictions with populations of 100,000 or more. In 1986, 46 percent of these departments indicated they had a pro-arrest policy in cases of domestic violence, as compared with 31 percent in 1985 and 10 percent in 1984. In addition, the percent of urban police departments reporting more actual domestic violence arrests appears to have risen from 24 percent in 1984 to 47 percent in 1986 (Cohn and Berk, 1987).

Other components of the criminal justice system have also begun to take a tougher stance on domestic violence. Many district attorneys' offices have established separate domestic violence units to encourage more vigorous prosecution of offenders. Judicial training on domestic violence has been promoted so that stronger court sanctions are imposed against abusive men.

The changes in the criminal justice system's response to domestic violence are quite new, however, and have not occurred universally. Although states have enacted various types of statutes to promote more aggressive treatment of domestic violence as a crime, whether this approach is upheld by individual actors within the system varies from jurisdiction to jurisdiction.

In many jurisdictions, courts can order batterers to attend special counseling programs either before the case is adjudicated or as a condition of probation. Frequently, criminal charges are dismissed if the defendant "successfully" completes the program. Unfortunately, the effectiveness of special programs for abusive men is hard to measure, and little information exists on the effectiveness of intervention.

Legal Protection for the Victim

In the early 1970s, few legal remedies existed for the battered woman seeking protection from abuse. If married, she could file for divorce, separation, or custody, and in some states obtain an injunction ordering her husband not to abuse her while domestic relations proceedings were pending.

Since that time, 47 states and the District of Columbia have enacted legislation allowing battered women to obtain civil protection or restraining orders. Depending on the state, through such legislation the court can order the abuser to move out of the residence, refrain from abuse of or contact with the victim, enter a batterers' treatment program, or pay support, restitution, or attorney's fees (Lerman and Livingston, 1983). However, "a protection or restraining order is meaningful only if violation of the order constitutes a crime and police are able to verify the existence of an order when a violation is alleged" (Goolkasian, 1986: 67).

The ability of such orders to protect all domestic violence victims is inconsistent across jurisdictions. Some areas require the victim to be married to and currently cohabitating with the abuser. Abuse may be narrowly defined as an attempt or infliction of bodily injury or serious bodily injury, providing no protection from threats of violence or destruction of property. The duration of protection orders can range from 15 days to no more than one year, thereby forcing many women to relocate to avoid abuse. Moreover, it is believed that protection orders are poorly implemented and enforced. It may be quite difficult for low-income women, women of color, and women who have defended themselves against physical abuse to obtain this type of protection. The use and enforcement of civil protection orders is now under study through funding from the Justice Department.

The Importance of Prevention

Clearly, just responding to domestic violence is not sufficient. An improved criminal justice response and the development of court-ordered programs for abusive men are not panaceas for the problem. Battered women's advocates believe that to bring an end to domestic violence, it is necessary to examine how the culture teaches young men and women to play roles that lead to such violent behavior, and how restricted access to economic resources can trap women in the potentially lethal cycle of violence.

If the cycle of violence is to be broken, advocates on behalf of battered women stress that young women must be encouraged to go beyond traditionally passive, dependent roles, while young men must be taught that abusive, violent, and controlling behavior is never acceptable. To this end, battered women's advocates have established children's programs in many shelters, as well as curricula on domestic violence for use in elementary, middle, and high schools.

Finally, equal access to employment, housing, and economic resources must be available to all women. This situation is particularly acute for battered women, who frequently remain in abusive relationships simply because of economics. Thus, a critical determinant of whether a battered woman will live without violence or be forced to return to an abusive partner often is the availability of decent affordable housing, adequate pay, and other forms of economic assistance.

Violence in the home is a problem with serious repercussions for the battered woman, her children, and the entire community. Breaking the cycle of violence requires financial support for services to battered women, a strong criminal justice response that holds abusive men accountable for their violence, and, most important, ongoing social activism that focuses on improving the status of all women.

Women in Prison

JANE ROBERTS CHAPMAN

THE GENERAL PERCEPTION of the prison population is that it is male. Indeed, the vast majority—95 percent in 1986—of prison inmates are men. Males are not only much more likely than females to commit crimes, they are a great deal more likely to commit violent crimes. Even though arrests do not necessarily result in convictions, much less in prison sentences, it is significant that the ratio of males to females among all those arrested in 1986 was nearly four to one; among arrests for violent crimes, the ratio was more than eight to one (Federal Bureau of Investigation, 1987). But women offenders and alleged offenders are increasing in the criminal justice system. The decade 1976–86 showed female arrests up 30 percent, while male arrests increased 15 percent.

Males are still far more likely to be sentenced to prison than females: males who have been convicted and sentenced are 21 times as likely to be incarcerated as their female counterparts. Nevertheless, although women accounted for only 4.9 percent of the prison population overall, 26,610 women were in prison (23,777 in state institutions; 2,833 in federal prisons) in this country at the end of 1986, and their numbers have been growing faster than those of male prisoners. Between 1976 and 1986, the number of women in prison increased by 138 percent, while the male prison population grew by 94 percent (U.S. Department of Justice, May 1987). Moreover, the percentage of women among prisoners has been creeping up (it was 4.2 percent in 1981), as has the female incarceration rate (the number of female prisoners per 100,000 females in the U.S. population), which increased by 15 percent between 1985 and 1986 (nearly double the eight percent increase for males). Fourteen states have at least 500 women in prison. Women are being sentenced to longer terms than in previous years, possibly as a by-product of the movement toward equal treatment of women and men in our society. And women convicted of capital crimes are more likely than in earlier times to end up on death row, where the female population increased from three in 1973 to 18 in 1986 (U.S. Department of Justice, September 1987).

The female offender is typically young, poor, and undereducated. She is likely to be a single parent. Sixty-two percent of female offenders are under 30 and the majority (58 percent) have neither a high school degree nor the equivalent (Ryan, 1984; Goetting and Howsen, 1983). Although most had some work experience before going to prison, it was generally in low-skill, low-paying occupations, and may have been sporadic. According to unpublished data from the Bureau of Justice Statistics, in 1979 (the most recent year for which the Bureau would provide such data) nearly three-fourths (74 percent) of women in state prisons had children, although only about one-fifth (21 percent) were currently married. Half of adult female offenders are minority women (Ryan, 1984).

Women offenders typically have much more in common with poor women in general than with male offenders. Moreover, while women in prison have been convicted of criminal acts and may have victimized others, they have very often been the victims of physical and psychological abuse themselves, and been affected by the kind of sex discrimination that affects all women (Chapman, 1980; Valente and Decostanzo, 1982; Goetting, 1985; Feinman, 1983; Ryan, 1984).

The majority of women's offenses are nonviolent and are in a category that could be called "economic crimes" (Chapman, 1980), that is, property crimes (which are the most common offenses among women), forgery and counterfeiting, fraud, embezzlement, prostitution, and commercialized vice and vagrancy. Male offenders have a much higher incidence of both violent crime and repetitive involvement in criminal lifestyles. In contrast, the woman incarcerated for murder very often has a single crime—the killing of her husband—on her record. Although there has not been a thorough study of the matter, available evidence suggests that the majority of homicides committed by women result from domestic violence. Frequently, the crime follows an extended period of physical and psychological abuse by a man whom the woman kills or attempts to kill in self-defense (Browne, 1987; Committee on Domestic Violence and Incarcerated Women, 1987).

Analysis of historical trends has shown a strong connection between female poverty and female crime (Chapman, 1980). In 1960, one-quarter of all female arrests were for economic crimes; by 1985, that proportion had increased to 40 percent. It is no coincidence that this is the same period that has seen the feminization of poverty. Although more women are working now than ever before, and there is apparently a wider range of employment opportunities for them, women's earning power remains inferior to men's even as social and economic changes have made more women responsible for supporting children.

The link between female poverty and female crime is exacerbated by the criminal justice system's treatment of the female offender (Bershad, 1985). As noted earlier, the typical woman in prison has held only marginal kinds of jobs—low-skilled and low-paying. Ironically, when what she needs is training for the kind of job necessary to support herself and her children, the corrections system implicitly treats her as though she will live out her days as a homemaker supported by a husband. Almost without exception, women prisoners in this country have substantially fewer rehabilitative opportunities, make less money in prison industries, and have fewer prison job opportunities than men.

Women are subject to correctional policies that reject realistic vocational rehabilitation and services promoting independence. A far greater range of programs is generally available in facilities for men (Goetting, 1985; Weisheit, 1985; Mahan, 1984; Goetting and Howsen, 1983). Historically, correctional authorities have claimed that it is difficult to provide adequate or comparable services and programs for female offenders because there are so few of them. Their relatively small number has also been the justification in most states for providing only one correctional facility for women when a range of facilities emphasizing rehabilitation opportunities (including work farms, work-release centers, halfway houses, etc.) are provided for men (Nesbitt and Argenta, 1984).

Women's correctional institutions are usually in rural areas. They not only lack access to community-based work or training opportunities, they generally lack even minimally adequate vocational, educational, and pre-release programs. Men in prison are often without job skills and education, but men's prisons generally offer training in a range of occupations, including some higher-paying, skilled jobs—welding, auto mechanics, and building trades, for example. Women's institutions, on the other hand, not only offer fewer choices but usually concentrate on entry-level jobs in sex-stereotyped and lower-paying occupations such as nurse's aide, clerical worker, cosmetician, and food service worker—not the types of jobs that can support a family.

Moreover, female offenders have all too often experienced a lifelong cycle of dependency—on males, on public welfare, on alcohol or drugs (Valente and Decostanzo, 1982; Mahan, 1984; Chapman, 1980). Incarceration fosters further dependency on the correctional institution itself. Thus, most of these women leave prison even less able to function independently than they were before they entered.

If female offenders are to break the bonds of dependency and reenter society as self-sufficient heads of families, they must have access to a full range of vocational programs and work opportunities (Bershad, 1985). This means all levels of education, including higher education directed to degree programs, vocational counseling, and training in higher-paying occupations.

A continuum of pre- and post-training services is particularly necessary for women because they tend to be less familiar with work procedures or with a wide range of occupations and work settings. What skills and self-esteem they may have erode easily in the confinement of a penal institution. Women offenders often need confidence-building orientation programs such as, for example, hands-on introduction to tools, if they are to succeed at formal training programs and compete in the job market (Chapman, 1980; Ryan, 1984). Prerelease training in personal finance, parenting, and job-seeking are sorely needed, as well.

Prolonged separation of mother and child is the source of

untold pain, and further strains prospects for an intact family when the mother is released. Several prisons have parent support groups and programs that provide mothers with regular visits from their children. But these programs are not widely available.

It is clearly in the interest of society to support vocational and parenting programs for women offenders. The female offender who leaves prison better equipped to meet her responsibilities as custodial parent and breadwinner is less likely to be dependent on public assistance or illegal income. But because the female offender population is relatively small and relatively passive, it has been overlooked both by departments of corrections and, until recently, by community-based advocacy programs. Efforts to provide women with decent educational and vocational programs have been limited; decisionmakers such as governors and state legislators have placed the needs of female offenders on their agendas sporadically or not at all (Ross and Fabiano, 1986).

As a result, in the past decade, litigation has become a major avenue for addressing the deficiencies of women's correctional institutions. Class action suits have been brought on behalf of women offenders in at least 27 states (Ryan, 1984) and on a variety of grounds—violation of constitutional as well as legislatively mandated rights. Many cases are still pending, but particularly important judgments for the plaintiffs have been rendered by courts in Michigan and Kentucky. Some state departments of corrections have been ordered to increase the number and range of women's training programs as well as to provide new facilities for training or educating women.

Litigation at the state level has proven to be a slow means of securing equity for women offenders (Leonard, 1983), but it is likely to be necessary as long as governors and state legislatures do not act to ensure that the women in their prisons are provided the preparation they need for living independent lives on the outside.

The Congressional Caucus for Women's Issues in the 100th Congress

THE MEMBERS OF CONGRESS who belong to the Congressional Caucus for Women's Issues are involved individually, as well as collectively, in efforts on behalf of women and families. The 18 women in the caucus—two senators and 16 representatives—constitute the caucus's executive committee in the 100th Congress. These women of achievement hail from 13 states. Eleven are Democrats, seven are Republicans. In all, their committee assignments involve 20 House committees, eight Senate committees, and one joint committee.

This section begins with a report from Representatives Patricia Schroeder and Olympia Snowe, in their capacity as its cochairs, on the caucus's collective activities and concerns, particularly in the first session of the 100th Congress. Following the cochairs' report, each of the 18 Congresswomen who belong to the caucus reports briefly on her particular activities and perspectives on matters of concern to women. All the women and men (95 as of March 1988) in the caucus are listed alphabetically at the end of the section.

The Cochairs Report . . .

The Honorable Patricia Schroeder and the Honorable Olympia J. Snowe: The 100th Congress may yet prove to be the Congress that moved family issues to the top of the legislative agenda where they belong. We should have known that the momentum was swinging our way by all the media attention commanded last year with the release of the first edition of *The American Woman.* The demand for this invaluable reference book exceeded everyone's expectations. Obviously, the public and the media were starving for a comprehensive compendium of statistics on the lives of women.

With these facts and figures about American women, the members of the Congressional Caucus for Women's Issues proceeded to get down to the real business at hand—passing legislative initiatives that would enhance the economic well-being of women and families.

Our progress was slow but steady during the first session of the 100th Congress (1987), as we attempted to shape a fair and practical family agenda given the current fiscal restraints faced by Congress. Despite the need to reduce the budget deficit, priorities can and must be established to free up the resources required to meet the needs of our nation's families.

Founded in 1977, the Congressional Caucus for Women's Issues is a bipartisan legislative organization of more than 100 members of Congress united in the goal of improving the status of women and families. Eighteen Congresswomen compose the executive committee, which sets the caucus's priorities and objectives.

Since 1981, the caucus has introduced its legislative agenda in a package of bills collectively entitled the Economic

Equity Act (EEA). In June 1987, we introduced the EEA for the 100th Congress. The package contains 17 bills divided into two broad titles: Work and Family. Surely, no two words can better describe our current priorities.

Two of the EEA provisions were enacted during 1987. We were able to achieve both an increase in the authorization level of the Title XX Social Services Block Grant and funding to establish child care programs in public housing. We were ahead of our pace in the 99th Congress, when we had enacted only one of our equity provisions by the end of the first session (1985).

The caucus has played a vital role in moving major pieces of work and family legislation through Congress. The Family and Medical Leave Act, first introduced in April of 1985, was favorably reported out of the House Education and Labor Committee in November 1987 after a bipartisan compromise had been reached. For the first time, the Senate is also moving on parental leave legislation, having held seven hearings across the country to bring the issue to the public.

In 1987, we witnessed a Senate breakthrough in the area of pay equity. While it had passed the House twice, legislation simply to require a *study* of the federal wage and job classification system had never before moved in the Senate until the its Governmental Affairs Committee favorably reported out the measure in November 1987.

At the close of 1987, child care was stealing the spotlight from other family issues, with the introduction of the Act for Better Child Care Services (ABC) in both the House and the Senate. At a press conference to announce the bill's introduction, enthusiasm was contagious as key members pledged to put the legislation on the fast track.

As we begin 1988, the consensus on Capitol Hill is that

this is the year of the family and that passage of comprehensive federal child care legislation is just around the corner. That corner has taken us a long time to reach; Congress last addressed comprehensive child care legislation in 1971.

We also look forward to the enactment of a major welfare reform bill. In 1987, the House passed a far-reaching overhaul of our welfare system that would emphasize job training and education to move families off the welfare rolls and into the workforce.

After being bottled up in the Senate for more than three years, the Civil Rights Restoration Act was approved by the Senate in early 1988 and awaits House action. The Act would reinstate institution-wide coverage of a federal law banning sex discrimination in colleges and universities that receive federal aid.

Given the concern over the deficit, some programs of importance to women, such as the Title X family planning program, the Women's Education Equity Act (WEEA), and the Family Violence Prevention and Services Act, were funded at lower levels for fiscal year 1988 than for 1987. Funding for the Title XX Social Services Block Grant remained the same as in fiscal year 1987. However, funding was increased for three programs: the Dependent Care Block Grant, the Maternal and Child Health Care Block Grant, and the Special Supplemental Food Program for Women, Infants, and Children (WIC).

Aside from legislation, the caucus was involved in other activities during 1987. We kept a careful eye on the hearings for the nominees to the U.S. Supreme Court, providing information to our members about where the nominees stood with regard to issues of importance to women and families.

Fifty-nine caucus members signed a letter to Secretary Otis Bowen of the Department of Health and Human Services (HHS), expressing concern over proposed regulations that would prohibit funding of family planning programs that provide abortion counseling and referral. Unfortunately, HHS decided to issue the final regulations.

A caucus letter paved the way for congressional approval of language to require the Federal Communications Commission to reinstate its program of granting broadcast licensing preferences for women and minorities.

And last but not least, we are very excited about a new caucus initiative—the Child Care Challenge. At its launching in June 1987, the congresswomen challenged their colleagues in the House and Senate to go to their districts and states and find model employer-sponsored child care programs. Approximately 170 employer programs were submitted. A caucus report on the employers and their programs is due out in 1988.

Despite the large number of entries to the Child Care Challenge, recent statistics from the Bureau of Labor Statistics indicate that only two percent of employers nationwide offer any child care services. Obviously, much education still needs to be done.

The bottom line is that budgetary constraints have forced us to be more creative in our approaches to solving the problems confronting women and their families, but we are by no means out of business. From our colleagues we are receiving looks of renewed interest, where before we encountered blank stares when we discussed family issues. As a caucus, we have a renewed sense of bipartisan commitment. Family issues have become the congressional epiphany of the 1980s. And it's about time.

The Congresswomen Report . . .

Representative Lindy (Mrs. Hale) Boggs (Democrat; Louisiana, 2d District): As a member of the executive committee of the Congressional Caucus for Women's Issues, I strongly supported the Economic Equity Act and its component parts, including H.R. 1897 (of which I am primary cosponsor), which is designed to ensure equal access to commercial credit for women.

The interests of women receive special consideration in all of my congressional work. In 1987, I strived to include women-owned businesses among minority-owned businesses sought out by the Federal Home Loan Bank Board for participation in the sale of bonds for its recapitalization; earmarked funds within the HUD budget to initiate a program establishing child care centers in public housing developments; required progress reports from public officials on hiring women for and promoting them to middle- and upper-income positions and on contracts with women-owned businesses; addressed the women parliamentarians and, subsequently, submitted a report on the status of women in the U.S. to the Interparliamentary Union Meeting in Nicaragua.

Representative Barbara Boxer (Democrat; California, 6th District): The Select Committee on Children, Youth and Families, of which I am a member, held a series of hearings of interest to women and families in 1987, addressing such issues as child abuse, domestic violence, eating disorders, AIDS and young children, and homeless families. I am optimistic that the hearings will lead to strategies for addressing these very serious problems.

Work and family have become the focus of many of the legislative initiatives facing the 100th Congress. The Congressional Caucus for Women's Issues established a "Child Care Challenge," and I scoured my district for examples of employer-provided child care. The Act for Better Child Care Services, of which I am an original cosponsor, will help the states make quality child care available and affordable. And welfare reform finally passed the House. I am hopeful that, with the bipartisan compromise, we will be able to pass the Family and Medical Leave Act in 1988. It is time for Congress to establish a minimum labor standard to help millions of American families bridge the gap between work and family responsibilities. I am optimistic that we will also be able to move on the Economic Equity Act of 1987, which focuses on several work and family issues. On another front, we celebrated March as Women's History Month in 1987, and I reintroduced legislation to create a Federal Council on Women (H.R. 1636) to study the unique economic problems of women, especially women in poverty.

Representative Cardiss Collins (Democrat; Illinois, 7th District): I have recently been involved in a number of legislative issues of particular concern to women and families. For example, I have declared war on infant mortality: the House Subcommittee on Health and the Environment adopted my amendment to H.R. 1326, the Public Health Service Infant Mortality Act. The amendment specifically targets funds for reducing infant mortality to communities with a high incidence of such deaths.

I offered a successful amendment to H.R. 1861, a bill to reauthorize preventive health services at $100 million, that would allow states to provide women with screening services to detect breast and uterine cancer.

To make sure that teens do not do without needed medical care, I introduced H.R. 324, to establish health clinics in high schools. These clinics would provide diet and personal cleanliness counseling; health care related to sports; family planning information and services; and alcohol and drug abuse education and treatment.

I have long been an advocate of child care. As the author of two child care bills, H.R. 95 and H.R. 2644, I have sought to increase attention to the issue by making speeches on the House floor, doing a Chicago-area cable television show, and fighting to pass legislation. In January, I personally lobbied House Speaker Jim Wright and convinced him to include day care language in the Welfare Reform Act which was taken up by the House.

As chair of the Subcommittee on Government Activities and Transportation, I recently conducted an extensive investigation into the failure of the General Services Administration to provide federal employees with adequate child care facilities.

Representative Nancy L. Johnson (Republican; Connecticut, 6th District): The American dream is one of independence and fulfillment. Ironically, present law does not support those families who are struggling the hardest to achieve this goal.

Government offers child care assistance to affluent families through the Dependent Care Tax Credit, and child care subsidies to very poor families through the Social Services Block Grant. To others, the working poor for whom the burden of child care is very great, we offer no help at all. That is why I have proposed child care assistance legislation that specifically targets this income group through a system of child care certificates.

When Congress tackled the issue of welfare reform, I worked hard for a child care subsidy that declines only as a former welfare beneficiary's salary increases. While I am very pleased that an amendment to the House welfare bill incorporated much of my day care subsidy proposal, this important reform must be extended to families of equally low income who are not former welfare recipients.

Since my first term as a U.S. Representative, I have proposed support subsidies that are based on income and not limited to a short period when a woman is making a transition from welfare to work. It was victory for American women when the House took the first step and passed welfare reform legislation allowing states to offer such open-ended child care subsidies to women who are struggling to break free of welfare. The next challenge is income-related day care subsidies that will help all families until their incomes reach a level at which the tax credit for dependent care can assist them.

Representative Marcy Kaptur (Democrat; Ohio, 9th District): I am pleased to report that the Congressional Caucus for Women's Issues has made some headway in addressing the crying need for additional child care in this nation. I was able to include a provision in the Housing, Community Development and Homelessness Prevention Act of 1987 to authorize a program for child care in public housing. My provision directs HUD to offer grants to nonprofit organizations for the establishment of day care centers. All-day and after-school care will be provided to allow parents to find work or pursue education or vocational training.

The caucus and Representative Lindy Boggs were instrumental in securing full funding—$5 million for fiscal 1988—from the Appropriations Committee for this important program.

Senator Nancy Landon Kassebaum (Republican; Kansas): In 1987, I renewed my efforts to strengthen international family planning programs. The Senate Foreign Relations Committee adopted my amendment to overturn the so-called Mexico City policy that had led to the cutoff of U.S. aid to experienced and effective family planning organizations. However, because the full Senate did not consider this legislation, the policy remains in effect.

My amendment to another Foreign Relations Committee bill provided Foreign Service spouses divorced prior to 1984 with an entitlement to pension benefits. This measure was signed into law. In addition, the Overseas Education Fund presented me with its Women in Development Award in recognition of my long-standing support.

I am also a member of the Carnegie Council on Adolescent Development. Currently, this group is focusing on the middle school as a means of identifying and assisting youth who are likely to drop out, become pregnant, or get involved with drugs or alcohol.

Representative Barbara B. Kennelly (Democrat; Connecticut, 1st District): One major and two minor steps were taken in 1987 by the Ways and Means Committee, of which I am the only woman member, to better the lives of women and children.

The two minor steps were contained in the 1987 reconciliation bill. First, the Title XX block grant program was increased by $50 million for one year. Second, low-income disabled widows and widowers will be allowed to retain Medicaid coverage until age 65; under previous law, they would have lost it by suddenly qualifying for Social Security survivors benefits at age 60.

The major step, of which I am most proud, is House passage of welfare reform. This bill lays the foundation for a comprehensive overhaul of the welfare system by promoting jobs, education, and child care instead of dependency on a system flawed to the core.

Welfare is no "tender trap." House passage offers hope to millions of women and children. In 1988 and beyond, we must fulfill those expectations.

Representative Jan Meyers (Republican; Kansas, 3d District): It has been my pleasure to participate in several congressional groups looking into constructive, workable, and innovative solutions to concerns of the American woman.

I chaired the 92 Group's Task Force on Welfare Reform (a group comprised of moderate Republicans), and cosponsored Representative Roukema's child support enforcement bill. Currently, I am a member of the Task Force on Child Care sponsored by the Congressional Caucus for Women's Issues. My office participated in the Child Care Challenge project in which we identified major employers from the third district of Kansas with innovative and effective child care programs. Also, I am serving on the Task Force on Women's Issues sponsored by the House Republican Research Committee. Additionally, I am actively participating in the Congressional Institute's "Women in the 21st Century" project which seeks to increase the political involvement and power of women in America.

My legislative priorities during the remainder of the 100th Congress and future Congresses include teen pregnancy, child care, welfare reform, domestic violence, spousal impoverishment, long-term health care, passage of the Equal Rights Amendment, and preserving family planning programs.

These are challenging times for women. Of course, that never changes. The federal government is not a panacea for all our problems. Meaningful reforms and solutions will require the best efforts and cooperation of all levels of government and the private sector. Without the depth of common effort, many of our concerns will remain unaddressed and unresolved.

Senator Barbara A. Mikulski (Democrat; Maryland): As the only Democratic woman in the Senate, and the first Democratic woman elected who did not succeed her husband, I have "at-large" status as a representative of women across the country. My agenda as a senator is deeply rooted in the values of our culture and the need for public policy to manifest those values. It also comes from listening to and learning about the day-to-day needs of people.

An important part of my agenda is to use public policy to remove the barriers which all too often prevent and inhibit women from participating in the marketplace, the professions, the arts, or wherever. That is why I'm working on issues of economic security and family security, from child and dependent care to pay equity to spousal impoverishment to welfare reform.

Great challenges face us in addressing today's problems as we prepare for the future. Working together I know we can meet those challenges.

Representative Constance A. Morella (Republican; Maryland, 8th District): As a member of the Committee on Post Office and Civil Service and the Select Committee on Aging, I have devoted my time to issues affecting federally employed women and the aging. My legislative priorities emphasize pay equity, family and medical leave, the need for protection against the costs of long-term and home health care services and spousal impoverishment, and the expansion of quality health care (including increased use of nursing services). I have also worked to sensitize federal agencies to the necessity for upward mobility for women and the practice of affirmative action.

I have extended my efforts on behalf of women and families to the international arena. In a recent trip to the Soviet Union, I met with government officials to grant exit visas to divided spouses and families, and have worked with women refuseniks.

I am an original cosponsor of the Act for Better Child Care Services and the Economic Equity Act. These comprehensive packages address the need for affordable and accessible high-quality child care and issues of equity for women in such areas as pay, business, and pension benefits.

Representative Mary Rose Oakar (Democrat; Ohio, 20th District): Pay equity has always been one of my paramount concerns, and I have been encouraged by progress made in this area in the 100th Congress. Since the 98th Congress, I have worked to pass legislation that would mandate a study of the federal government's pay and classification systems to determine whether or not they are marred by discrimination. Each time, the House has passed the bill by a wide margin, only to see it die in the Senate.

The Senate finally took action with S. 552, the Federal Employee Compensation Equity Act of 1987, which was marked up by the Senate Governmental Affairs Committee, and floor action is expected in the near future.

I introduced H.R. 2935, which would amend Medicare to provide coverage for annual mammograms for women age 65 and older. This bill was incorporated into H.R. 2762, Congressman Pepper's long-term health care bill, which is expected to see action in early 1988.

I have also proposed legislation establishing an earnings sharing program that would require that all earning credits be combined and divided equally between spouses upon retirement or divorce. This system would replace the concept of female dependency with equality, recognizing women's contribution to the economic well-being of the family, whether as a member of the labor force or as a homemaker.

The year 1987, while not without its pain, included some promising developments for women. I look forward to even more progress in the future.

Representative Elizabeth J. Patterson (Democrat; South Carolina, 4th District): As one of 24 women in the House of Representatives, I have been a strong supporter of issues of interest to women and families. Through my work on the Veterans Affairs Committee, I introduced a bill to establish child care centers at veterans' medical centers for the employees' children. The bill was incorporated into a veterans health care bill, which the House has approved. As a member of the Congressional Caucus for Women's Issues, I have worked on several bills addressing the concerns of women, including the Economic Equity Act, of which I am a cosponsor. I have also taken an interest in efforts to protect our children from the influences of pornography, and I am a cosponsor of a bill to make the use of 1–900 telephone lines for pornographic telephone calls illegal. I look forward to continuing to work on these issues.

Representative Nancy Pelosi (Democrat; California, 5th District): As the newest congresswoman elected to the 100th Congress, I am pleased to be included in the 1988–89 edition of *The American Woman*. It is a privilege to work as an executive committee member of the Congressional Caucus for Women's Issues. In my own district of San Francisco, California, I have formed a women's advisory committee which meets periodically to discuss the legislative agenda of the

Congressional Caucus for Women's Issues, as well as to share with me problems and solutions which may be of interest to my colleagues on the caucus. We look forward to an exciting and productive year in San Francisco and in Washington, D.C. as we champion the goals of equality.

Representative Patricia Saiki (Republican; Hawaii, 1st District): If we could choose only one family issue to focus our legislative attention on, I believe it would have to be child care.

Without adequate child care options, the 71 percent of working mothers with children under the age of 18 who work full time cannot hope to realize their dreams. Without adequate child care, the millions of families headed by females who live in poverty cannot hope to break the cycle of despair that grips their lives.

As the mother of five children, I know what is involved in trying to raise a family and pursue a professional career. It is not easy, even under the best of circumstances. For most families, the best of circumstances is simply out of reach.

Seventeen years ago, the Congress tried to address the need for child care. Unfortunately, an ambitious legislative effort was vetoed.

The 100th Congress has an historic opportunity to act by approving H.R. 3660 and its Senate companion bill, S. 1885, the Act for Better Child Care Services, and the Economic Equity Act of 1987. Both legislative initiatives are necessary steps to establish quality child care options for American families. That is why I am proud to be an original cosponsor of both measures.

We have learned much in the past 17 years. We know that America's families need child care assistance. The debate now is about implementing such a program, not whether we need to act.

Representative Claudine Schneider (Republican; Rhode Island, 2d District): Many seeds of legislation that affect today's women first take root on the executive committee of the Congressional Caucus for Women's Issues, where I have served since coming to Congress. I have cultivated bills to ensure proper leave following childbirth (Family and Medical Leave Act), provide for adequate child care (Act for Better Child Care Services), enhance the status of women at home and in the workplace (Economic Equity Act), and improve women's access to federal dollars (Civil Rights Restoration Act).

In 1987, I cofounded and currently cochair the Congressional Competitiveness Caucus, where I have been addressing the need to improve women's access to training and child care. Last year, one of my provisions earmarking a percentage of African training funds strictly to that continent's women passed Congress.

I hold leadership posts in two international women's organizations, World Women Parliamentarians for Peace and Women for a Meaningful Summit, which are groups dedicated to raising women's voices for the cause of global harmony.

Representative Patricia Schroeder (Democrat; Colorado, 1st District): Working on behalf of women and families has long been a top priority for me. As cochair of the Congressional Caucus for Women's Issues, I have brought critical issues like parental leave, child care, pension rights, and pay equity into sharp focus by introducing, along with my colleagues, the Economic Equity Act (EEA), an omnibus bill containing 17 separate pieces of legislation to improve the lives of women. In 1987, for the first time, the EEA focused exclusively on work and family issues. Issues such as parental leave have gained national attention and become a major legislative priority for the historic 100th Congress.

During the summer months of 1987, when I explored the possibility of running for president, I found that families all across the country felt that many of their concerns weren't being heard. Therefore, I have launched the "Great American Family Tour," which began in January 1988, to involve parents, as well as teenagers and grandparents, in the development of a national family policy.

Representative Louise M. Slaughter (Democrat; New York, 30th District): On November 4, 1986, I was elected to represent the 30th congressional district of New York, which includes Rochester, the home of Susan B. Anthony, Emma Goldman, and the Second Women's Right's Convention in 1848. I am the only female member of the New York congressional delegation and was appointed by the House leadership to serve as a Majority Whip-at-Large. To represent the needs of my district adequately, I serve on the Committee on Public Works and Transportation, the Committee on Government Operations and was one of three freshman appointed to serve on the Select Committee on Aging. As chair of the Advisory Board of the Women's Economic Justice Center at the National Center for Policy Alternatives, I am working to identify legislative priorities for family support, income support, and job security issues. My commitment to women's issues continues to be a priority for me in the 100th Congress where I have cosponsored numerous pieces of legislation affecting women, including the Economic Equity Act, the Civil Rights Restoration Act, the Family and Medical Leave Act, and the Reproductive Health Equity Act.

Representative Olympia J. Snowe (Republican; Maine, 2d District): In the first session of the 100th Congress, I continued my work to eliminate the many obstacles preventing American women from equal participation in our society.

I have introduced legislation to address the lack of quality child care, the need for pay equity, the concerns of elderly women, and the restoration of civil rights. In addition, I have worked to ensure that women have the ability to make informed family planning decisions.

The need for quality child care in our country is reaching crisis proportions, and I am pleased to be an original cosponsor of the Act for Better Child Care Services. By developing standards, increasing the supply, and helping lower-income families afford care, this bill takes the first step in providing a national solution to this immense problem.

Much still needs to be done, and as cochair of the Congressional Caucus for Women's Issues, I will continue to emphasize policies beneficial to American women.

The Congressional Caucus for Women's Issues

Gary Ackerman (D-NY)
Michael Andrews (D-TX)
Les Aspin (D-WI)
Chester Atkins (D-MA)
Les AuCoin (D-OR)
Jim Bates (D-CA)
Anthony Beilenson (D-CA)
Howard Berman (D-CA)
Sherwood Boehlert (R-NY)
*Lindy (Mrs. Hale) Boggs (D-LA)
Don Bonker (D-WA)
Robert Borski (D-PA)
*Barbara Boxer (D-CA)
George Brown Jr. (D-CA)
Benjamin Cardin (D-MD)
Thomas Carper (D-DE)
Rod Chandler (R-WA)

Tony Coelho (D-CA)
Ronald Coleman (D-TX)
*Cardiss Collins (D-IL)
Silvio Conte (R-MA)
John Conyers (D-MI)
George Crockett (D-MI)
Peter DeFazio (D-OR)
Ronald Dellums (D-CA)
Julian Dixon (D-CA)
Thomas Downey (D-NY)
Richard Durbin (D-IL)
Bernard Dwyer (D-NJ)
Don Edwards (D-CA)
Ben Erdreich (D-AL)
Lane Evans (D-IL)
Dante Fascell (D-FL)
Vic Fazio (D-CA)
Hamilton Fish Jr. (R-NY)
Thomas Foglietta (D-PA)
Thomas Foley (D-WA)
Harold Ford (D-TN)
Barney Frank (D-MA)
Martin Frost (D-TX)
Jaime Fuster (Del-D-PR)
Robert Garcia (D-NY)
Sam Gejdenson (D-CT)
Richard Gephardt (D-MO)
Kenneth Gray (D-IL)
Bill Green (R-NY)
Frank Guarini (D-NJ)
Steve Gunderson (R-WI)
Augustus Hawkins (D-CA)
Charles Hayes (D-IL)
Steny Hoyer (D-MD)
*Nancy Johnson (R-CT)
*Marcy Kaptur (D-OH)
*Nancy Kassebaum (Sen-R-KS)
*Barbara Kennelly (D-CT)
John LaFalce (D-NY)
Tom Lantos (D-CA)
Jim Leach (R-IA)
William Lehman (D-FL)
Mickey Leland (D-TX)
Sander Levin (D-MI)
Mel Levine (D-CA)
Mike Lowry (D-WA)
Frank McCloskey (D-IN)
Matthew McHugh (D-NY)
Thomas McMillen (D-MD)
Edward Markey (D-MA)
Robert Matsui (D-CA)
*Jan Meyers (R-KS)
Kweisi Mfume (D-MD)
*Barbara Mikulski (Sen-D-MD)
George Miller (D-CA)
John Miller (R-WA)
Jim Moody (D-WI)
*Constance Morella (R-MD)
Bruce Morrison (D-CT)
Sid Morrison (R-WA)
Robert Mrazek (D-NY)
Stephen Neal (D-NC)
*Mary Rose Oakar (D-OH)
Wayne Owens (D-UT)
*Elizabeth Patterson (D-SC)
*Nancy Pelosi (D-CA)
Claude Pepper (D-FL)
Carl Pursell (R-MI)
Charles Rangel (D-NY)
Peter Rodino Jr. (D-NJ)
Robert Roe (D-NJ)
Martin Sabo (D-MN)
*Patricia Saiki (R-HI)
Thomas Sawyer (D-OH)

James Scheuer (D-NY)
*Claudine Schneider (R-RI)
*Patricia Schroeder (D-CO)
Gerry Sikorski (D-MN)
David Skaggs (D-CO)
Jim Slattery (D-KS)
*Louise Slaughter (D-NY)
Larry Smith (D-FL)
*Olympia Snowe (R-ME)
Harley Staggers Jr. (D-WV)
Gerry Studds (D-MA)
Al Swift (D-WA)
Mike Synar (D-OK)
Edolphus Towns (D-NY)
Morris Udall (D-AZ)
Bruce Vento (D-MN)
Ted Weiss (D-NY)
Alan Wheat (D-MO)
Pat Williams (D-MT)
Howard Wolpe (D-MI)
Ron Wyden (D-OR)
Sidney Yates (D-IL)

*Executive committee member.

Appendices

American Women Today: A Statistical Portrait

Highlights of Tables and Figures

Figure 1. *Population of the United States by Race and Sex, 1970 and 1986*

In 1986, the population of the United States stood at 241.6 million people, up 36.5 million (approximately 18 percent) since 1970. The 123.8 million females were 51.2 percent of the total population, about the same percentage as in 1970. The distribution of the population by race, however, has changed somewhat since then, with the result that people of color accounted for a greater proportion of the population in 1986 (15.3 percent) than in 1970 (12.3 percent).

Table 1. *Female Population by Age and Race, 1986*

On average, minority females are considerably younger than white females, as is evident in the age distribution of the population and, at least in the case of whites and blacks, the median age. For example, one-fourth of all women of color, but only one-fifth of all white women, were under the age of 15 in 1986. At the other end of the age continuum, differences remain pronounced: 15 percent of white females, but only nine percent of black and seven percent of all other females were over the age of 65. The median age of black females was nearly six years lower than that of white females.

Table 2. *Family Type by Race and Hispanic Origin, 1970, 1980, 1984, and 1986*

The total number of families in the United States rose by almost 1.8 million between 1984 and 1986. Numerically, the increase was greatest for married-couple families, which, by a wide margin, remain the dominant family type. The greatest percentage increase, however, was in families headed by men. Although these families were only 3.9 percent of the total in 1986, their number had increased by more than 280,000 (almost 13 percent) since 1984.

The number of female-headed families also increased over this two-year period, but at a less rapid rate than it had been increasing. The result is that the percentage of families headed by women remained stable at 16.2. However, differences by race are apparent. Among white families, for example, there was a barely perceptible decline in the percentage of married-couple families, and a correspondingly slight increase in the percentage of families headed by women. Among blacks, the opposite occurred: the percentage of married-couple families increased, and female-headed families decreased, their shares of the total.

Figure 2. *Marital Status of Persons Age 15 and Over by Sex, Race, and Hispanic Origin, 1986*

In the population (age 15 and over) as a whole, marital status varies enormously by sex. In general, men in 1986 were more likely than women to be either single (never married) or currently married and living with a spouse. (The exception involved persons of Hispanic origin, among whom the percentage married with spouse present was almost the same for both sexes.) Women, on the other hand, were more likely than men to be widowed, divorced, or separated—especially widowed. Because of life expectancy and mortality differences that favor women over men and because women typically marry older men, women in 1986 were—depending on race or ethnic origin—three to five times as likely as men to be widowed.

Figure 3. *Number of Marriages Among Currently Married Women and Men Age 15 and Over, 1985*

Despite the well-publicized high divorce rates of recent years, multiple marriages remain atypical—at least where currently married women and men are concerned. In 1985, more than 80 percent of currently married women and men had not been wed before; less than three percent had been married three or more times.

Table 3. *Births to Unmarried Women by Age of Mother and Race of Child, 1985*

In 1985, over 800,000 babies were born to unwed mothers. Although Table 3 does not show it, these births were 22 percent of all births that year, up from 18.4 percent in 1980. Perhaps surprisingly, given the publicity about teenage pregnancy, a majority of unwed mothers of all races were in their twenties and, depending on the race of the mother, from 11 to 16 percent were 30 or older.

Figure 4. *Percent of Homeowners and Renters, by Household Type, 1983*

Home ownership—the great American dream—remained an elusive goal for many households in 1983, the latest year for which data are available. Fewer than half of all one-person households, for example, owned their own homes. Rates of home ownership were also below average among larger households headed by nonelderly males or females, many of whom were single parents. The elderly, however, tend to have high rates of homeownership; this was also true for older women living alone, 61 percent of whom owned their homes in 1983. Widows retaining the house after the death of a husband surely accounted for a large percentage of elderly female homeowners.

Table 4. *Monthly Housing Costs as a Percent of Household Income, 1983*

For one-person households overall, housing costs consumed about the same median percentage of the total income of both homeowners and renters. What did make a difference was gender: in 1983, single female householders had housing costs averaging nearly one-third of income, compared to about one-fourth for male householders.

Among larger households, however, renters saw a greater proportion of their incomes go for housing costs than owners did, regardless of the sex of the householder. Female householders reported median rental housing costs amounting to 41 percent of income, the highest figure for any household group listed in Table 4.

Table 5. *Child Support Awards and Payments, 1978 and 1985*

Although, at any one time, the majority of children reside in two-parent families, a growing number of children are living, or will at some point live, with only one parent, generally the mother. For single-parent families, child-support payments might mean the difference between economic self-sufficiency and welfare.

In 1985, 8.8 million women (1.7 million more than in 1978) were responsible for children whose fathers did not live with them. Of these women, just over 60 percent had been awarded child-support payments and half were entitled to receive payments that year.

Of the women who had been awarded payments, nearly three-fourths received at least some, and more frequently, all, of what they were due. However, it should be noted that these women represented a little more than one-third of all mothers caring for minor children whose fathers lived elsewhere. The other two-thirds received nothing, either because (1) benefits had not been awarded (39 percent of the 8.8 million women), (2) the mothers were not—for one reason or another—supposed to receive payments that year (12 percent), or (3) the father did not pay any of what he had been ordered or had agreed to pay (13 percent).

Figure 5. *Percent of High School Graduates Among Women and Men, Age 25 and Over, Selected Years, 1940-March 1987*

As of March 1987, three-fourths of the population age 25 and over had graduated from high school—an increase of approximately 50 percentage points since 1940. Through 1970, graduation rates were higher among women than they were among men, but by 1980, men had a slight edge over women.

Figure 6. *Women as a Percent of All Students and All Part-time Students Enrolled in Institutions of Higher Education, 1970, 1975, 1980, and 1985*

The number of women enrolled in institutions of higher learning increased by nearly 82 percent between 1970 and 1985, while men posted a mere 15 percent gain. By 1985, women were somewhat more than half of all college and university students.

Part-time students accounted for nearly 60 percent of the increase in female college/university enrollment between 1970 and 1985; as of 1985, 57 percent of all part-time students were women.

Table 6. *First Professional Degrees Awarded in Selected Fields, 1973–74 and 1985–86*

Over the past decade, women have made impressive gains among degree recipients in a number of fields, most notably dentistry where their numbers have increased by over 1,200 percent. Women received over 20 percent of all dental degrees in 1985–86, up from less than two percent in 1973–74. Other dramatic gains have been in law, medicine, business, and veterinary medicine. In fact, women were nearly half of the recent recipients of degrees in veterinary medicine—a more than fourfold increase in 12 years.

Figure 7. *Percent of Women and Men Who Reported Having Voted in Presidential Elections, 1964–84*

Between 1964 and 1984, the percentages of adult women and men who reported having voted in presidential elections declined, but the drop was greater among men. As of 1984, women were somewhat more likely than men to say they had cast their votes in the presidential election of 1984; they were also a majority of reported voters in that election.

Table 7. *Percent of Persons Who Reported Voting in the 1984 Presidential Election by Age, Sex, Race, and Hispanic Origin*

The gender difference in voting behavior in the presidential election of 1984 was widest in the case of blacks, among whom 59 percent of the women but only 52 percent of the men reported voting. Voting tends to increase with age, with rates typically highest among both women and men in their mid-50s to mid-70s.

Table 8. *Political Party Identification of Women and Men, 1976, 1980, 1984, and November 1987*

According to *The New York Times*/"CBS News" polls, women are somewhat more likely than men to identify with the Democratic party—39 versus 33 percent in November of 1987—although the percentage of both sexes who did so in 1987 was lower than it was in 1976. Since 1976, smaller proportions of adults of either sex have been calling themselves Independents or claiming no party preference, while identification with the Republican party has risen sharply—from 19 to 29 percent among women and from 21 to 33 percent among men.

Table 9. *Civilian Labor Force Participation Rates For Persons Age 16 and Over by Sex, Race, and Hispanic Origin, Selected Years, 1950–86 and June 1987*

One of the most pronounced developments of the post-World War II era has been the steady influx of women into the workforce. By June 1987, the civilian female labor force participation rate stood at nearly 56 percent, compared to just over 76 percent for males. Among women, blacks had the highest and Hispanics the lowest rates, but regardless of race or Hispanic origin, the trend toward greater participation is unmistakable. Among men, specifically white men, attachment to the labor force has been weakening, largely because of the wider availability of pension coverage and early retirement benefits.

Table 10. *Civilian Labor Force Participation Rates by Age and Sex, Selected Years, 1950–86 and May 1987*

The increase in female labor force participation is characteristic of women of almost all ages, but most notably those between the ages of 25 and 44, whose civilian participation rate has increased by over 35 percentage points since 1950. Only among women 65 and over, who have never been particularly well represented in the labor force, have participation rates dropped over the past three and a half decades.

Table 11. *Labor Force Status of the Civilian Noninstitutional Population of Mexican, Puerto Rican, and Cuban Origin, Age 16 and Over, by Sex, 1986*

Within the Hispanic population, labor force participation, employment, and unemployment rates vary by country of origin as well as by sex. Not surprisingly, both labor force and employment rates are far higher among men, but so are unemployment rates. Of all Hispanic women in 1986, Cubans were the most likely to be in the labor force and least likely to be unemployed, while Puerto Rican women were considerably more likely than their counterparts to be out of the labor force.

Figure 8. *Civilian Labor Force Participation Rates by Age and Sex, Actual 1986 and Projected 1995*

The Bureau of Labor Statistics projects that between 1986 and 1995, the civilian labor force participation rates of adult women of all age groups except the very oldest (65-plus) will continue to increase. The picture for men, however, is considerably different: rates for all but the youngest age groups (ages 16–24) are projected to decline by 1995.

Table 12. *Number of Persons in the Civilian Labor Force by Age and Sex, Actual 1986 and Projected 1995*

Of the projected 13.8 million increase in the total labor force by 1995, nearly two-thirds (64 percent) will be women between the ages of 35 and 54.

Table 13. *Unemployment Rates for Persons Age 16 and Over by Sex, Race, and Hispanic Origin, Selected Years, 1950–86, and Second Quarter 1987*

For most of the past 35 years, female unemployment rates have been higher than those of males. (One exception, not presented in Table 13, was during the recession of 1981–82. Figures for the second quarter of 1987 also showed a higher male rate, but those figures are not seasonally adjusted and do not necessarily represent a reversal of the more common pattern.) Racial variations are apparent, however, with unemployment rates among black males typically higher than they are among black females.

Figure 9. *Reasons for Unemployment Among Women and Men, Age 20 and Over, 1986*

Sharp differences by sex are evident in reasons given for being unemployed. Nearly 70 percent of the unemployed men in 1986, for example, had lost their jobs. While the problems of the 40 percent of unemployed women who had lost their jobs should not be dismissed lightly, the majority of unemployed women had either left their last job voluntarily or were looking for work after a period out of the labor force.

Figure 10. *Reasons for Not Being in the Labor Force by Sex, 1975 and 1986*

Over three-quarters of a million *fewer* women (as compared to over four million *more* men) were out of the labor force by choice in 1986 than had been the case 11 years earlier. As in 1975, the majority of women voluntarily out of the labor force in 1986 gave keeping house as their reason, but their percentage was considerably lower in 1986 (67 percent) than in 1975 (79 percent). On the other hand, the percentage of women who reported being retired increased from less than four percent in 1975 to just over 14 percent in 1986.

More than half (55 percent) of the men voluntarily out of the labor force in 1986 were retired. Only 2.1 percent gave keeping house as their reason for being out of the workforce. Nevertheless, the 383,000 men who gave that reason in 1986 represented a 75 percent increase over the number who did so in 1975.

Table 14. *Families by Labor Force Status of Husband and Wife and Presence of Children, 1980 and 1985*

The so-called "traditional" family in which the husband is the wage earner and the wife stays at home to care for the children may not be a vanishing breed, but it definitely represents a shrinking proportion of all families; only 14 percent of American families could be so classified in 1985. This figure represents a drop of four percentage points in just five years. At 40 percent of the total, the dual-earner family in which both spouses are in the paid labor force has become the modal, or most common, family type.

Figure 11. *Labor Force and Employment Experience of Women with Young Children, 1960 and 1986*

Regardless of marital status or the presence of young children, labor force participation has become the norm for women. As of 1986, just over half of all women with children under the age of three were in the labor force, up from 16 percent in 1960.

In 1960, widowed, divorced, and separated women with young children were more than twice as likely as women living with their husbands to be in the labor force. By 1986, this differential had narrowed dramatically.

Women who work tend to work full time. Nonetheless, full-time workers are still a minority of women with small children. Overall, only about three women in 10 who had children under the age of three were employed full time in 1986.

Table 15. *Work Experience of Householders in All Families and Female-headed Families, by Race and Hispanic Origin, 1986*

Work experience rates for any one year, which measure whether someone did any work at all for pay during the year, are typically higher than average annual labor force participation rates. Over three-fourths of household heads worked at some time in 1986, the majority of them year round and full time. Female family heads were somewhat less likely to have had work experience, but still, nearly two-thirds (63 percent) did work at some time during that year, and over one-third (38 percent) were year-round, full-time workers. Work experience rates were lowest for Hispanic women who headed families.

Figure 12. *Primary Child Care Arrangements for Children with Employed Mothers, 1984–85*

Given the rapid growth in the labor force participation rates of women with children, ensuring adequate child care has become a growing concern. Most working mothers have arranged for some type of home care for their youngest children (under the age of 5): some two-thirds (68 percent) of those children were cared for in their own or another person's home in 1984–85. An organized child care facility was the primary care arrangement for a minority—23 percent—of young children of working mothers. Child care arrangements tend to be quite different in the case of older children (between the ages of 5 and 14), for three-fourths of whom school was the primary source of child care.

Figure 13. *Primary Caregiver for Children With Employed Mothers, 1984–85*

As was shown in Figure 12, less than one-quarter of the children under age five who had working mothers were cared for by organized child care facilities while their mothers worked in 1984–85. Relatives—parents, grandparents, or other kin—were the primary care providers of nearly half (48 percent) of these children; the remaining 28 percent were looked after by nonrelatives or, in a few instances, a child's school. Very few children (three percent) were apparently left to fend for themselves, and none of these was reported to be under the age of five.

Table 16. *Work Interruptions Lasting Six Months or Longer By Worker's Sex, Education, and Reason for Interruption, 1984*

It is not uncommon for workers of either sex to experience rather lengthy work interruptions, although such interruptions are, not surprisingly, more common among women than among men. In 1984, for example, nearly half (47 percent) of all working women between the ages of 21 and 64 had had at least one six-month or longer work interruption. The comparable figure for men was only 13 percent. When women leave the labor force, it is typically for family reasons. Nearly 41 percent of all working women in 1984, but less than one percent of all working men, had been out of the labor force at least once for "family reasons."

Figure 14. *Occupational Distribution of Employed Women and Men, by Race, 1986*

In 1986, nearly half (47 percent) of all employed white women and over half (55 percent) of all employed black women worked in jobs in just three of the Census Bureau's 11 broad occupational categories: administrative support, private household, and other services.

Men, in contrast, were somewhat more evenly distributed across industries.

Table 17. *Occupational Distribution of Employed Hispanic Women, 1986*

Employed Hispanic women, regardless of their country of origin, tend to be concentrated in (1) technical, sales, administrative support and (2) service occupations: nearly two-thirds of all Hispanic women were in these occupations in 1986. Nonetheless, some differences by country of origin are apparent. Cuban and Puerto Rican women, for example, were more likely than other Hispanic women to be employed in managerial and professional occupations, while Puerto Rican and Central and South American women had the highest percentages of operators, fabricators, and laborers.

Table 18. *Women as a Percent of All Workers in Selected Occupations, 1975 and 1986*

Despite continuing and sometimes increasing segregation in many occupations, women's representation in a number of predominantly male preserves is on the rise. In 1986, women accounted for 18 percent of all lawyers and judges, up from seven percent in 1975; 21 percent of all mail carriers versus nine percent in 1975; and 39 percent of all economists, as opposed to 13 percent 11 years earlier. Even some of the nation's employed airplane pilots are women—admittedly not many at 1.5 percent in 1986—but in 1975 there were apparently too few even to classify.

Table 19. *Women as a Percent of the Federal Workforce by Race and Ethnic Origin, 1982–85*

Although their proportion is increasing, women are less well represented in the federal government than they are in the total civilian labor force. In 1985, for example, women were 44 percent of the civilian labor force but only 37 percent of the federal workforce, a difference predominantly explained by an underrepresentation of white women. White women were nearly 38 percent of the civilian labor force but only 25 percent of the federal workforce. Hispanic women were also proportionately underrepresented among federal workers, while blacks and American Indians (of whom there were very few) were better represented. Asian women, whose numbers were also few, appeared to be proportionately represented.

Figure 15. *Women as a Percent of Federal Professional, Clerical, and Blue-collar Workers, by Race and Ethnic Origin, 1985*

As is the case in the workforce as a whole, women were overrepresented among the federal government's clerical workers (86 percent female) in 1985 and underrepresented among its professional workers (26 percent) and its blue-collar workers (less than 10 percent).

Figure 16. *Industry Distribution of Employed Women and Men, 1986*

Women workers tend to be concentrated in a few industries. In fact, over 60 percent of all female workers worked in just two industries—"other" (nonprivate household) service and retail trade—in 1986. Male workers were better distributed across industries, but the service industry employed the largest percentage of them as well as of females.

Table 20. *Service Industry Employment of Women and Men, 1986*

Within the broad classification known as the "service" industry, the particular industry in which workers are employed varies considerably by sex. In 1986, women were twice as likely as men to be employed in hospitals and other health services, but less than half as likely to be in business and repair. Since so many women are employed as teachers, and teaching is largely a female-dominated occupation, it is not surprising that a substantial proportion of women employed in the service sector were in educational industries (26 percent in 1986). However, 21 percent of all men employed in the service industry were also in education.

Table 21. *Median Usual Weekly Earnings of Full-time Wage and Salary Workers by Sex, Race, and Hispanic Origin, 1987*

The median weekly earnings of white men continue to exceed, by a wide margin, the earnings of minority men and all women. In 1987, white women who worked full time had median weekly earnings of $307, approximately 68 percent of the $450 median earnings of fully employed white men. Black and Hispanic women fared even worse, earning, respectively, only 61 percent and 56 percent of what white men earned. (When the 1986 usual median earnings of all women are compared to the earnings of all men, one finds a wage ratio of 70 percent, a slight improvement over the figure for 1986.)

Table 22. *Median Weekly Earnings of Full-time Wage and Salary Workers by Sex and Age, 1986*

In general, the earnings of females and males are most comparable at the younger ages when workers are just starting out: in 1986, full-time working women between the ages of 16 and 24 earned some 89 percent of what men in that age group were earning. Among workers 25 to 34, however, the female-male wage ratio was 76 percent, and by middle age, it dropped to 61 percent.

Table 23. *Median Weekly Earnings of Full-time Wage and Salary Workers by Sex and Occupation, 1986*

The ratio of female to male earnings varies considerably across occupations. Among full-time workers, women fare least well compared to men in sales, where their median weekly earnings in 1986 were only 54 percent of the earnings of men. Except among mechanics and repairers, where women actually did better than men (104 percent), the 1986 female to male wage ratio did not exceed 85 percent in any of the broad occupational classifications utilized by the Bureau of Labor Statistics.

Table 24. *Occupations with the Highest and Lowest Median Weekly Earnings for Women and Men, 1986*

With median weekly earnings of $624, the best paid women in 1986 were lawyers. Law was also the most highly paid occupation for men, but it paid men considerably more—$806 per week. In fact, none of the five most remunerative occupations for women paid as well as any of the five most remunerative occupations for men.

The most poorly paid females are child care workers employed in private households. These women had median earnings of only $90 a week in 1986.

Table 25. *Average (Mean) Earnings of Year-round, Full-time Workers by Sex and Educational Attainment, 1985*

At every educational level, women who work year round, full time earn less than their male counterparts. In fact, female college graduates who worked full time for all of 1985 earned less, on average, than fully employed men with no more than a high school diploma—$21,362 versus $22,852.

Table 26. *Mean Hourly Earnings of Full-time Workers by Tenure on Current Job, 1984*

It is argued that one reason why women earn less than men is that they are less experienced and/or have fewer years on the job, but the fact is that in 1984, the female-male earnings ratio was least favorable (66 percent) among workers with 20 or more years of work experience and most favorable (82 percent) among those with fewer than five years of experience. However, the ratio does generally improve somewhat as years on a *particular* job increase.

Figure 17. *Workers with Earnings At or Below the Minimum Wage by Sex and Age, 1986*

As of 1986, 5.1 million workers—two-thirds of them women—were employed in jobs that paid them at or below the minimum wage of $3.35 per hour.

Figure 18. *Selected Characteristics of Workers with Earnings At or Below the Minimum Wage, 1986*

Most minimum-wage workers appear to be supplementing other family earnings. Nonetheless, in 1986, nearly seven percent—or 337,000—were women maintaining families.

Figure 19. *Median Annual Income of Persons by Age, Sex, and Year-round, Full-time Employment Status, 1986*

As would be expected, year-round, full-time workers report incomes well above the incomes of all workers and nonworkers of the same age and sex. This is true for both women and men; however, the median income of year-round, full-time women workers was just under $17,000 in 1986, in contrast to their male counterparts' median of almost $26,000.

Table 27. *Median Annual Income of Families by Family Type, Race, and Hispanic Origin, 1986*

Working wives contribute substantially to family income. In 1986, married-couple families in which the wife was in the paid labor force had a median income of $38,346, some 50 percent higher than the median $25,803 for families in which the wife stayed at home. Among black couples, the median family income of those families with a wife in the paid labor force was not quite double that of families where the wife stayed at home. Not surprisingly, the financial status of female-headed families is far more precarious than that of either married couples or male-headed families. Families headed by women had a median income of only $13,647 in 1986, which, although not shown in Table 27, was actually $13 lower than their 1985 median.

Table 28. *Poverty Rates of All Families and Female-headed Families, by Work Experience of Householder, 1986*

While people who work normally have higher earnings than those who do not, work experience on the part of one or more family members does not necessarily lift a family out of poverty.

Among families whose head did *not* work in 1986, the poverty rate was over 24 percent, a figure that more than doubled when the head of the household was black or of Hispanic origin. The poverty rate was still over seven percent when the householder worked in 1986 and doubled again when the head was black or Hispanic. Nor can everyone who works year round, full time escape poverty: over three percent of all families whose heads were fully employed in 1986 had incomes below the poverty level; once more the rate was substantially higher for blacks (6.6 percent) and Hispanics (9.3 percent).

Among families headed by women, the situation was considerably bleaker. Over one-fifth of all such families were below the poverty level in 1986, even though the householder had worked at some point during the year. Even when these women worked year round, full time, the poverty rate was nearly eight percent, and higher still in the case of black and Hispanic female-headed families—13.1 and 11.5 percent.

Table 29. *Trends in Poverty Rates of Persons by Family Type, Race, and Hispanic Origin, 1960–86*

Living in a female-headed family increased one's chances of being poor by more than 300 percent in 1986. Regardless of race, the poverty rates of persons in female-headed families are, and long have been, far above those in other family types, but members of minority female-headed families are especially at risk of poverty.

Figure 20. *Households Receiving Noncash Benefits, 1985*

For many families, but especially for those headed by women, noncash benefits are an important income supplement. In 1985, such families were far more likely than other families to be recipients of those benefits. For example, in 1985, female-headed families were less than 12 percent of the 88.5 million households (which include families and single people), but they were 28 percent of the food stamp recipients, 32 percent of the Medicaid households, 26 percent of the households receiving free or reduced price school lunches, and 14 percent of the households residing in public or subsidized housing.

Table 30. *Number of Families on and Recipients of AFDC, Selected Years, 1936-December 1985*

As of December 1985, 3.7 million families, including 7.2 million children, were receiving Aid to Families with Dependent Children (AFDC), the country's major means-tested cash benefit program. The program grew steadily from the year benefits were first paid in 1936 until 1981, after which the AFDC caseload began to drop as changes in federal law made fewer families eligible for benefits. 1984 witnessed another slight increase in the number of AFDC families, but the 1985 figure of 3.7 million was still below the 1981 high of 3.8 million.

The Tables and Figures

Figure 1 • POPULATION OF THE UNITED STATES[1] BY RACE AND SEX, 1970 AND 1986

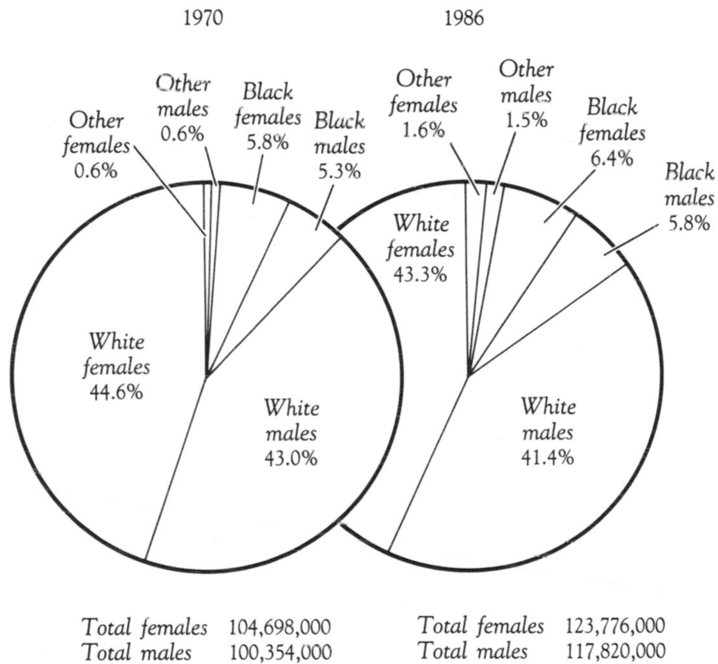

	1970		1986
Total females	104,698,000	*Total females*	123,776,000
Total males	100,354,000	*Total males*	117,820,000

[1]Includes Armed Forces overseas.

Source: Bureau of the Census, Current Poplulation Reports, Series P-25, No. 917, 1982, Table 1; and Series P-25, No. 1,000, 1987, Table 1.

Table 1 • FEMALE POPULATION BY AGE AND RACE, 1986 (numbers in thousands)

	White		*Black*		*Other*	
Age	*Number*	*Percent*	*Number*	*Percent*	*Number*	*Percent*
Under 5	7,148	6.8	1,341	8.7	365	9.6
5–14	13,296	12.7	2,596	16.8	625	16.4
15–19	7,451	7.1	1,385	9.0	295	7.7
20–24	8,429	8.1	1,463	9.5	318	8.3
25–34	17,868	17.1	2,807	18.2	742	19.5
35–44	14,299	13.7	1,907	12.4	580	15.2
45–54	10,039	9.6	1,346	8.7	352	9.2
55–64	10,349	9.9	1,154	7.5	271	7.1
65 and over	15,649	15.0	1,434	9.3	268	7.0
Total	104,528	100.0	15,433	100.0	3,816	100.0
Median age	33.9		28.2		NA	

Source: Bureau of the Census, Current Population Reports, Series P-25, No. 1,000, 1987, Table 1.

Table 2 • FAMILY TYPE BY RACE AND HISPANIC ORIGIN, 1970, 1980, 1984, AND 1986 (in percentages)

Family Type	*1970*	*1980*	*1984*	*1986*
ALL RACES				
Married-couple families	86.7	81.7	80.3	79.9
Wife in paid labor force	NA	(50.2)	(53.5)	(55.3)
Wife not in paid labor force	NA	(49.8)	(46.5)	(44.7)
Female householder, no husband present	10.9	15.1	16.2	16.2
Male householder, no wife present	2.4	3.2	3.6	3.9
Total percent	100.0	100.0	100.0	100.0
Total number of families (in thousands)	51,237	60,309	62,706	64,491
WHITE				
Married-couple families	88.6	85.1	83.9	83.4
Wife in paid labor force	NA	(49.3)	(52.5)	(54.3)
Wife not in paid labor force	NA	(50.6)	(47.5)	(45.7)
Female householder, no husband present	9.1	11.9	12.8	13.0
Male householder, no wife present	2.2	3.0	3.3	3.7
Total percent	100.0	100.0	100.0	100.0
Total number of families (in thousands)	46,022	52,710	54,400	55,676
BLACK				
Married-couple families	68.0	53.7	51.2	52.7
Wife in paid labor force	NA	(59.6)	(64.0)	(65.4)
Wife not in paid labor force	NA	(40.4)	(36.0)	(34.6)
Female householder, no husband present	28.2	41.7	43.7	41.8
Male householder, no wife present	3.7	4.6	5.1	5.4
Total percent	100.0	100.0	100.0	100.0
Total number of families (in thousands)	4,774	6,317	6,778	7,096
HISPANIC ORIGIN[1]				
Married-couple families	NA	73.1	71.7	70.8
Wife in paid labor force	NA	(46.2)	(49.1)	(50.8)
Wife not in paid labor force	NA	(53.8)	(50.9)	(49.2)
Female householder, no husband present	NA	21.8	23.0	23.4
Male householder, no wife present	NA	5.1	5.3	5.7
Total percent		100.0	100.0	100.0
Total number of families (in thousands)	NA	3,235	3,939	4,403

[1]Persons of Hispanic origin may be of any race.

Source: Bureau of the Census, Current Population Reports, Series P-20, No. 218, 1971, Table 6; Series P-60, No. 127, 1981, Table 1; Series P-60, No. 149, 1985, Table 1; and Series P-60, No. 157, 1987, Table 1.

Figure 2 • MARITAL STATUS OF PERSONS AGE 15 AND OVER BY SEX, RACE, AND HISPANIC ORIGIN,[1] 1986

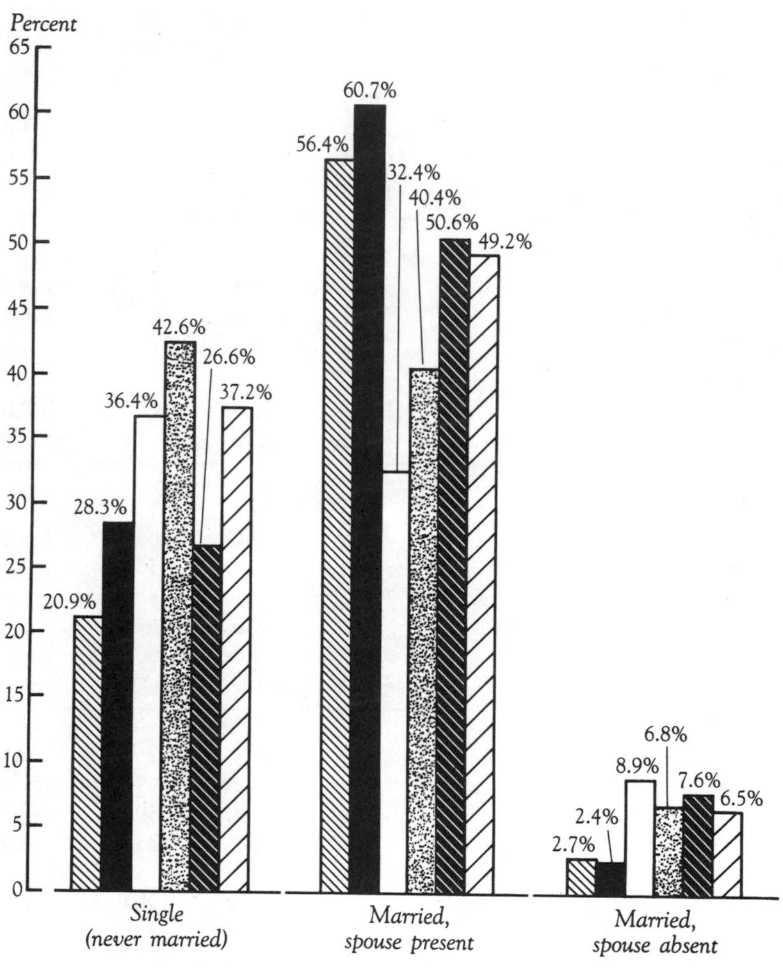

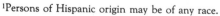

[1]Persons of Hispanic origin may be of any race.

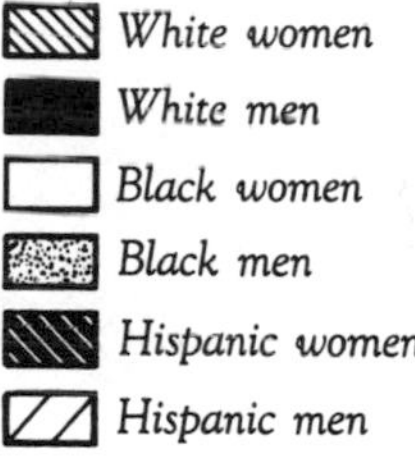

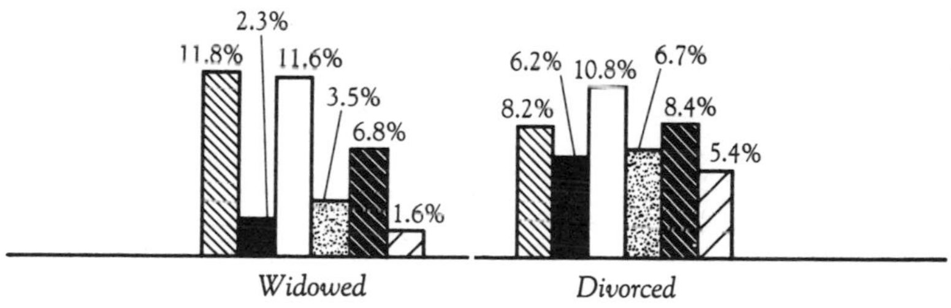

Source: Bureau of the Census, unpublished data.

Figure 3 • NUMBER OF MARRIAGES AMONG CURRENTLY MARRIED WOMEN AND MEN AGE 15 AND OVER, 1985

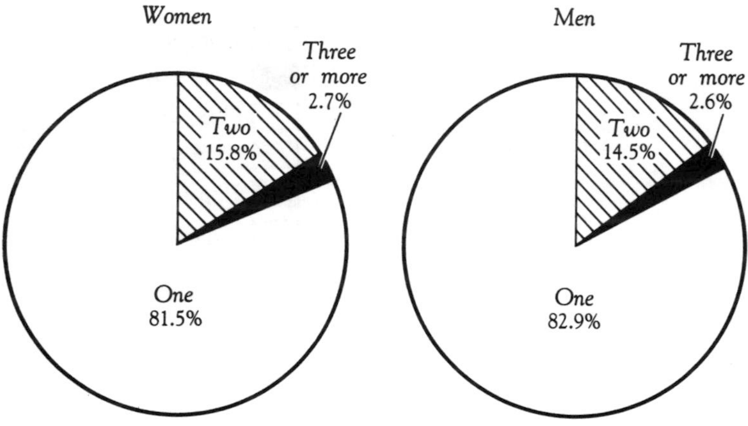

Source: Bureau of the Census, unpublished data.

Table 3 • BIRTHS TO UNMARRIED WOMEN BY AGE OF MOTHER AND RACE OF CHILD, 1985

	Race of Child							
	All Races		*White*		*Black*		*Other*	
Age of Mother	*Number*	*Percent*	*Number*	*Percent*	*Number*	*Percent*	*Number*	*Percent*
Under 15	9,386	1.1	3,380	0.8	5,783	1.6	223	0.8
15–19	270,922	32.7	142,131	32.8	120,378	32.9	8,413	28.3
20–24	300,365	36.3	156,568	36.2	133,360	36.5	10,437	35.2
25–29	152,024	18.4	78,834	18.2	67,300	18.4	5,890	19.8
30–34	67,315	8.1	35,871	8.3	28,305	7.7	3,139	10.6
35–39	24,038	2.9	13,714	3.2	9,027	2.5	1,297	4.4
40 and over	4,124	0.5	2,471	0.6	1,374	0.4	279	0.9
Total	828,174	100.0	432,969	100.0	365,527	100.0	29,678	100.0

Source: National Center for Health Statistics, *Monthly Vital Statistics Report*, 36, 4, Supplement, 1987, Table 18.

Figure 4 • PERCENT OF HOMEOWNERS AND RENTERS, BY HOUSEHOLD TYPE, 1983

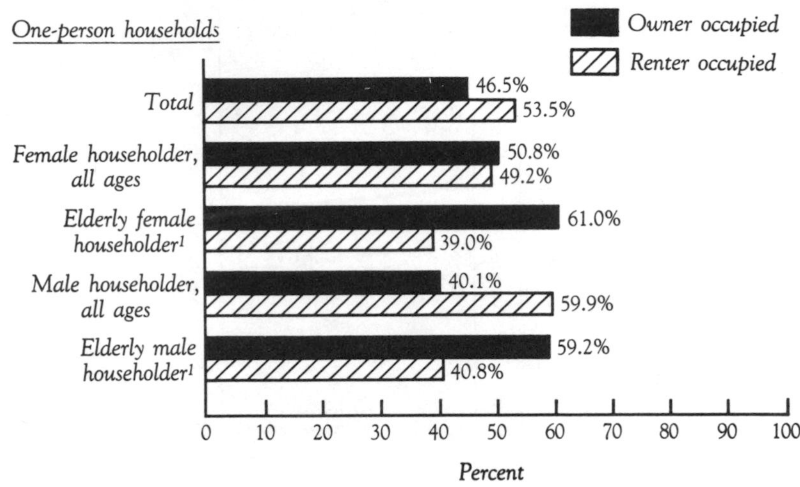

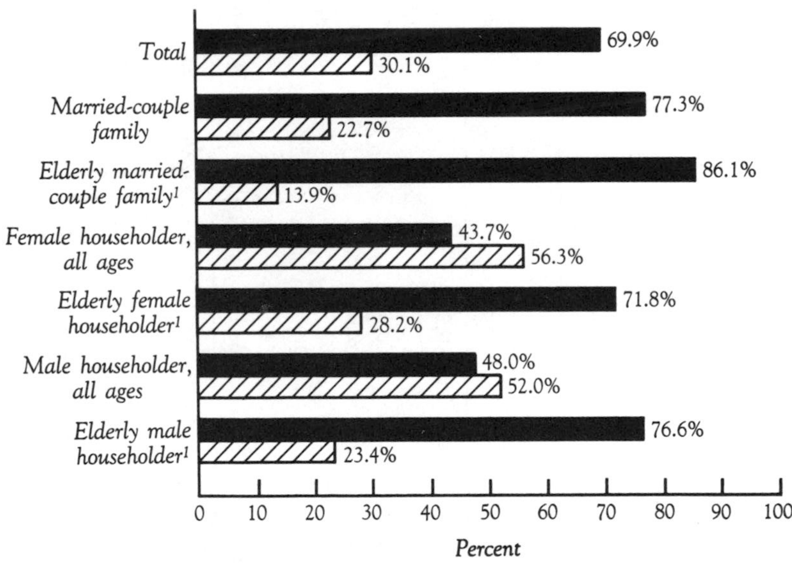

[1]Elderly householders are age 65 or over.

Source: Bureau of the Census, Current Housing Reports, Series H-150-83, 1984, Table A-1.

Table 4 • MONTHLY HOUSING COSTS[1] AS A PERCENT OF HOUSEHOLD INCOME, 1983

	Total Number (in thousands)	Less Than 10	10–24	25–49	50 or More	Not Computed or Not Reported	Median
		Cost as a Percent of Income					
Units with Mortgages							
One-person households							
Female householder	993	2.3	27.0	37.1	20.9	12.8	32.0
Male householder	989	4.8	38.4	34.2	10.7	11.8	25.3
Two or more person households							
Married-couple family	22,500	10.9	52.7	22.0	5.1	9.4	18.8
Female householder	2,245	3.3	33.1	35.6	18.6	9.4	28.9
Male householder	1,030	6.9	38.9	30.5	8.6	15.1	23.8
Rental Units							
One-person households							
Female householder	5,537	1.6	28.2	38.8	26.2	5.2	31.0
Male householder	4,510	6.2	41.8	29.4	16.8	5.8	24.0
Two or more person households							
Married-couple family	11,069	5.0	46.7	30.0	11.7	6.7	23.0
Female householder	5,725	1.1	20.2	36.2	37.5	4.9	41.0
Male householder	2,373	3.8	31.3	33.3	26.6	5.0	32.0

[1]Limited to one-unit structures on less than 10 acres and no business on property.

Source: Bureau of the Census, unpublished data.

Table 5 • CHILD SUPPORT AWARDS AND PAYMENTS, 1978 AND 1985 (numbers in thousands)

	1978		*1985*	
Award and Recipient Status[1]	*Number*	*Percent*	*Number*	*Percent*
Awarded	4,196	59.2	5,396	61.3
Should have received payments	3,424	48.3	4,381	49.7
Received full amount	1,675	23.6	2,112	24.0
Received partial amount	779	11.0	1,131	12.8
Did not receive payments	969	13.7	1,138	12.9
Not supposed to receive payments	772	10.9	1,015	11.5
Not awarded[2]	2,898	40.9	3,411	38.7
Total	7,094		8,808	

[1]Payments from absent fathers to women with children under age 21.

[2]Reasons for nonaward include: final agreement pending; property settlement in lieu of award; joint custody granted; did not want child support.

Source: Bureau of the Census, Current Population Reports, Series P-23, No. 112, 1981, Table A; and Series P-23, No. 152, 1987, Table A.

Figure 5 • PERCENT OF HIGH SCHOOL GRADUATES AMONG WOMEN AND MEN, AGE 25 AND OVER, SELECTED YEARS, 1940–MARCH 1987

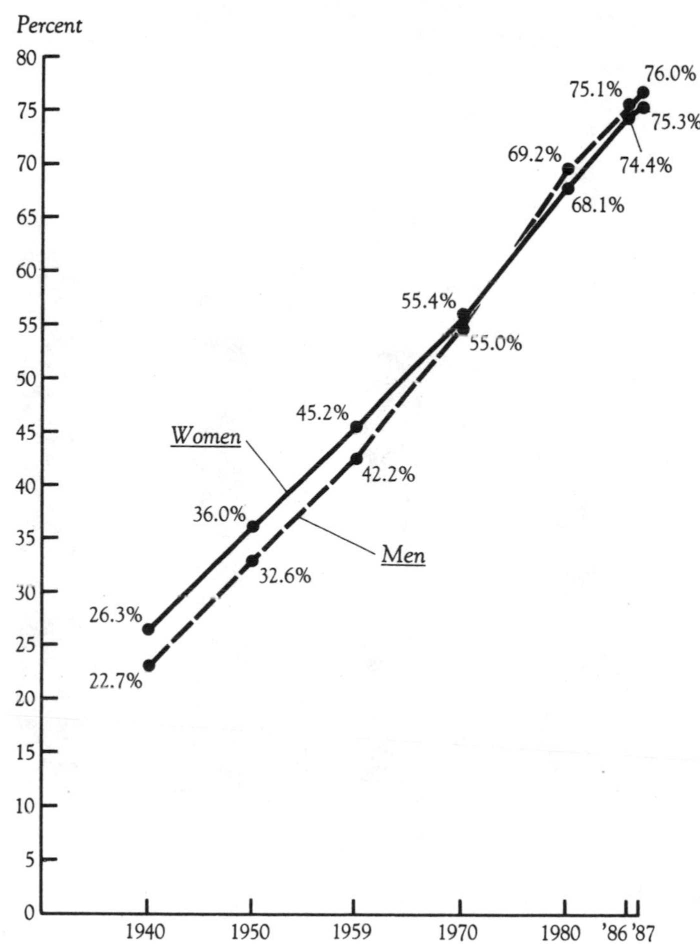

Source: Bureau of the Census, unpublished data.

Figure 6 • WOMEN AS A PERCENT OF ALL STUDENTS AND ALL PART-TIME STUDENTS ENROLLED IN INSTITUTIONS OF HIGHER EDUCATION, 1970, 1975, 1980, AND 1985

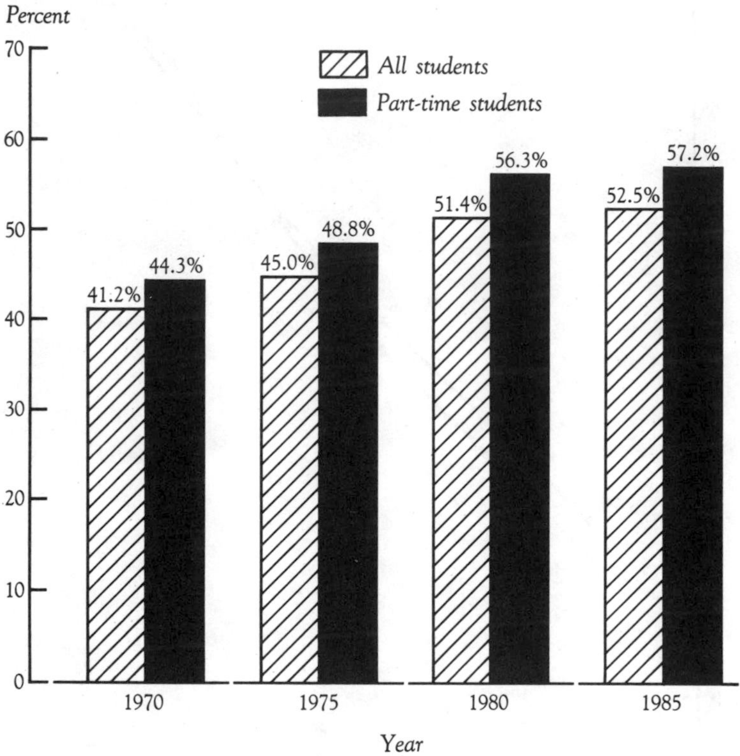

Source: U.S. Department of Education, Center for Education Statistics, *Digest of Education Statistics, 1987,* Table 103.

Table 6 • FIRST PROFESSIONAL DEGREES AWARDED IN SELECTED FIELDS, 1973–74 AND 1985–86

	1973–74			*1985–86*		
	Both Sexes, Total	*Women*		*Both Sexes, Total*	*Women*	
Field		*Number*	*Percent*		*Number*	*Percent*
Dentistry	4,440	85	1.9	5,046	1,139	22.6
MBA's	32,644	2,153	6.6	66,967	20,795	31.0
Medicine	11,356	1,263	11.1	15,938	4,916	30.8
Veterinary medicine	1,384	155	11.2	2,270	1,079	47.5
Law	29,326	3,340	11.4	35,844	13,970	39.0

Source: U.S. Department of Education, *Digest of Education Statistics,* 1987, Table 164 and unpublished data.

Figure 7 • PERCENT OF WOMEN AND MEN WHO REPORTED HAVING VOTED IN PRESIDENTIAL ELECTIONS, 1964–84

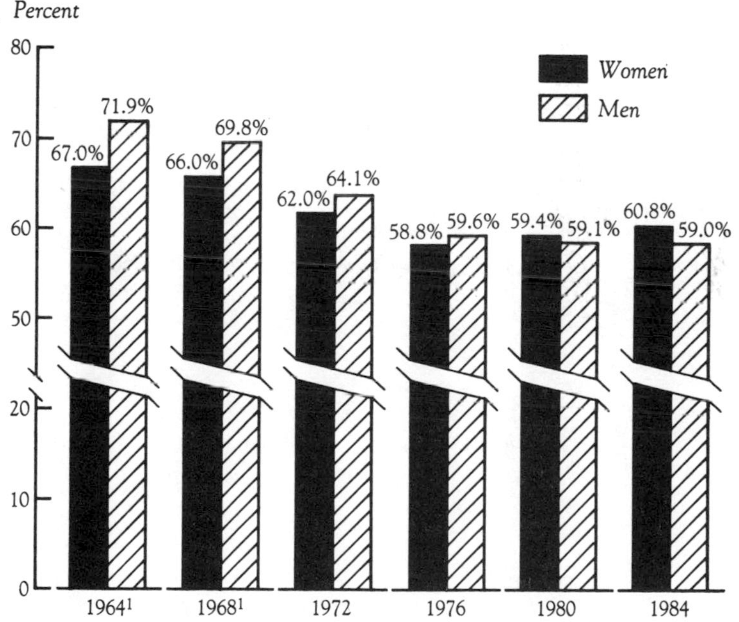

[1]Data are for persons of voting age, 21-years-old and over in most states prior to 1972.

Source: Bureau of the Census, Current Population Reports, Series P-20, No. 405, 1986, Table C.

Table 7 • PERCENT OF PERSONS WHO REPORTED VOTING IN THE 1984 PRESIDENTIAL ELECTION BY AGE, SEX, RACE, AND HISPANIC ORIGIN

	White		*Black*		*Hispanic Origin*[1]	
Age	*Women*	*Men*	*Women*	*Men*	*Women*	*Men*
18–20	39.5	35.4	41.3	30.0	20.7	13.9
21–24	45.8	42.9	47.1	40.6	26.2	23.7
25–34	58.2	53.9	57.7	47.2	29.9	26.2
35–44	66.2	63.7	65.2	55.9	36.7	33.8
45–54	69.1	68.4	68.4	61.5	40.4	45.9
55–64	72.5	74.0	67.8	66.3	41.6	50.3
65–74	71.2	75.0	64.0	65.9	44.6	49.7
75 and over	57.8	69.6	55.0	57.9	29.2	30.3
Total percent	62.0	60.8	59.2	51.7	33.1	32.1
Total number (in thousands)	47,716	42,435	6,058	4,235	1,667	1,425

[1]Persons of Hispanic origin may be of any race.

Source: Bureau of the Census, Current Population Reports, Series P-20, No. 405, 1986, Table 2.

Table 8 • POLITICAL PARTY IDENTIFICATION OF WOMEN AND MEN, 1976, 1980, 1984, AND NOVEMBER 1987 (in percentages)

	1976		*1980*		*1984*		*November 1987*	
Party	*Women*	*Men*	*Women*	*Men*	*Women*	*Men*	*Women*	*Men*
Democratic	43.0	38.0	42.0	40.0	40.0	33.0	39.0	33.0
Republican	19.0	21.0	22.0	23.0	27.0	27.0	29.0	33.0
Independent[1]	38.0	41.0	36.0	37.0	33.0	40.0	32.0	34.0
Total	100.0	100.0	100.0	100.0	100.0	100.0	100.0	100.0

[1]Independents include those with no preference.

Source: *The New York Times*/CBS News polls, 1976: February–November; 1980: January–November; 1984: January–December; and 1987: November. Data provided to the Women's Research and Education Institute by the *New York Times.*

Table 9 • CIVILIAN LABOR FORCE PARTICIPATION RATES FOR PERSONS AGE 16 AND OVER BY SEX, RACE, AND HISPANIC ORIGIN, SELECTED YEARS, 1950–86 AND JUNE 1987

	Total		*White*		*Black*		*Hispanic Origin*[1]	
Year	*Women*	*Men*	*Women*	*Men*	*Women*	*Men*	*Women*	*Men*
1950	33.9	86.4	—	—	—	—	—	—
1955	35.7	85.4	34.5	85.4	—	—	—	—
1960	37.7	83.3	36.5	83.4	—	—	—	—
1965	39.3	80.7	38.1	80.8	—	—	—	—
1970	43.3	79.7	42.6	80.0	—	—	—	—
1975	46.3	77.9	45.9	78.7	48.8	70.9	43.2	80.7
1980	51.5	77.4	51.2	78.2	53.1	70.3	47.8	81.6
1985	54.5	76.3	54.1	77.0	56.5	70.8	49.4	80.4
1986	55.3	76.3	55.0	76.9	56.9	71.2	50.1	81.0
June 1987[2]	55.8	76.4	55.6	77.1	57.1	71.1	52.3	80.6

[1]Persons of Hispanic origin may be of any race.

[2]Not seasonally adjusted; averages from April, May, and June 1987.

Source: Bureau of Labor Statistics (BLS), *Handbook of Labor Statistics,* 1985, Table 5; *Employment and Earnings,* January 1986, Table 39; January 1987, Table 39; July 1987, Table 58; and unpublished BLS data.

Table 10 • CIVILIAN LABOR FORCE PARTICIPATION RATES BY AGE AND SEX, SELECTED YEARS, 1950–86 AND MAY 1987

	Age and Sex													
	16–19		*20–24*		*25–34*		*35–44*		*45–54*		*55–64*		*65 and Over*	
Year	*Women*	*Men*	*Women*	*Men*	*Women*	*Men*	*Women*	*Men*	*Women*	*Men*	*Women*	*Men*	*Women*	*Men*
1950	41.0	63.2	46.0	87.9	34.0	96.0	39.1	97.6	37.9	95.8	27.0	86.9	9.7	45.8
1955	39.7	58.9	45.9	86.9	34.9	97.6	41.6	98.1	43.8	96.4	32.5	87.9	10.6	39.6
1960	39.3	56.1	46.1	88.1	36.0	97.5	43.4	97.7	49.9	95.7	37.2	86.8	10.8	33.1
1965	38.0	53.8	49.9	85.8	38.5	97.2	46.1	97.3	50.9	95.6	41.1	84.6	10.0	27.9
1970	44.0	56.1	57.7	83.3	45.0	96.4	51.1	96.9	54.4	94.3	43.0	83.0	9.7	26.8
1975	49.1	59.1	64.1	84.5	54.9	95.2	55.8	95.6	54.6	92.1	40.9	75.6	8.2	21.6
1980	52.9	60.5	68.9	85.9	65.5	95.2	65.5	95.5	59.9	91.2	41.3	72.1	8.1	19.0
1985	52.1	56.8	71.8	85.0	70.9	94.7	71.8	95.0	64.4	91.0	42.0	67.9	7.3	15.8
1986	53.0	56.4	72.4	85.8	71.6	94.6	73.1	94.8	65.9	91.0	42.3	67.3	7.4	16.0
May, 1987[1]	52.2	55.0	72.1	85.2	72.4	94.7	75.0	94.2	67.6	91.1	42.9	68.3	7.1	16.6

[1]Rates for May, 1987 are not seasonally adjusted.

Source: Bureau of Labor Statistics, *Handbook of Labor Statistics,* 1985, Table 5; *Employment and Earnings,* January 1986, Table 3; January 1987, Table 3; and June 1987, Table A-4.

Table 11 • LABOR FORCE STATUS OF THE CIVILIAN NONINSTITUTIONAL POPULATION OF MEXICAN, PUERTO RICAN, AND CUBAN ORIGIN, AGE 16 AND OVER, BY SEX, 1986 (in percentages)

	Women				*Men*			
Labor Force Status	*Total Hispanic Origin*[1]	*Mexican Origin*	*Puerto Rican Origin*	*Cuban Origin*	*Total Hispanic Origin*[1]	*Mexican Origin*	*Puerto Rican Origin*	*Cuban Origin*
In labor force	50.1	50.5	38.1	56.9	81.0	82.7	73.5	78.4
Employed	44.7	44.6	32.3	53.3	72.5	73.7	63.6	73.5
Unemployed	5.4	5.9	5.7	3.6	8.5	9.1	9.8	5.0
Not in labor force	49.9	49.5	62.0	43.1	19.0	17.3	26.5	21.6
Total number (in thousands)	6,238	3,605	829	420	6,106	3,771	665	422

[1]Includes persons of Central, South American or other Hispanic origin, not shown separately.

Source: Bureau of Labor Statistics, *Employment and Earnings,* January 1987, Table 40.

Figure 8 • CIVILIAN LABOR FORCE PARTICIPATION RATES BY AGE AND SEX, ACTUAL 1986 AND PROJECTED 1995

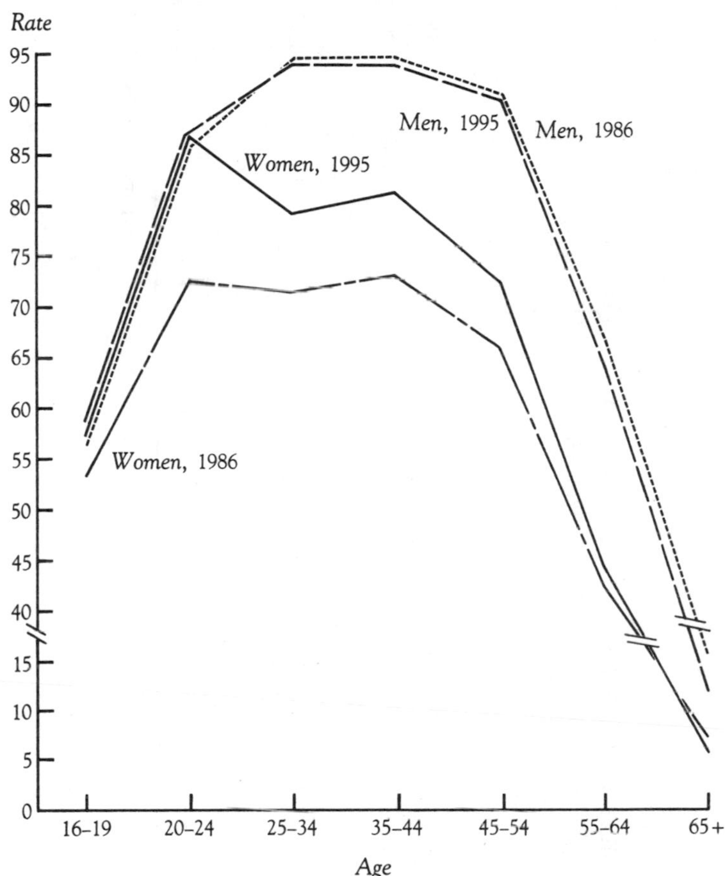

Source: Bureau of Labor Statistics (BLS), *Employment and Earnings,* January 1987, Table 3; and unpublished BLS data (middle growth path).

Table 12 • NUMBER OF PERSONS IN THE CIVILIAN LABOR FORCE BY AGE AND SEX, ACTUAL 1986 AND PROJECTED 1995
(numbers in thousands)

	Women		*Change 1986–95*		*Men*		*Change 1986–95*	
Age	*1986*	*1995*	*Number*	*Percent*	*1986*	*1995*	*Number*	*Percent*
16–19	3,824	3,849	25	0.6	4,102	3,977	−125	−3.0
20–24	7,293	6,528	−765	−10.5	8,148	6,904	−1,244	−15.3
25–34	15,208	16,021	813	5.3	19,383	18,386	−997	−5.1
35–44	12,204	17,149	4,945	40.5	15,029	19,394	4,365	29.0
45–54	7,746	11,589	3,843	49.6	9,994	13,708	3,714	37.2
55–64	4,940	4,915	−25	−0.5	6,954	6,438	−516	−7.4
65 and over	1,199	1,155	−44	−3.7	1,811	1,585	−226	−12.5
Total, age 16 and over	52,414	61,206	8,792	16.8	65,421	70,392	4,971	7.6

Source: Bureau of Labor Statistics (BLS), *Employment and Earnings,* January 1987, Table 3; and unpublished BLS data (middle growth path).

Table 13 • UNEMPLOYMENT RATES FOR PERSONS AGE 16 AND OVER BY SEX, RACE, AND HISPANIC ORIGIN, SELECTED YEARS, 1950–86 AND SECOND QUARTER 1987

	All Races		*White*		*Black*		*Hispanic Origin*[1]	
Year	*Women*	*Men*	*Women*	*Men*	*Women*	*Men*	*Women*	*Men*
1950	5.7	5.1	—	—	—	—	—	—
1955	4.9	4.2	4.3	3.7	—	—	—	—
1960	5.9	5.4	5.3	4.8	—	—	—	—
1965	5.5	4.0	5.0	3.6	—	—	—	—
1970	5.9	4.4	5.4	4.0	—	—	—	—
1975	9.3	7.9	8.6	7.2	14.8	14.8	13.5	11.4
1980	7.4	6.9	6.5	6.1	14.0	14.5	10.7	9.7
1985	7.4	7.0	6.4	6.1	14.9	15.3	11.0	10.2
1986	7.1	6.9	6.1	6.0	14.2	14.8	10.8	10.5
Second quarter 1987[2]	6.1	6.3	5.1	5.4	13.2	13.5	8.4	8.6

[1]Persons of Hispanic origin may be of any race.

[2]Rates for second quarter 1987 are quarterly averages and are not seasonally adjusted.

Source: Bureau of Labor Statistics (BLS), *Handbook of Labor Statistics,* 1985, Table 27; *Employment and Earnings,* January 1986, Table 39; January 1987, Table 39; July 1987, Table A-63; and unpublished BLS data.

Figure 9 • REASONS FOR UNEMPLOYMENT AMONG WOMEN AND MEN, AGE 20 AND OVER, 1986

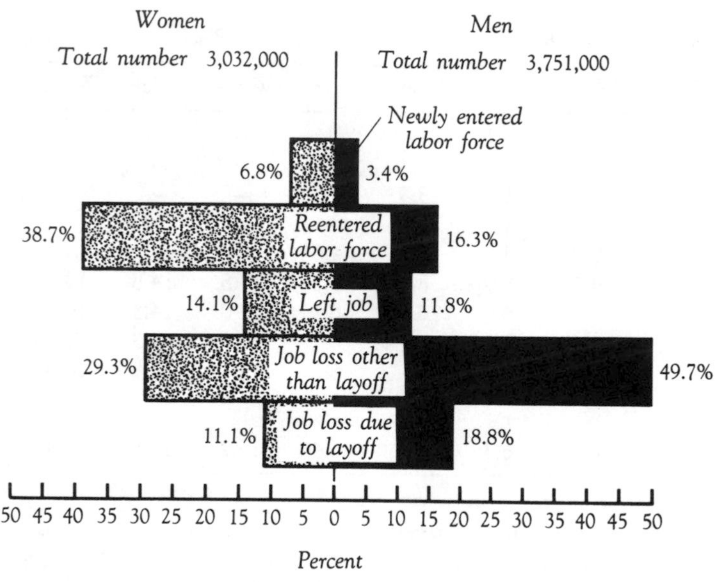

Source: Bureau of Labor Statistics, *Employment and Earnings,* January 1987, Table 12.

Figure 10 • REASONS FOR NOT BEING IN THE LABOR FORCE[1] BY SEX, 1975 AND 1986

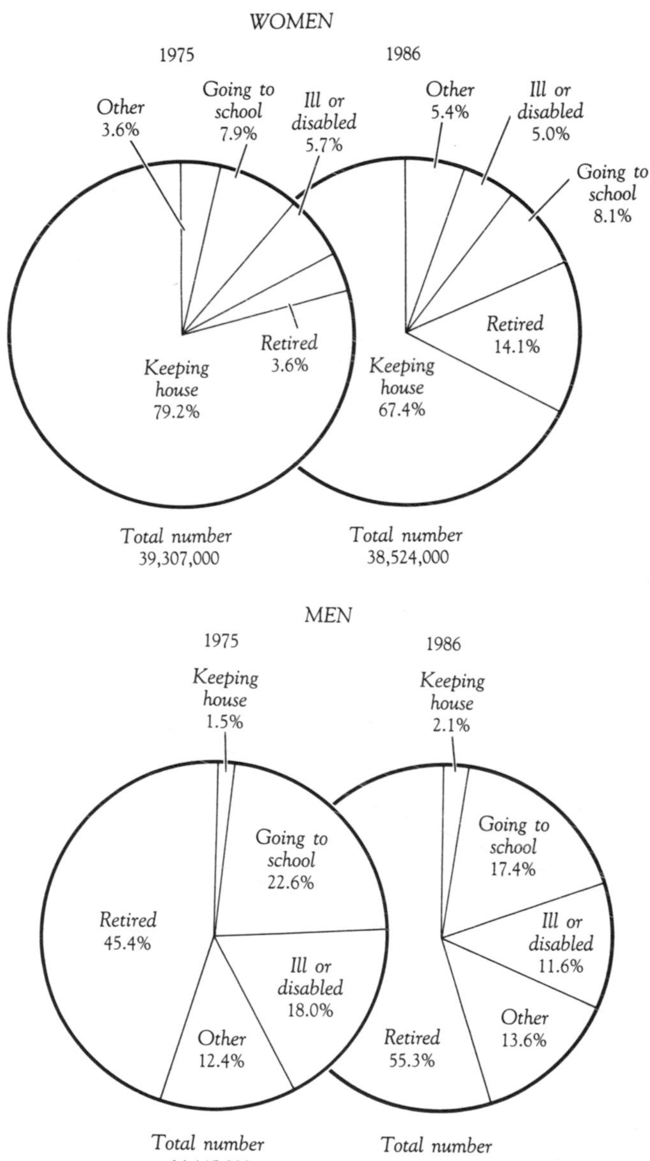

[1]Includes only persons out of the labor force by choice.

Source: Bureau of Labor Statistics, *Employment and Earnings,* January 1976, Table 29; and January 1987, Table 35.

Table 14 • FAMILIES BY LABOR FORCE STATUS OF HUSBAND AND WIFE AND PRESENCE OF CHILDREN, 1980 AND 1985 (in percentages)

Family Type	*1980*	*1985*
Married couples		
Husband working, wife not in labor force	28.8	23.5
Without children	10.7	9.4
With children	18.2	14.2
Husband and wife in labor force	38.2	39.9
Without children	16.1	17.1
With children	22.1	22.8
Other family type[1]	32.9	36.6
Total percent	100.0	100.0
Total number (in thousands)	58,426	62,706

[1]Includes families headed by a single parent, married-couple families with wife only in the labor force, and married-couple families with neither spouse in the labor force.

Source: Bureau of the Census, Current Population Reports, Series P-20, No. 366, 1981, Tables 1 and 18; Series P-20, No. 411, 1986, Tables 1 and 17.

Figure 11 • LABOR FORCE AND EMPLOYMENT EXPERIENCE OF WOMEN WITH YOUNG CHILDREN, 1960 AND 1986

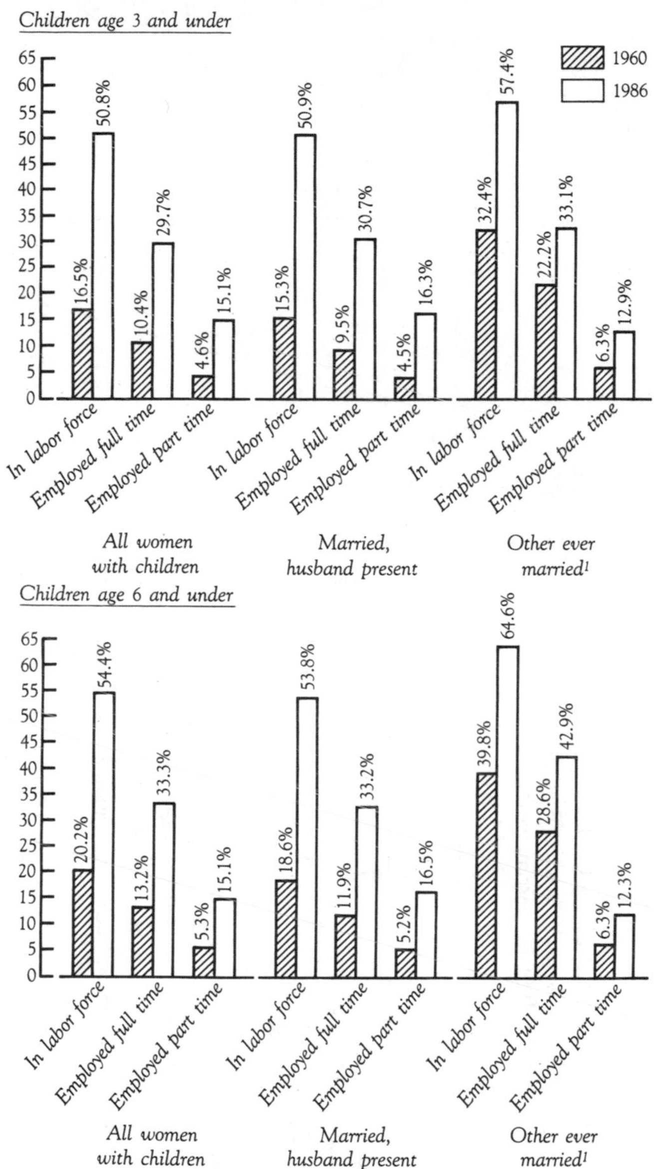

[1]Includes widowed, divorced, and married with an absent spouse.

Source: Bureau of Labor Statistics (BLS), *Marital and Family Characteristics of Workers, March 1960,* 1961, Tables G and I; and unpublished BLS data.

Table 15 • WORK EXPERIENCE OF HOUSEHOLDERS IN ALL FAMILIES AND FEMALE-HEADED FAMILIES, BY RACE AND HISPANIC ORIGIN, 1986 (in percentages)

	All Families				*Female-Headed Families*			
Work Experience of Householder[1]	*Total*	*White*	*Black*	*Hispanic Origin*[2]	*Total*	*White*	*Black*	*Hispanic Origin*[2]
Worked	77.4	78.4	69.3	77.7	62.7	64.3	58.9	50.1
Worked 50–52 weeks	61.0	62.4	49.8	57.0	43.1	45.5	37.5	33.2
Full time	58.0	59.4	46.3	54.2	37.5	39.4	32.8	28.7
Worked 1–49 weeks	16.4	16.0	19.4	20.6	19.6	18.8	21.4	16.9
Did not work	22.6	21.6	30.7	22.3	37.3	35.7	41.1	49.9
Total number (in thousands)	63,707	55,041	6,962	4,366	10,445	7,227	2,967	1,032

[1]Restricted to families with civilian householders.

[2]Persons of Hispanic origin may be of any race.

Source: Bureau of the Census, Current Population Reports, Series P-60, No. 157, 1987, Table 19.

Figure 12 • PRIMARY CHILD CARE ARRANGEMENTS FOR CHILDREN WITH EMPLOYED MOTHERS, 1984–85

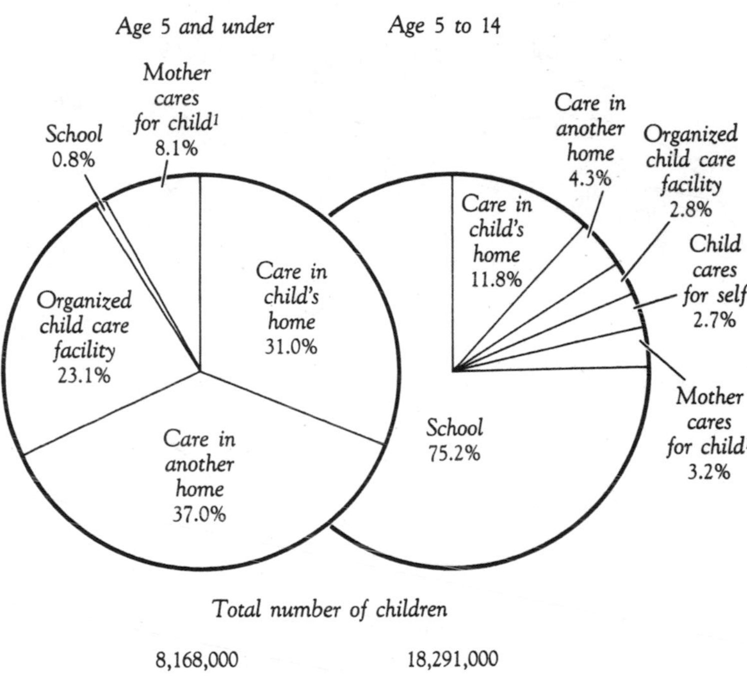

[1]Includes mothers working at home or away from home.

Source: Bureau of the Census, Current Population Reports, Series P-70, No. 9, 1987, Table B.

Figure 13 • PRIMARY CAREGIVER FOR CHILDREN WITH EMPLOYED MOTHERS, 1984–85

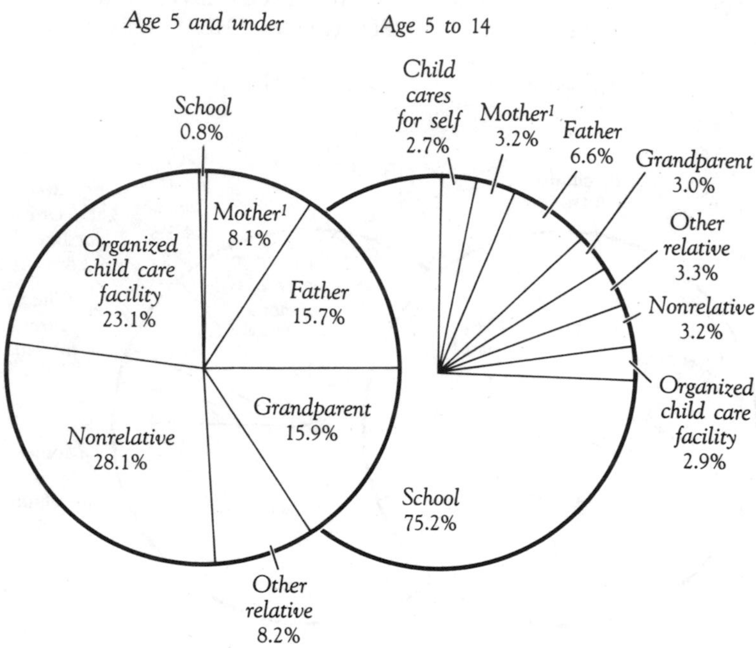

Total number of children

8,168,000 18,291,000

[1]Includes mothers working at or away from home.

Source: Bureau of the Census, Current Population Reports, Series P-70, No. 9, 1987, Table B.

Table 16 • WORK INTERRUPTIONS LASTING SIX MONTHS OR LONGER BY WORKER'S SEX, EDUCATION, AND REASON FOR INTERRUPTION, 1984 (in percentages)

	Women					*Men*				
Age by Years of School Completed	*All Reasons*	*Inability to Find Work*	*Family Reasons*	*Illness or Disability*	*Other*	*All Reasons*	*Inability to Find Work*	*Family Reasons*	*Illness or Disability*	*Other*
Workers 21–29	19.9	4.4	13.5	0.6	2.3	11.5	8.6	0.1	1.1	2.0
Less than 12	34.5	5.7	25.5	0.6	3.8	22.3	16.7	0.7	1.9	4.1
12 to 15	21.6	4.6	15.1	0.7	2.4	11.0	8.3	0.1	0.9	1.9
16 or more	8.1	3.1	3.3	0.5	1.6	5.0	3.3	—	1.0	0.8
Workers 30–44	53.1	4.7	46.0	2.7	3.7	14.1	8.5	0.4	2.2	3.6
Less than 12	65.2	9.7	51.1	6.8	4.6	20.8	12.9	0.5	4.5	4.4
12 to 15	57.0	4.3	50.8	2.5	3.7	14.8	9.1	0.3	2.4	3.5
16 or more	36.7	3.2	30.5	1.3	3.4	9.7	5.3	0.6	0.9	3.4
Workers 45–64	69.2	3.2	64.2	3.6	4.6	13.6	6.4	0.2	3.2	4.5
Less than 12	65.7	4.5	58.5	5.4	5.5	16.2	8.9	0.1	4.1	3.8
12 to 15	72.0	3.0	67.6	3.2	4.2	13.8	6.1	0.2	3.0	5.2
16 or more	63.2	1.9	60.0	2.3	4.3	9.8	4.0	0.2	2.3	3.8
Total, 21–64	47.0	4.2	40.7	2.3	3.5	13.2	7.9	0.3	2.2	3.4

Source: Bureau of the Census, Current Population Reports, Series P-23, No. 136, 1984, Tables A and B; and Series P-70, No. 10, 1987, Table 1.

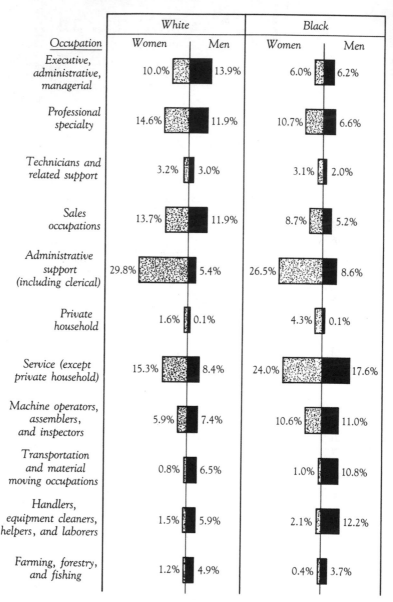

Figure 14 • OCCUPATIONAL DISTRIBUTION OF EMPLOYED WOMEN AND MEN, BY RACE, 1986

Occupation	White Women	White Men	Black Women	Black Men
Executive, administrative, managerial	10.0%	13.9%	6.0%	6.2%
Professional specialty	14.6%	11.9%	10.7%	6.6%
Technicians and related support	3.2%	3.0%	3.1%	2.0%
Sales occupations	13.7%	11.9%	8.7%	5.2%
Administrative support (including clerical)	29.8%	5.4%	26.5%	8.6%
Private household	1.6%	0.1%	4.3%	0.1%
Service (except private household)	15.3%	8.4%	24.0%	17.6%
Machine operators, assemblers, and inspectors	5.9%	7.4%	10.6%	11.0%
Transportation and material moving occupations	0.8%	6.5%	1.0%	10.8%
Handlers, equipment cleaners, helpers, and laborers	1.5%	5.9%	2.1%	12.2%
Farming, forestry, and fishing	1.2%	4.9%	0.4%	3.7%

Source: Bureau of Labor Statistics, *Employment and Earnings,* January 1987, Table 21.

Table 17 • OCCUPATIONAL DISTRIBUTION OF EMPLOYED HISPANIC WOMEN,[1] 1986 (in percentages)

Occupation	*Total*	*Mexican*	*Puerto Rican*	*Cuban*	*Central and South American*	*Other Hispanic*
Managerial and professional specialty	13.7	11.3	18.7	20.7	13.7	17.2
Technical, sales, and administrative support	40.8	42.1	38.6	47.5	30.4	44.7
Service occupations	23.6	24.6	19.7	13.9	29.4	20.7
Farming, forestry, and fishing	1.4	2.1	0.3	1.1	0.6	0.2
Precision production, craft, and repair	3.7	4.0	2.0	2.6	4.0	3.4
Operators, fabricators, and laborers	16.9	15.8	20.7	14.2	22.0	13.9
Total percent	100.0	100.0	100.0	100.0	100.0	100.0
Total number (in thousands)	2,736	1,572	268	218	387	292

[1]Persons of Hispanic origin may be of any race.

Source: Bureau of the Census, Current Population Reports, Series P-20, No. 416, 1987, Table 6.

Table 18 • WOMEN AS A PERCENT OF ALL WORKERS IN SELECTED OCCUPATIONS, 1975 AND 1986

	Women as Percent of Total Employed	
Occupation	*1975*	*1986*
Airline pilot	—	1.5
Architect	4.3	9.7
Auto mechanic	0.5	1.0
Bartender	35.2	48.8
Bus driver	37.7	50.4
Cab driver, chauffeur	8.7	12.5
Carpenter	0.6	1.4
Child care worker	98.4	97.4
Computer programmer	25.6	34.0
Computer systems analyst	14.8	34.4
Data entry keyer	92.8	91.1
Data-processing equipment repairer	1.8	11.1
Dentist	1.8	4.4
Dental assistant	100.0	99.0
Economist	13.1	39.3
Editor, reporter	44.6	50.5
Elementary school teacher	85.4	85.2
College/university teacher	31.1	36.0
Garage, gas station attendant	4.7	5.8
Lawyer, judge	7.1	18.1
Librarian	81.1	85.9
Mail carrier	8.7	20.6
Office machine repairer	1.7	1.6
Physician	13.0	17.6
Registered nurse	97.0	94.3
Social worker	60.8	65.0
Telephone installer, repairer	4.8	13.3
Telephone operator	93.3	87.9
Waiter/waitress	91.1	85.1
Welder	4.4	5.1

Source: Bureau of Labor Statistics, *Employment and Earnings,* January 1976, Table 2, and January 1987, Table 22.

Table 19 • WOMEN AS A PERCENT OF THE FEDERAL WORKFORCE BY RACE AND ETHNIC ORIGIN, 1982–85

Race and Ethnic Origin	*Federal Workforce*				*Civilian Labor Force*
	1982	*1983*	*1984*	*1985*	*1985*
White (not of Hispanic origin)	24.3	24.3	24.9	25.2	37.6
Black (not of Hispanic origin)	8.2	8.4	8.6	9.0	5.3
Hispanic[1]	1.3	1.4	1.5	1.6	2.6
Asian	0.8	0.9	1.0	1.1	0.8 (1980)[2]
American Indian	0.4	0.4	0.5	1.1	0.2 (1980)[2]
Total percent	35.1	35.7	36.3	37.4	44.2
Total number (in thousands)	2,550	2,574	2,607	2,680	

[1]Persons of Hispanic origin may be of any race.

[2]More recent data on Asian and American Indian women are not available.

Source: Equal Employment Opportunity Commission, *Annual Report on the Employment of Minorities, Women, and Individuals with Handicaps in the Federal Government, Fiscal Year 1985*, 1987, Table I-1; and Bureau of Labor Statistics, *Employment and Earnings*, 1987, Table 39.

Figure 15 • WOMEN AS A PERCENT OF FEDERAL PROFESSIONAL, CLERICAL, AND BLUE-COLLAR WORKERS, BY RACE AND ETHNIC ORIGIN, 1985

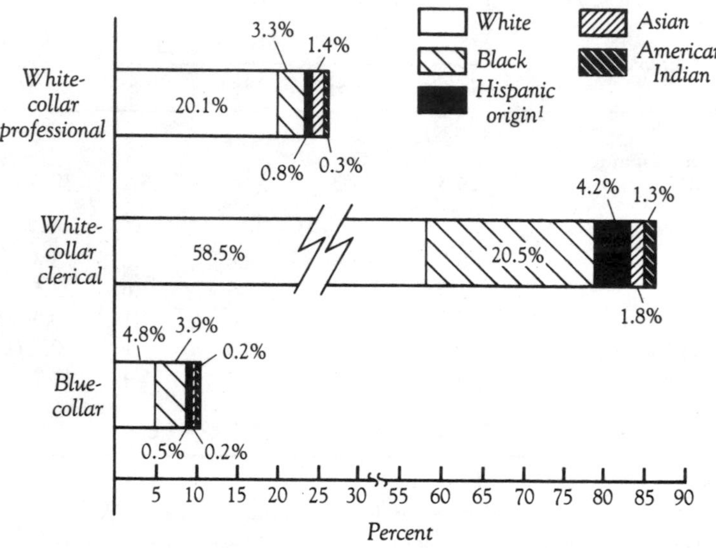

[1]Persons of Hispanic origin may be of any race.

Source: Equal Employment Opportunity Commission, *Annual Report on the Employment of Minorities, Women, and Individuals with Handicaps in the Federal Government, Fiscal Year 1985,* 1987, Table I-1.

Figure 16 • INDUSTRY DISTRIBUTION OF EMPLOYED WOMEN AND MEN, 1986

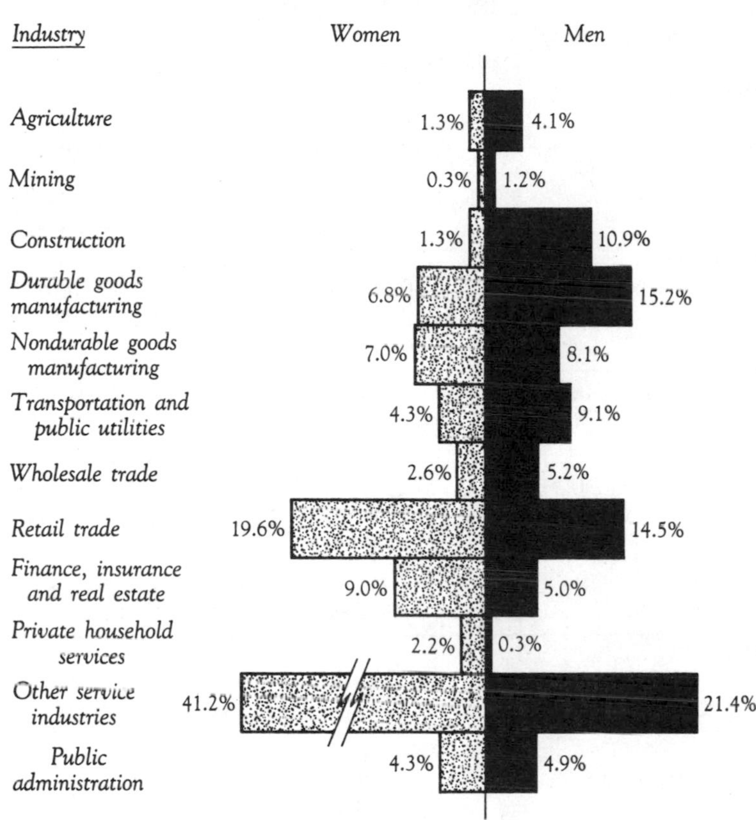

Source: Bureau of Labor Statistics, *Employment and Earnings,* January 1987, Tables 19, 24 and 25.

Table 20 • SERVICE INDUSTRY EMPLOYMENT OF WOMEN AND MEN, 1986 (numbers in thousands)

	Women		*Men*		
Industry	*Number*	*Percent*	*Number*	*Percent*	*Women as Percent of Total Industry*
Private household	1,057	5.0	184	1.4	85.2
Business and repair	2,366	11.2	3,845	29.1	38.1
Personal (except private household)	2,207	10.4	1,024	7.8	68.3
Entertainment and recreation	527	2.5	765	5.8	40.8
Hospitals	3,343	15.8	1,025	7.8	76.5
Health services (except hospitals)	2,901	13.7	860	6.5	77.1
Educational	5,449	25.8	2,808	21.3	66.0
Social services	1,741	8.2	798	6.0	68.6
Forestry and fisheries	34	0.2	153	1.2	18.2
Other	1,511	7.1	1,738	13.2	46.5
Total	21,136	100.0	13,200	100.0	61.6

Source: Bureau of Labor Statistics, *Employment and Earnings,* January 1987, Table 24.

Table 21 • MEDIAN USUAL WEEKLY EARNINGS OF FULL-TIME WAGE AND SALARY WORKERS BY SEX, RACE, AND HISPANIC ORIGIN, 1987

Sex, Race, and Hispanic Origin[1]	*Earnings (in dollars)*	*Earnings as a Percent of White Men's Earnings*
White		
Women	307	68.2
Men	450	—
Black		
Women	275	61.1
Men	326	72.4
Hispanic origin		
Women	251	55.8
Men	306	68.0

[1]Persons of Hispanic origin may be of any race.

Source: Bureau of Labor Statistics, *News,* USDL 88-43, 1988, Table 5.

Table 22 • MEDIAN WEEKLY EARNINGS OF FULL-TIME WAGE AND SALARY WORKERS BY SEX AND AGE, 1986

	Median Weekly Earnings (in dollars)		
Age	*Women*	*Men*	*Women's Earnings as a Percent of Men's Earnings*
16–24	218	245	89.0
25–34	305	401	76.1
35–44	319	498	64.1
45–54	308	505	61.0
55–64	295	484	61.0
65 and over	255	358	71.2
Total, age 16 and over	290	419	69.2

Source: Bureau of Labor Statistics, *Employment and Earnings*, January 1987, Table 61.

Table 23 • MEDIAN WEEKLY EARNINGS OF FULL-TIME WAGE AND SALARY WORKERS BY SEX AND OCCUPATION, 1986

	Median Weekly Earnings (in dollars)		
Occupational Category	*Women*	*Men*	*Female/Male Wage*
Managerial and professional specialty	414	608	68.1
Executive, administrative, and managerial	395	620	63.7
Professional specialty	428	599	71.4
Technical, sales, and administrative support	282	437	64.5
Technicians and related support	343	490	70.0
Sales occupations	239	447	53.5
Administrative support (including clerical)	284	403	70.5
Service Occupations	191	284	67.2
Private household	119	NA	NA
Protective service	292	402	72.6
Service (except private household and protective)	195	239	81.6
Precision production, craft, and repair	277	418	66.3
Mechanics and repairers	431	413	104.4
Construction trades	333	401	83.0
Other precision production, craft, and repair	258	448	57.6

Occupational Category	Median Weekly Earnings (in dollars) Women	Men	Female/Male Wage
Operators, fabricators, and laborers	225	332	67.8
Machine operators, assemblers, and inspectors	223	354	63.0
Transportation and material moving occupations	287	372	77.2
Handlers, equipment cleaners, helpers, and laborers	226	271	83.4
Farming, forestry, and fishing	187	220	85.0

Source: Bureau of Labor Statistics, *Employment and Earnings,* January 1987, Table 56.

Table 24 • OCCUPATIONS WITH THE HIGHEST AND LOWEST MEDIAN WEEKLY EARNINGS FOR WOMEN AND MEN, 1986

Occupations	*Median Weekly Earnings (in dollars)*[1]
Highest for Women	
Lawyers	624
Engineers	580
Computer systems analysts and scientists	537
Physicians	505
Administrators, education and related fields	495
Highest for Men	
Lawyers	806
Economists	794
Airplane pilots and navigators	760
Personnel and labor relations managers	759
Managers, marketing, advertising, and public relations	751

Occupations	*Median Weekly Earnings (in dollars)*[1]
Lowest for Women	
Waitresses	168
Farm workers	165
Food counter, fountain, and related occupations	149
Private household cleaners and servants	146
Child care workers, private households	90
Lowest for Men	
Textile sewing machine operators	205
Garage and service station related occupations	202
Farm workers	195
Miscellaneous food preparation	165
Assistants for waiters and waitresses	162

[1]Median weekly earnings for workers who usually work full time.

Source: Bureau of Labor Statistics, unpublished data.

Table 25 • AVERAGE (MEAN) EARNINGS OF YEAR-ROUND, FULL-TIME WORKERS[1] BY SEX AND EDUCATIONAL ATTAINMENT, 1985 (in dollars)

Educational Attainment	*Women*	*Men*
Fewer than 8 years	9,681	15,039
1–3 years of high school	12,317	19,241
High school graduates	14,903	22,852
1–3 years of college	17,229	26,705
College graduates	21,362	35,400
1 or more years postgraduate	26,348	44,478
All education levels	17,033	27,430

[1]Persons age 25 and over.

Source: Bureau of the Census, Current Population Reports, Series P-60, No. 156, Table 36.

Table 26 • MEAN HOURLY EARNINGS OF FULL-TIME WORKERS BY TENURE ON CURRENT JOB, 1984

Years of Work Experience by Tenure on Current Job	*Hourly Earnings (in dollars)*		*Ratio of Women's Earnings to Men's*
	Women	*Men*	
Experience less than 5 years	5.88	7.19	.82
On job less than 2 years	5.72	7.07	.81
On job 2 years or more	6.07	7.33	.83
Experience 5 to 9 years	6.95	8.35	.83
On job less than 2 years	6.36	7.74	.82
On job 2 to 4 years	6.91	8.45	.82
On job 5 years or more	7.45	8.89	.84
Experience 10 to 19 years	8.07	10.95	.74
On job less than 2 years	6.56	9.50	.69
On job 2 to 4 years	7.69	10.39	.74
On job 5 to 9 years	8.71	11.15	.78
On job 10 years or more	8.53	12.01	.71
Experience 20 years or more	8.15	12.41	.66
On job less than 2 years	6.12	10.20	.60
On job 2 to 4 years	6.92	11.27	.61
On job 5 to 9 years	7.42	11.96	.62
On job 10 years or more	9.10	13.02	.70

Source: Bureau of the Census, Current Population Reports, Series P-70, No. 10, 1987, Table F.

Figure 17 • WORKERS[1] WITH EARNINGS AT OR BELOW THE MINIMUM WAGE BY SEX AND AGE, 1986

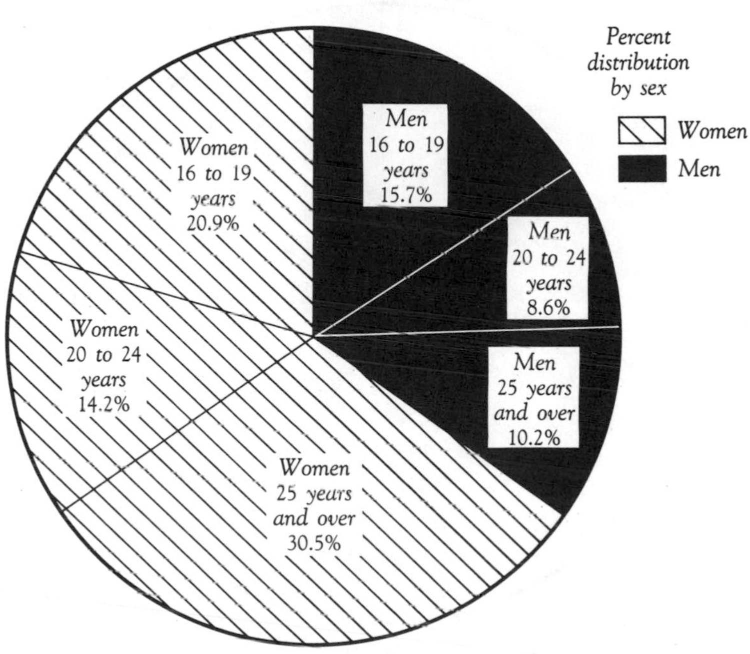

Total number 5,060,000

[1]For wage and salary workers paid hourly rates.

[2]Also includes persons in families where the husband, wife or other person maintaining the family is in the Armed Forces, and persons in unrelated subfamilies.

Source: Earl Mellor, *Monthly Labor Review* 110 (July 1987), Table 1.

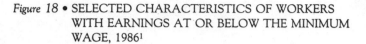

Figure 18 • SELECTED CHARACTERISTICS OF WORKERS WITH EARNINGS AT OR BELOW THE MINIMUM WAGE, 1986[1]

Percent distribution by family relationship

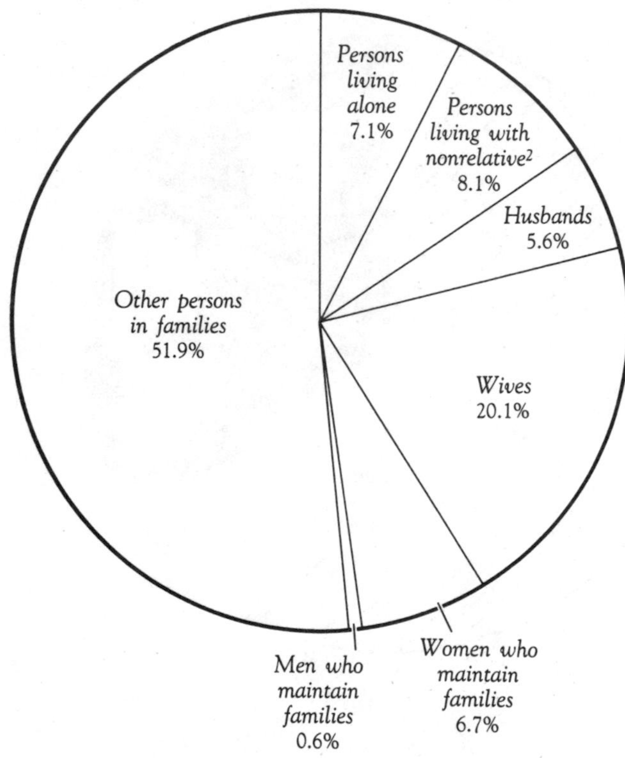

[1]For wage and salary workers paid hourly rates.

[2]Also includes persons in families where the husband, wife or other person maintaining the family is in the Armed Forces, and persons in unrelated subfamilies.

Source: Earl Mellor, *Monthly Labor Review* 110 (July 1987), Table 1.

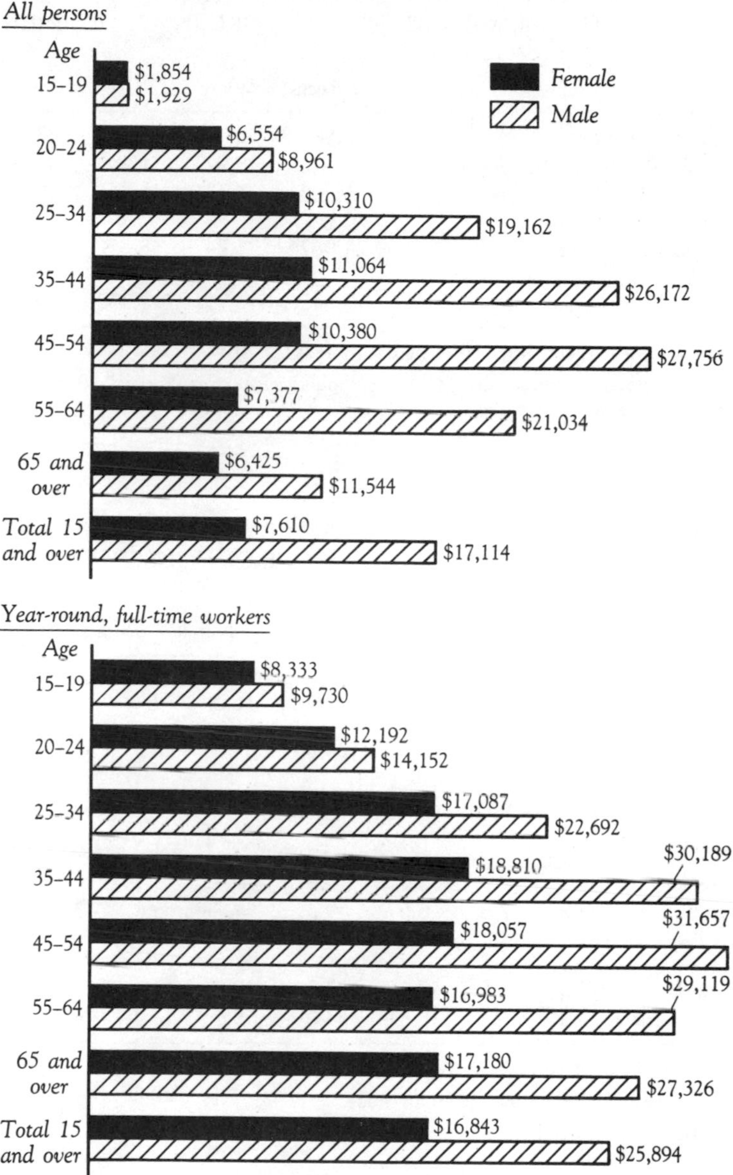

Figure 19 • MEDIAN ANNUAL INCOME OF PERSONS BY AGE, SEX, AND YEAR-ROUND, FULL-TIME EMPLOYMENT STATUS, 1986

Source: Bureau of the Census, Current Population Reports, Series P-60, No. 157, 1987, Table 7.

Table 27 • MEDIAN ANNUAL INCOME OF FAMILIES BY FAMILY TYPE, RACE, AND HISPANIC ORIGIN, 1986 (in dollars)

	All Races	*White*	*Black*	*Hispanic Origin*[1]
Married couple	32,805	33,426	26,583	23,912
Wife in paid labor force	38,346	38,972	31,949	30,206
Wife not in paid labor force	25,803	26,421	16,766	17,507
Male householder, no wife present	24,962	26,247	18,731	20,894
Female householder, no husband present	13,647	15,716	9,300	9,432

[1]Persons of Hispanic origin may be of any race.

Source: Bureau of the Census, Current Population Reports, Series P-60, No. 157, 1987, Table 1.

Table 28 • POVERTY RATES OF ALL FAMILIES AND FEMALE-HEADED FAMILIES, BY WORK EXPERIENCE OF HOUSEHOLDER, 1986 (in percentages)

Work Experience of Householder[1] *in 1986*	*All Families*				*Families Headed by Women*			
	Total	*White*	*Black*	*Hispanic Origin*[2]	*Total*	*White*	*Black*	*Hispanic Origin*[2]
Total	11.0	8.7	28.5	24.9	34.6	28.2	50.1	51.2
Worked in 1986	7.1	6.0	16.4	16.5	22.1	18.4	32.1	29.6
Worked 50–52 weeks	3.7	3.2	8.3	10.4	10.4	8.3	16.4	17.1
Full time	3.2	2.8	6.6	9.3	7.7	5.6	13.1	11.5
Worked 1–49 weeks	19.6	16.9	37.3	33.3	48.0	42.8	59.6	54.2
Did not work	24.3	18.3	55.8	54.0	55.6	46.0	76.0	72.8

[1]Restricted to families with civilian householders.

[2]Persons of Hispanic origin may be of any race.

Source: Bureau of the Census, Current Population Reports, Series P-60, No. 157, 1987, Table 19.

Table 29 • TRENDS IN POVERTY RATES OF PERSONS BY FAMILY TYPE, RACE, AND HISPANIC ORIGIN, 1960–86

	All Races		*White*		*Black*		*Hispanic Origin*[1]	
Year	*Female-Headed*	*All Others*	*Female-Headed*	*All Others*	*Female-Headed*	*All Others*	*Female-Headed*	*All Others*
1960	49.5	18.5	42.3	14.9	70.0[2]	50.7[2]	NA	NA
1965	46.0	13.2	38.5	10.3	65.1[3]	33.4[3]	NA	NA
1970	38.2	8.2	31.4	6.8	58.8	21.7	NA	NA
1976	34.4	7.1	27.3	6.0	54.7	16.9	54.3	17.9
1977	32.8	6.9	25.5	5.9	53.9	16.6	53.3	15.3
1978	32.3	6.6	24.9	5.7	53.1	15.1	53.3	14.6
1979	32.0	7.0	24.9	5.9	52.2	16.2	48.9	15.5
1980	33.8	8.0	27.1	6.9	53.1	17.9	52.5	18.5
1981	35.2	8.8	28.4	7.6	55.8	19.4	54.0	18.6
1982	36.2	9.8	28.7	8.7	57.4	20.0	57.4	22.0
1983	35.6	10.1	28.3	8.8	55.9	20.5	53.2	20.9
1984	34.0	9.3	27.3	8.2	52.9	19.1	54.3	20.9
1985	33.5	8.9	27.3	7.9	51.8	16.4	54.2	21.1
1986	34.2	8.2	27.9	7.3	52.9	15.2	51.3	19.9

[1]Persons of Hispanic origin may be of any race.

[2]1959.

[3]1966.

Source: Bureau of the Census, Current Population Reports, Series P-60, No. 157, 1987, Table 16.

Figure 20 • HOUSEHOLDS RECEIVING NONCASH BENEFITS, 1985 (as percent of all households of a specific category)

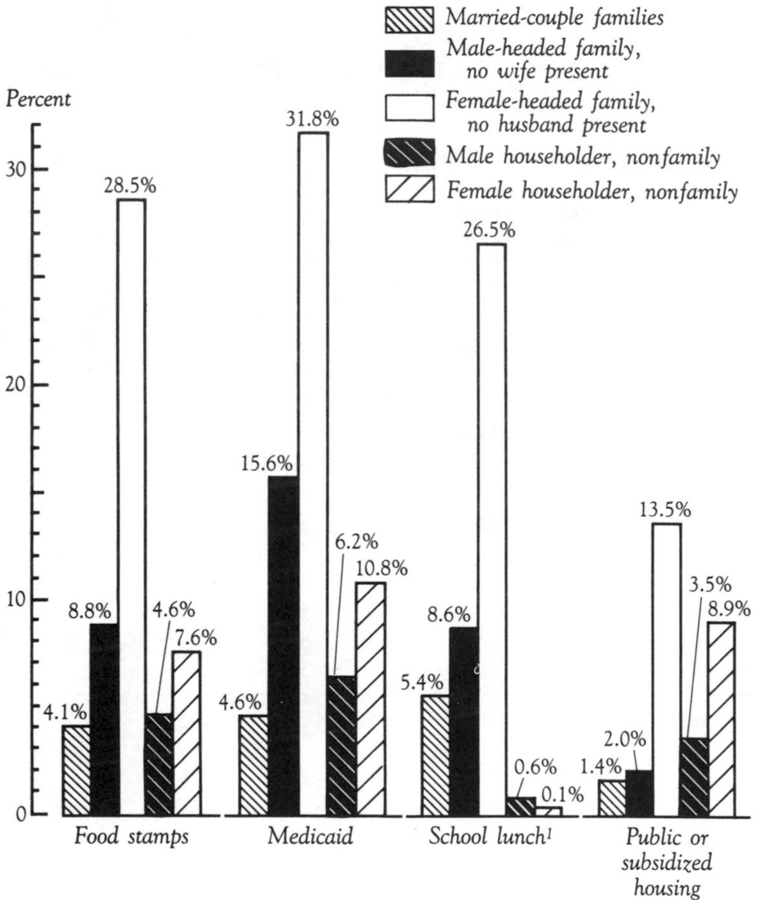

[1]Children 5- to 18-years-old receiving free or reduced price school lunches.

Source: Bureau of the Census, Current Population Reports, Series P-60, No. 155, 1987, Tables 1, 5, 6, 7, and 8.

Table 30 • NUMBER OF FAMILIES ON AND RECIPIENTS OF AFDC, SELECTED YEARS, 1936-DECEMBER 1985 (numbers in thousands)

		Recipients[1]	
Year	*Families*	*Total*	*Children*
December 1985	3,721	10,924	7,247
1984	3,714	10,832	7,144
1983	3,686	10,761	7,098
1982	3,542	10,358	6,903
1981	3,835	11,079	7,527
1980	3,712	10,774	7,419
1975	3,498	11,346	8,095
1970	2,208	8,466	6,214
1965	1,039	4,329	3,256
1960	787	3,005	2,314
1955	612	2,214	1,673
1950	644	2,205	1,637
1945	259	907	656
1940	349	1,182	840
1936	149	534	361

[1]Includes Alaska and Hawaii beginning in 1943, Puerto Rico and Virgin Islands beginning in October 1950, and Guam beginning in July 1959.

Source: Social Security Administration, *Social Security Bulletin* 50 (November 1987), Table M-27; Annual Statistical Supplement, 1986, Table 5.3.

Chapter Notes

TWO The Political Woman

1. "In her own right" became a common way of describing the achievement of a growing number of political women who have come into office directly as a result of their own personal aspirations, initiative, and political career paths. The phrase distinguishes these women from others, usually of an earlier generation, who arrived in office via "matrimonial connection," typically as widows, often only serving a short time to fill out the term of a deceased husband, although sometimes then running for the seat themselves and remaining in office for many terms. Until recently, the "widow's route" to office was common among women in Congress. Moreover, the only three women who had served as state governors before Ella Grasso's election in 1974 had reached office via the matrimonial connection: Nellie Tayloe Ross, governor of Wyoming from 1925–27, was elected to replace her deceased husband; both Miriam ("Ma") Ferguson, governor of Texas in 1925–27 and again in 1933–35, and Lurleen Wallace, governor of Georgia 1967–68, were elected as surrogates for husbands barred under state law from seeking reelection.
2. In broad outline and approach, the following profile of the new political woman (both numbers and demographics) is an adapted, expanded, and updated version of a similar discussion in Mandel (1983, Chapter 1).
3. Women's entry into politics since the early 1970s has taken place on a system-wide basis from local to national levels, in appointive as well as elective office, in political parties as well as in governmental positions, on campaign staffs and in political consulting firms, on lobbying and legislative staffs, in bureaucratic and administrative positions. Because elective office is the most visible part of the political system and most directly asks for a vote of approval from the general public, this profile of the new political woman is concentrated there. However, many of the observations and conclusions about trends and challenges faced by women seeking elective office apply generally to other areas of political life.
4. School boards are not included in this account of legislative and executive elective office.

5. In 1987, 716 black women were serving in elective offices as members of Congress, state legislatures, county and municipal governing bodies, and as mayors, according to figures compiled by the Joint Center for Political Studies (JCPS) in Washington, D.C. This number represents 18.6 percent of black elected officials and approximately four percent of women in these offices.
6. Two relatively new efforts in Minnesota illustrate the type of activity that has taken place out of a commitment to increase the numbers of female candidates and to provide support to political women. One project, Women Candidates Development Coalition, was established in 1986 to build a statewide, bipartisan women's network to identify and develop female candidates. Officers of the Coalition have gone from community to community to speak with women who lost their races in order to discover what would have helped them to win, whether they plan to run again, and who else might be available for future candidacies. The second project, the Minnesota Women's Political Assembly, is a bipartisan coalition of various women's political groups (for example, the Minnesota Women's Political Caucus, the Minnesota Political Congress of Black Women, the GOP Feminist Caucus of Minnesota, and the DFL Feminist Caucus) which come together to promote and highlight women in politics through informal talent banks, education and information-sharing projects, and public relations efforts.

THREE **Women's Paid Work, Household Income, and Household Well-being**

1. The author wishes to thank Ann Harrison for her excellent research assistance.

FOUR **Women and Health Care**

1. The author wishes to thank Jane Andrews, Suzanne Griffith, Barbara Lyons, and Lydia Taghavi for research assistance.
2. Unless otherwise noted, all comparisons are based on data reported in National Center for Health Statistics (1986).

References

Introduction

D'Arusmont, Frances Wright. *Life, Letters and Lectures, 1834–1844.* New York: Arno Press, 1972.

ONE A Richer Life: A Reflection on the Women's Movement

Astin, Alexander W., Kenneth C. Green, and William S. Korn. *The American Freshman: Twenty-Year Trends.* Los Angeles: Higher Education Research Institute, UCLA, 1987.

Basler, Barbara. "Putting a Career on Hold." *New York Times Magazine*, December 7, 1986, 152–153, 158, 160.

Becraft, Carolyn. "Women in the Military." In *The American Woman 1987–88*, edited by Sara E. Rix. New York: W. W. Norton and Company, 1987.

Bianchi, Suzanne and Daphne Spain. *American Women in Transition.* New York: Russell Sage Foundation, 1986.

Bureau of the Census, Current Population Reports, Series P-23, No. 146. *Women in the American Economy,* by Cynthia M. Taueber and Victor Valdisera. Washington, D.C.: U.S. Government Printing Office, November 1986.

———. *Statistical Abstract of the United States: 1987*, 107th Edition. Washington, D.C.: U.S. Government Printing Office, 1987.

———, Current Population Reports, Series P-23, No. 152. *Child Support and Alimony: 1985.* Washington, D.C.: U.S. Government Printing Office, August 1987.

Bureau of Labor Statistics (BLS). "Usual Weekly Earnings of Wage and Salary Workers." *News*. USDL88–43. Washington, D.C.: BLS, February 1, 1988.

Cherlin, Andrew. "Women and the Family." In *The American Woman, 1987–88*, edited by Sara E. Rix. New York: W. W. Norton and Company, 1987.

Coser, Rose Laub and Gerald Rokoff. "Women in the Occupational World: Social Disruption and Conflict." In *Women and Work: Prob-*

lems and Perspectives, edited by Rachel Kahn-Hut, Arlene Kaplan Daniels, and Richard Colvard. New York: Oxford University Press, 1982.

Ehrenreich, Barbara. "The Next Wave." *Ms.*, July/August 1987, 166, 168, 216–218.

"14 Years of Women as Federal Agents." *New York Times*, September 26, 1986.

Hood, Jane C. *Becoming a Two-Job Family.* New York: Praeger, 1983.

McGlen, Nancy and Karen O'Connor. *Women's Rights: The Struggle for Equality in the Nineteenth and Twentieth Centuries.* New York: Praeger, 1983.

Mellor, Earl. "Shift Work and Flexitime: How Prevalent Are They?" *Monthly Labor Review* 109 (November 1986): 14–21.

Mortimer, Jeylan T. and Gloria Sorensen. "Men, Women, Work, and Family." In *Women in the Workplace: Effects on Families*, edited by Kathryn M. Borman, Sarah Gideonse, and Daisy Quarm. Norwood, New Jersey: Ablex Publishing Company, 1984.

National Committee on Pay Equity (NCEP). *State Update*. Washington, D.C.: NCEP, August 1987.

Ross, Susan Deller and Ann Barcher. *The Rights of Women*, Revised Edition. New York: Bantam Books, 1983.

Shaw, Lois. *Older Women at Work.* Washington, D.C.: Women's Research and Education Institute, 1985.

Shreve, Anita. "The Group, 12 Years Later." *New York Times Magazine*, July 6, 1986.

Skrzycki, Cindy and Frank Swoboda. "Child Care Issue Emerges as Focus of Legislative Efforts." *Washington Post*, February 8, 1988.

U.S. Department of Education, Office of Educational Research and Statistics, Center for Education Statistics. *Digest of Education Statistics.* Washington, D.C.: U.S. Government Printing Office, 1987.

Weitzman, Lenore J. *The Divorce Revolution: The Unexpected Social and Economic Consequences for Women and Children in America.* New York: The Free Press, 1985.

TWO **The Political Woman**

Baxter, Sandra and Marjorie Lansing. *Women and Politics: The Visible Majority.* Ann Arbor, Michigan: University of Michigan Press, 1983.

Carroll, Susan J. *Women as Candidates in American Politics.* Bloomington, Indiana: Indiana University Press, 1985.

Carroll, Susan J. and Wendy S. Strimling. *Women's Routes to Elective Office: A Comparison with Men's.* New Brunswick, New Jersey: Center for the American Woman and Politics, Eagleton Institute of Politics, Rutgers University, 1983.

Center for the American Woman and Politics (CAWP). *Bringing More Women Into Public Office* (fact sheet), 1983; *Women's Routes to Elective Office* (fact sheet), 1984; *Black Women Officeholders* (fact sheet), 1985; *Women in Municipal Office* (fact sheet), 1987; *Women in Elective Office* (fact sheet), 1988; *Women in State Legislatures* (fact sheet), 1988. New Brunswick, New Jersey: CAWP, selected dates.

———. *News & Notes About Women Public Officials* 4 (August 1986); 5 (December 1986). New Brunswick, New Jersey: CAWP, 1986.

Chisholm, Shirley. *The Good Fight.* New York: Harper and Row, 1973.

Douglass College/Center for the American Woman and Politics (CAWP). *Women in Government Around the World* (fact sheet). New Brunswick, New Jersey: Douglass College/CAWP, Rutgers University, 1987.

Evans, Sara. *Personal Politics.* New York: Vintage, 1980.

Freeman, Jo. *The Politics of Women's Liberation.* New York: McKay, 1975.

Gallup, George Jr. "Women in Politics" (Survey 239-G). *The Gallup Poll: Public Opinion 1984.* Wilmington, Delaware: Scholarly Resources Inc., 1985.

Gertzog, Irwin N. *Congressional Women: Their Recruitment, Treatment, and Behavior.* New York: Praeger, 1984.

Gruberg, Martin. *Women in American Politics: An Assessment and Sourcebook.* Oshkosh, Wisconsin: Academia Press, 1968.

Ivins, Molly. "Woman in the News: Kathy Whitmire." *Working Woman,* March 1987, 120–124.

Johnson, Marilyn and Susan J. Carroll. "Profile of Women Holding Office, 1977." In *Women in Public Office: A Biographical Directory and Statistical Analysis,* Second Edition, compiled by the Center for the American Woman and Politics. Metuchen, New Jersey: The Scarecrow Press, 1978.

Johnson, Marilyn and Kathy Stanwick. "Profile of Women Holding Office, 1975." In *Women in Public Office: A Biographical Directory and Statistical Analysis,* First Edition, compiled by the Center for the American Woman and Politics. New York: R. R. Bowker Company, 1976.

Kirkpatrick, Jeane J. *Political Woman.* New York: Basic Books, 1974.

Kleeman, Katherine E. and Ruth B. Mandel. "Women Officials: A Singular Bond." In *The Women's Economic Justice Agenda.* Washington, D.C.: The National Center for Policy Alternatives, 1987.

Klein, Ethel. *Gender Politics: From Consciousness to Mass Politics.* Cambridge, Massachusetts: Harvard University Press, 1984.

Lynn, Naomi. "American Women and the Political Process." In *Women: A Feminist Perspective,* edited by Jo Freeman. Palo Alto, California: Mayfield, 1979.

McGlen, Nancy E. and Karen O'Connor. *Women's Rights: The Struggle for Equality in the 19th and 20th Centuries.* New York: Praeger, 1983.

Mandel, Ruth B. *In the Running: The New Woman Candidate.* Boston: Beacon Press, 1983.

Not One of the Boys. (A documentary film about women in politics.) New Brunswick, New Jersey: Center for the American Woman and Politics, 1984.

Sivard, Ruth Leger. *Women . . . A World Survey.* Washington, D.C.: World Priorities, 1985.

Stanwick, Kathy A. and Katherine E. Kleeman. *Women Make a Difference.* New Brunswick, New Jersey: Center for the American Woman and Politics, 1983.

Tolchin, Susan and Martin Tolchin. *Clout: Womanpower and Politics.* New York: Coward, McCann and Geoghegan, 1974.

"Women Legislators Lead Stunning Revolt in WV." *National NOW Times,* May/June 1987, 4, 7.

THREE **Women's Paid Work, Household Income, and Household Well-being**

Barrett, Nancy. "Women and the Economy." In *The American Woman 1987–88,* edited by Sara E. Rix. New York: W. W. Norton and Company, 1987.

Bergmann, Barbara. *The Economic Emergence of Women.* New York: Basic Books, 1986.

Betson, David and Jacques van der Gaag. "Working Married Women and the Distribution of Income." *Journal of Human Resources* XIX (December 1984): 532–543.

Brown, Clair. "Home Production for Use in a Market Economy." In *Rethinking the Family: Some Feminist Questions,* edited by Barrie Thorne and Marilyn Yalom. White Plains, New York: Longman Press, 1982.

Bureau of the Census, Current Population Reports. Series P-23, No. 117. *Trends in Child Care Arrangements of Working Mothers.* Washington, D.C.: U.S. Government Printing Office, June 1982.

———, Current Population Reports. Series P-23, No. 129. *Child Care Arrangements of Working Mothers.* Washington, D.C.: U.S. Government Printing Office, November 1983.

———. *Statistical Abstract of the United States 1986,* 106th Edition. Washington, D.C.: U.S. Government Printing Office, 1985.

———, Current Population Reports. Series P-70, No. 9. *Who's Minding the Kids?* Washington, D.C.: U.S. Government Printing Office, May 1987.

Bureau of Labor Statistics. *Handbook of Labor Statistics 1985*. Washington, D.C.: U.S. Government Printing Office, 1985.

———. *Employment and Earnings.* Washington, D.C.: U.S. Government Printing Office, January 1987.

Cain, Glen G. "Welfare Economics of Policies Toward Women." *Journal of Labor Economics* 3, Part 2 (January 1985): S375–S396.

Danziger, Sheldon. "Do Working Wives Increase Family Income Inequality?" *Journal of Human Resources* XV (Summer 1980): 444–451.

Danziger, Sheldon and Peter Gottschalk. *How Have Families with Children Been Faring?* Discussion Paper No. 801–86. Madison, Wisconsin: Institute for Research on Poverty, January 1986.

Davis, Kingsley. "Wives and Work: The Sex Role Revolution and Its Consequences." *Population and Development Review* 10 (September 1984): 397–417.

Fuchs, Victor R. "His and Hers: Gender Differences in Work and Income, 1959–1979." *Journal of Labor Economics* 4, 3, Part 2 (July 1986): S245–S272.

Hartmann, Heidi. "The Family as the Locus of Gender, Class and Political Struggle: The Example of Housework." *Signs* 6 (Spring 1981): 366–394.

Hill, C. Russell and Frank P. Stafford. "Parental Care of Children: Time Diary Estimates of Quantity, Predictability, and Variety." In *Time, Goods, and Well-Being,* edited by F. Thomas Juster and Frank P. Stafford. Ann Arbor, Michigan: University of Michigan Survey Research Center, 1984.

Hill, Martha S. "Patterns of Time Use." In *Time, Goods, and Well-Being,* edited by F. Thomas Juster and Frank P. Stafford. Ann Arbor, Michigan: University of Michigan Survey Research Center, 1984.

Hofferth, Sandra L. "Long-term Economic Consequences for Women of Delayed Childbearing and Reduced Family Size." *Demography* 21 (May 1984): 141–155.

Johnson, William R. and Jonathan Skinner. "Labor Supply and Marital Separation." *American Economic Review* 76 (June 1986): 455–469.

Juster, F. Thomas. "A Note on Recent Changes in Time Use." In *Time, Goods, and Well-Being,* edited by F. Thomas Juster and Frank P. Stafford. Ann Arbor, Michigan: University of Michigan Survey Research Center, 1984.

Lazear, Edward P. and Robert T. Michael. "Real Income Equivalence Among One-Earner and Two-Earner Families." *American Economic Review* 70 (May 1980): 203–212.

———. "Estimating the Personal Distribution of Income with Adjustment for Within-Family Variation." *Journal of Labor Economics* 4, 3, Part 2 (July 1986): S216–S239.

Leibowitz, Arleen. "Women's Work in the Home." In *Sex Discrimination and the Division of Labor,* edited by Cynthia Lloyd. New York: Columbia University Press, 1975.

Levy, Frank. *Dollars and Dreams, The Changing American Income Distribution.* New York: Russell Sage Foundation, 1987.

Michael, Robert T. "Consequences of the Rise in Female Labor Force Participation Rates: Questions and Probes." *Journal of Labor Economics* 3, 1, Part 2 (January 1985): S117–S146.
Smith, James P. "The Distribution of Family Earnings." *Journal of Political Economy* 87, 5, Part 2 (October 1979): S163–S192.
Smith, James P. and Michael P. Ward. *Women's Wages and Work in the Twentieth Century.* Santa Monica, California: Rand Corporation, October 1984.
———. "Time Series Growth in the Female Labor Force." *Journal of Labor Economics* 3, 1, Part 2 (January 1985): S59–S90.
Stolzenberg, Ross M. and Linda J. Waite. "Local Labor Markets, Children and Labor Force Participation of Wives." *Demography* 21 (May 1984): 157–170.
Wolfe, Barbara and Robert Haveman. "Time Allocation, Market Work and Changes in Female Health." *American Economic Review* 73, 12 (May 1983): 134–139.

FOUR **Women and Health Care**

Berk, Marc L. and Amy K. Taylor. "Women and Divorce: Health Insurance Coverage, Utilization, and Health Care Expenditures." *American Journal of Public Health* 74 (November 1984): 1,276–1,278.
Bureau of the Census. *Statistical Abstract of the United States 1987*, 107th Edition. Washington, D.C.: U.S. Government Printing Office, 1986.
———. Current Population Reports, Series P-60, No. 157. *Money Income and Poverty Status of Families and Persons in the United States, 1986*. Washington, D.C.: U.S. Government Printing Office, July 1987.
Bureau of Labor Statistics. *Employment and Earnings.* Washington, D.C.: U.S. Government Printing Office, January 1986.
Commonwealth Fund Commission on Elderly People Living Alone. *Old, Alone, and Poor: A Plan for Reducing Poverty Among Elderly People Living Alone*. Baltimore, Maryland: Commonwealth Fund, 1987a.
———. *Medicare's Poor: Filling the Gaps in Medical Coverage for Low-Income Elderly Americans*. Baltimore, Maryland: Commonwealth Fund, 1987b.
Davis, Karen. *Child Health and Research Funding*. Testimony before the U.S. Congress, Joint Economic Committee, Subcommittee on Investment, Jobs, and Prices. August 14, 1986.
———. *Employment and Health Insurance Coverage*. Testimony before the U.S. Senate, Committee on Labor and Human Resources, May 19, 1987.
Davis, Karen and Diane Rowland. "Uninsured and Underserved: Inequi-

ties in Health Care in the United States." *Milbank Memorial Fund Quarterly* 61 (1983): 149–176.

Davis, Karen and Cathy Schoen. *Health and the War on Poverty: A Ten Year Appraisal*. Washington, D.C.: The Brookings Institution, 1978.

Freeman, Howard, Robert J. Blendon, Linda H. Aiken et al. "Americans Report on Their Access to Care." *Health Affairs* 6 (Spring, 1987): 6–18.

Hadley, Jack. *More Medical Care, Better Health?* Washington, D.C.: The Urban Institute, 1982.

Harris, Louis and Associates. *Problems of Elderly People Living Alone*. Report to the Commonwealth Fund Commission on Elderly People Living Alone. Baltimore, Maryland: Commonwealth Fund, 1987.

Health Care Financing Administration. *Medicare and Medicaid Data Book, 1984*, HCFA Pub. No. 03210. Washington, D. C.: U.S. Government Printing Office, June 1986.

ICF, Inc. *The Effects of Variations in Medicaid Programs on Older Women*. Report to the American Association of Retired Persons. Washington, D.C.: ICF, Inc., December 1986.

Institute of Medicine. *Preventing Low Birthweight*. Washington, D.C.: National Academy Press, 1985.

Lurie, Nicole, Nancy B. Ward, Martin F. Shapiro, and Robert H. Brook. "Termination from Medi-Cal: Does It Affect Health?" *New England Journal of Medicine* 311 (August 16, 1984): 480–484.

National Center for Health Statistics (NCHS). *National Health Interview Survey, 1984*. Washington, D.C.: NCHS, 1984.

———. *Health United States, 1986*. DHHS Pub. No. (PHS) 87–1232. Washington, D.C.: U.S. Government Printing Office, 1986.

Rowland, Diane, Barbara Lyons, and Jennifer Edwards, "Medicaid: Health Care for the Poor in the Reagan Era." *Annual Review of Public Health*, forthcoming, 1988.

Starfield. "Family Income, Ill Health and Medical Care of U.S. Children." *Journal of Public Health Policy* 3 (September 1982): 244–259.

Swartz, Katherine and Marilyn Moon. *The Health Insurance Status of Midlife Women: The Problem and Options for Alleviating It*. Report to the American Association of Retired People. Washington, D.C.: The Urban Institute, 1986.

Taylor, Amy K. and Walter R. Lawson, Jr. "Employer and Employee Expenditures for Private Health Insurance." National Center for Health Services Research, National Health Care Expenditure Study, Data Preview Series 7, DHHS Pub. No. (PHS) 81–3297. Rockville, Maryland: U.S. Department of Health and Human Services, 1981.

U.S. Congress. Office of Technology Assessment (OTA). *Smoking Related Deaths and Financial Costs*. Washington, D.C.: OTA, September, 1985.

———. House. Committee on Ways and Means. *Background Material and Data on Programs Within the Jurisdiction of the Committee on Ways and Means*. March 6, 1987.

Verbrugge, Lois M. "Gender and Health: An Update on Hypotheses and Evidence." *Journal of Health and Social Behavior* 26 (1985): 156–182.

Wilensky, Gail and Marc L. Berk. *Medicare and the Elderly Poor*. Testimony on the Future of Medicare before the U.S. Senate Special Committee on Aging. April 1983.

Women in Brief

American Academy of Nursing, Task Force on Nursing Practice in Hospitals. *Magnet Hospitals, Attraction and Retention of Professional Nurses.* Kansas City, Missouri: American Nurses' Association, 1983.

The American Baptist, July/August, 1987.

American Council on Education (ACE). *Minorities in Higher Education: Fifth Annual Status Report.* Washington, D.C.: ACE, 1986.

American Hospital Association (AHA). *Hospital Statistics*, 1987 Edition. Chicago: AHA, 1987.

American Nurses' Association (ANA). *Facts About Nursing: 76–77.* Kansas City, Missouri: ANA, 1977.

———. *Facts About Nursing: 84–85.* Kansas City, Missouri: ANA, 1985.

———. *The Scope of Nursing Practice.* Kansas City, Missouri: ANA, 1987.

American Symphony Orchestra League. Unpublished data for 1985 available through main office, Reston, Virginia.

American Women Composers, Inc. *News/Forum*, April-October, 1986.

Andrews, Emily. *The Changing Profile of Pensions in America.* Washington, D.C.: Employee Benefit Research Institute, 1985.

Beard, Charles A. and Mary R. Beard. *The Rise of American Civilization*, Vol. II. New York: Macmillan, 1927.

Benner, Patricia. *From Novice to Expert: Excellence and Power in Clinical Nursing Practice.* Menlo Park, California: Addison-Wesley Publishing Co., 1984.

Bennett, Neil G. and David E. Bloom. "Why Today's Women Aren't Marrying." *Boston Globe*, December 21, 1986.

Bennett, Neil G., David E. Bloom, and Patricia H. Craig. *Black and White Marriage Patterns: Why So Different?* Economic Growth Center Discussion Paper No. 500. New Haven, Connecticut: Yale University Economic Growth Center, March 1986.

Bergmann, Barbara. "Occupational Segregation, Wages and Profits When Employers Discriminate by Race or Sex." *Eastern Economic Journal* 1 (1974): 103–110.

Bershad, Lawrence. "Discriminatory Treatment of the Female Offender in the Criminal Justice System." *Boston College Law Review* 26 (1985).

Block, Adrienne (ed.). *Statistical Report on the Status of Women in College Music.* College Music Society Report No. 5, forthcoming.

Block, Adrienne and Carol Neuls-Bates (eds.). *Women in American Music: A Bibliography.* Westport, Connecticut: Greenwood Press, 1979.

Bowers, Jane and Judith Tick (eds.). *Women Making Music: The Western Art Tradition, 1150–1950.* Urbana, Illinois: University of Illinois Press, 1986.

Brix, Kelly and William Butler. "Reproductive Outcomes of Video Display Terminal Workers." University of Michigan, Ann Arbor, unpublished.

Browne, Angela. *When Battered Women Kill.* New York: The Free Press, 1987.

Bureau of the Census, Current Population Reports. Series P-27, No. 58. *Farm Population of the United States: 1984.* Washington, D.C.: U.S. Government Printing Office, December 1985.

———, Current Population Reports. Series P-20, No. 410. *Marital Status and Living Arrangements: March 1985.* Washington, D.C.: U.S. Government Printing Office, November 1986a.

———, Current Population Reports. Series P-23, No. 146. *Women in the American Economy* by Cynthia M. Taeuber and Victor Valdisera. Washington, D.C.: U.S. Government Printing Office, November 1986b.

———, Current Population Reports. Series P-60, No. 157. *Money Income and Poverty Status of Families and Persons in the United States: 1986.* Washington, D.C.: U.S. Government Printing Office, July 1987.

———, Current Population Reports. Series P-20, No. 416. *The Hispanic Population of the United States: March 1986 and 1987.* Washington, D.C.: U.S. Government Printing Office, August 1987.

Bureau of Labor Statistics. *Employment and Earnings.* Washington, D.C.: U.S. Government Printing Office, January 1978, January 1984, January 1987, October 1987.

———. "Usual Weekly Earnings of Wage and Salary Workers." *News.* USDL88–43. Washington, D.C.: Bureau of Labor Statistics, February 1, 1988.

Butler, William, University of Michigan School of Public Health. Letter to U.S. Rep. Ted Weiss, July 16, 1986.

Calabrese, Edward and P. Tastides. "A Health Study of Digital Equipment Corporation Workers." University of Massachusetts, Amherst, 1986.

Carroll, Jackson W., Barbara Hargrove, and Adair T. Lumis. *Women of the Cloth.* San Francisco: Harper and Row, 1983.

Centers for Disease Control. "Acquired Immunodeficiency Syndrome

(AIDS) Among Blacks and Hispanics—United States." *Morbidity and Mortality Weekly Report* 35 (1986): 655–658, 663–666.

———. *AIDS Weekly Surveillance Report—United States* 1 (November 1987).

Chapman, Jane Roberts. *Economic Realities and the Female Offender.* Lexington, Massachusetts: Lexington Books, 1980.

Chollet, Deborah. "Financing Retirement Today and Tomorrow: The Prospect for America's Workers." In *America in Transition: Benefits for the Future.* Washington, D.C.: Employee Benefit Research Institute, 1987.

Cohn, Ellen G. and Lawrence W. Sherman. *Police Policy on Domestic Violence, 1986: A National Survey.* Washington, D.C.: Crime Control Institute, March 1987.

Committee on Domestic Violence and Incarcerated Women. *Battered Women and Criminal Justice.* New York: Committee on Domestic Violence and Incarcerated Women, 1987.

Davidson, Terry. "Wifebeating: A Recurring Phenomenon Throughout History." In *Battered Women: A Psychosociological Study of Domestic Violence,* edited by Maria Roy. New York: Van Nostrand Reinhold Company, 1977.

Elinson, L., L. Rosenbaum, T. Hancock, and G. Caplen. *Health Effects of Video Display Terminals—A Report of the Health Advisory Unit.* Toronto, Canada: Department of Public Health, July 1980.

Employee Benefit Research Institute. "Women, Family and Pensions." *EBRI Issue Brief* 49 (December 1985).

Epstein, Stephen. "New Connecticut Law on Domestic Violence." *The Women's Advocate.* Newsletter of the National Center on Women and Family Law VIII (January 1987).

"Equal Opportunity—Assessing Women's Presence in the Exxon/Arts Endowment Conductors Program: An Interview with Jesse Rosen." In *The Musical Woman: An International Perspective,* Vol. II, edited by Judith Lang Zaimont. Westport, Connecticut: Greenwood Press, 1987, 91–119.

Evans, Sara M. "Women in Twentieth Century America: An Overview." In *The American Woman 1987–88,* edited by Sara E. Rix. New York: W. W. Norton and Company, 1987.

Fact Book on Theological Education, 1986–87. Vandalia, Ohio: Association of Theological Schools, 1987.

Federal Bureau of Investigation (FBI). Uniform Crime Reports. *Crime in the United States.* Washington, D.C.: FBI, 1985 and 1987.

Feinman, Clarice. "Historical Overview of the Treatment of Incarcerated Women: Myths and Realities of Rehabilitation." *The Prison Journal* 63 (Autumn/Winter 1983): 12–26.

Freidson, Eliot. *Professional Dominance: The Social Structure of Medical Science.* New York: Atherton Press, Inc., 1970.

Frolen, H., B. M. Svedenstal, and P. Bierke. "The Effect of Pulsed Magnetic Fields on the Development of Fetuses in Mice." Swedish Agricultural University, Upsaala, Sweden, 1987.

Goetting, Ann. "Racism, Sexism, and Ageism in the Prison Community." *Federal Probation* 49 (September 1985): 10–22.

Goetting, Ann and Roy Michael Howsen. "Women in Prison: A Profile." *The Prison Journal* 63 (Autumn/Winter 1983): 27–46.

Gondolf, E. and E. Fisher. *Battered Women as Survivors: An Empirical Study of Helpseeking.* Lexington, Massachusetts: Lexington Books, 1988.

Goolkasian, Gail A. *Confronting Domestic Violence: A Guide for Criminal Justice Agencies.* Washington, D.C.: U.S. Department of Justice, May 1986.

Green, Kenneth C. "The Educational 'Pipeline' in Nursing." *Journal of Professional Nursing*, July/August 1987, 247–257.

Guinan, Mary E. and Ann Hardy. "Epidemiology of AIDS in Women in the United States." *Journal of the American Medical Association* 257 (April 17, 1987): 2039–2042.

Hartmann, Heidi I. "Capitalism, Patriarchy, and Job Segregation by Sex." *Signs,* 1, Part 2 (Spring 1976): 137–169.

Hirschorn, Michael W. "Doctorates Earned by Blacks Decline 26.5 Pct. in Decade." *Chronicle of Higher Education,* February 3, 1988, A1, A32, A33.

Jacquet, Constant H. Jr. "Clergy Salaries and Income in 1982 in Eleven U.S. Denominations." In *Yearbook of Canadian and American Churches,* edited by Constant H. Jacquet Jr. Nashville, Tennessee: Abington Press, 1984.

——— (ed.). *Yearbook of American and Canadian Churches.* Nashville, Tennessee: Abington Press, 1987.

Jensen, Joan M. *Loosening the Bonds: Mid-Atlantic Farm Women, 1750–1850.* New Haven, Connecticut: Yale University Press, 1986.

Jones, Jacqueline. *Labor of Love, Labor of Sorrow: Black Women, Work and the Family From Slavery to the Present.* New York: Basic Books, 1985.

Kalbacher, Judith Z. *A Profile of Female Farmers in America.* Washington, D.C.: U.S. Department of Agriculture, Economic Research Service, RDRR-45, 1985.

Kalisch, Philip A. and Beatrice J. Kalisch. *The Advance of American Nursing,* Second Edition. Boston: Little, Brown and Co., 1986.

Knowles, Jane B. " 'It's Our Turn Now': Rural Women Speak Out, 1900–1920." In *Women and Farming: Changing Roles, Changing Structures,* edited by Wava G. Haney and Jane B. Knowles. Boulder, Colorado: Westview Press, 1988.

Ladyslipper Catalog and Resource Guide of Records and Tapes by Women. Durham, North Carolina: Ladyslipper, Inc., annual.

Langan, Patrick A. and Christopher A. Innes. *Preventing Domestic Violence Against Women.* Washington, D.C.: U.S. Department of Justice, Bureau of Justice Statistics Special Report, August 1986.

Lehman, Edward C. *Women Clergy: Breaking Through Gender Barriers.* New Brunswick, New Jersey: Transaction, 1985.

Leonard, Eileen B. "Judicial Decisions and Prison Reform—The Impact of Litigation on Women Prisoners." *Social Problems* 31 (October 1983): 45–58.

Lerman, Lisa G. and Franci Livingston. "State Legislation on Domestic Violence." *Response to Violence in the Family and Sexual Assault* 6 (September/October 1983).

McArdle, Frank B. "The Evolution of the U.S. Retirement Income System: Public Versus Private Funds." Paper prepared for a conference of the Camera di Commercio Industria Artigianato e Agricoltura, Rome, Italy, September 25–26, 1987.

Mahan, S. "Imposition of Despair—An Ethnography of Women in Prison." *Journal of Crime and Justice* 17 (1984): 101–129.

Mantell, J. E., S. H. Akabas, and S. P. Schinke. "Women and AIDS Prevention." *Journal of Primary Prevention*, forthcoming, 1988.

Melius, James. Internal memorandum from the director of the Division of Surveillance, Hazard Evaluation and Field Studies, National Institute for Occupational Safety and Health, June 23, 1986.

Mellor, Earl F. "Weekly Earnings in 1983: A Look at More Than 200 Occupations." *Monthly Labor Review* 108 (January 1985): 54–59.

Miller, Lorna and Mary Neth. "Farm Women in the Political Arena." In *Women and Farming: Changing Roles, Changing Structures,* edited by Wava G. Haney and Jane B. Knowles. Boulder, Colorado: Westview Press, 1988.

Mitchell, Olivia and Emily Andrews. "Scale Economies in Private Multiemployer Pension Systems." *Industrial and Labor Relations Review* 34 (July 1981): 522–530.

Mondanaro, Josette. "Strategies for AIDS Prevention: Motivating Health Behavior in Drug Dependent Women." *Journal of Psychoactive Drugs* 19 (April-June 1987): 143–149.

Moorman, Jeanne E. "The History and Future of the Relationship Between Education and Marriage." Draft, undated.

Moorman, Jeanne E., Campbell Gibson, and Robert E. Fay. "Higher Education and Marriage for Women: What Recent Data Show." Unpublished paper, April 1987.

National Academy of Sciences/National Research Council. *Video Displays, Work, and Vision.* Washington, D.C.: National Academy Press, 1983.

National Endowment for the Arts (NEA). *Changing Proportions of Men and Women in the Artist Occupations 1970–1980.* Report No. 9. Washington, D.C.: NEA, 1985.

National Institute for Occupational Safety and Health (NIOSH). *Health Hazard Evaluation—Southern Bell.* NIOSH Pub. No. 83–329. Cincinnati: NIOSH, 1983.

———. *Health Hazard Evaluation—United Airlines, San Francisco, California.* NIOSH Pub. No. 84–191. Cincinnati: NIOSH, 1984a.

———. *Health Hazard Evaluation—General Telephone Company of Michigan.* NIOSH Pub. No. 84–297. Cincinnati: NIOSH, 1984b.

National League for Nursing (NLN). *Nursing Student Census with Policy Implications, 1986.* Pub. No. 19–2175. New York: NLN, 1986.

———. *Nursing Data Review, 1986.* Pub. No. 19–2176. New York: NLN, 1987.

Nesbitt, Charlotte A. and Angela Argenta. *Female Classification, An Examination of the Issues.* College Park, Maryland: American Correctional Association, August 1984.

Pagelow, Mildred Daley. *Family Violence.* New York: Praeger Press, 1984.

Phipps, Polly A. "Occupational Resegregation: A Case Study of Insurance Adjusters, Examiners, and Investigators." Paper presented at the annual meetings of the American Sociological Association, New York, 1986.

Pinsky, Jane. "Congress Ends 1987 by Passing Budget Act." *American Nurse* 20 (February 1988): 2–5.

"Profile of a Warning." *Wall Street Journal*, January 13, 1987.

Reskin, Barbara and Heidi I. Hartmann. *Women's Work, Men's Work: Sex Segregation on the Job.* Washington, D.C.: National Academy Press, 1986.

Roos, Patricia. "Women in the Composing Room: The Determinants of Women's Entry into Typesetting and Composition." Paper presented at the annual meetings of the American Sociological Association, New York, 1986.

Rosenfeld, Rachel Ann. *Farm Women: Work, Farm, and Family in the United States.* Chapel Hill, North Carolina: University of North Carolina Press, 1985.

Ross, Robert R. and Elizabeth A. Fabiano. *Female Offenders: Correctional Afterthoughts.* Jefferson, North Carolina: McFarland and Company, Inc., 1986.

Rothenberg, Richard, Mary Woelfel, Rand Stoneburner, et al. "Survival with the Acquired Immunodeficiency Syndrome: Experience with 5833 Cases in New York City." *The New England Journal of Medicine* 317 (November 19, 1987): 1297–1302.

Ruether, Rosemary and Eleanor McLaughlin (eds.). *Women of Spirit: Female Leadership in the Jewish and Christian Traditions.* New York: Simon and Schuster, 1979.

Ryan, T. A. *Adult Female Offenders and Institutional Programs: A State of the*

Art Analysis. Columbia, South Carolina: University of South Carolina Press, 1984.

Sachs, Carolyn E. *The Invisible Farmers: Women in Agricultural Production.* Totowa, New Jersey: Rowman & Allanheld, 1983.

Selikoff, Irving, Mount Sinai School of Medicine. Letter to U.S. Rep. Ted Weiss, August 25, 1986.

Sherman, Lawrence W. and Richard A. Berk. "The Specific Deterrent Effects of Arrest for Domestic Assault." *American Sociological Review* 49 (1984): 261–272.

Stark, Evan and Ann Flitcraft. "Medical Therapy as Repression: The Case of Battered Women." *Health and Medicine,* Summer/Fall 1982, 29–32.

———. "Violence Among Intimates: An Epidemiological Review." In *Handbook of Family Violence,* edited by V. N. Haslett et al. New York: Plenum, 1987.

Stark, Evan, Ann Flitcraft, Diana Zuckerman, et al. *Wife Abuse in the Medical Setting: An Introduction for Health Professionals.* Rockville, Maryland: National Clearinghouse on Domestic Violence, April 1981.

Starr, Paul. *The Social Transformation of American Medicine.* New York: Basic Books, Inc., 1982.

Strober, Myra. "Toward a General Theory of Occupational Sex Segregation: The Case of Public School Teaching." In *Sex Segregation in the Workplace: Trends, Explanations, Remedies,* edited by Barbara F. Reskin. Washington, D.C.: National Academy Press, 1984.

Strober, Myra and Carolyn L. Arnold. "The Dynamics of Occupational Segregation among Bank Tellers." In *Gender in the Workplace,* edited by Clair Brown and Joseph Pechman. Washington, D.C.: The Brookings Institution, 1987.

Sulton, Cynthia G. and Roi D. Townsey. *A Progress Report on Women in Policing.* Washington, D.C.: Police Foundation, 1981.

Thomas, Barbara J. and Barbara F. Reskin. "Occupational Change and Sex Integration in Real Estate Sales." Paper presented at the annual meetings of the American Sociological Association, Chicago, 1987.

Tick, Judith. "Women and Music." In *The New Grove Dictionary of American Music,* Vol. 4, edited by S. Sadie and H. W. Hitchcock. New York: Macmillan, 1987.

Tigges, Leann M. and Rachel A. Rosenfeld. "Independent Farming: Correlates and Consequences for Women and Men." *Rural Sociology* 52 (1987): 345–364.

Umansky, Ellen M. "Women in Judaism: From the Reform Movement to Contemporary Jewish Religious Feminism." In *Women of the Spirit: Female Leadership in the Jewish and Christian Traditions,* edited by Rosemary Ruether and Eleanor McLaughlin. New York: Simon and Schuster, 1979.

U.S. Congress. House. Committee on Energy and Commerce. Subcommittee on Oversight and Investigations. 99th Congress, 2d Session. *OMB Review of CDC Research: Impact of the Paperwork Reduction Act.* Washington, D.C.: U.S. Government Printing Office, 1986.

———. Office of Technology Assessment. *Automation of America's Offices.* Washington, D.C.: U.S. Government Printing Office, 1985.

———. Office of Technology Assessment. *Nurse Practitioners, Physician Assistants, and Certified Nurse-Midwives: A Policy Analysis* (Health Technology Case Study 37). OTA-HCS-37. Washington, D.C.: U.S. Government Printing Office, December 1986.

U.S. Department of Education, Office of Educational Research and Statistics, Center for Education Statistics. *Digest of Education Statistics.* Washington, D.C.: U.S. Government Printing Office, 1987 and forthcoming.

U.S. Department of Health and Human Services (DHHS). *Fifth Report to the President and Congress on the Status of Health Personnel in the United States.* Washington, D.C.: DHHS, 1986.

U.S. Department of Justice. Attorney General's Task Force on Family Violence. *Final Report.* Washington, D.C.: U.S. Department of Justice, 1984.

———. *Report to the Nation on Crime and Justice: The Data.* Washington, D.C.: U.S. Department of Justice, 1985.

———. Bureau of Justice Statistics. Bulletin, *Prisoners in 1986.* Washington, D.C.: U.S. Department of Justice, May 1987.

———. Bureau of Justice Statistics. Bulletin, *Capital Punishment, 1986.* Washington, D.C.: U.S. Department of Justice, September 1987.

Valente, Janet and Elaine Decostanzo. *Female Offenders in the Eighties, A Continuum of Services.* Atlanta, Georgia: Georgia Department of Offender Rehabilitation, Office of Women's Services, January 1982.

Ver Steeg, Donna F. and Sydney H. Croog. "Hospitals and Related Health Care Delivery Settings." In *Handbook of Medical Sociology*, Third Edition, edited by Howard E. Freeman, Sol Levine, and Leo G. Reeder. Englewood Cliffs, New Jersey: Prentice-Hall Inc., 1979.

Weisheit, R. A. "Trends in Programs for Female Offenders: The Use of Private Agencies as Service Providers." *International Journal of Offender Therapy and Comparative Criminology* 29 (1985): 35–42.

Wofsy, Constance B. "Human Immunodeficiency Virus Infection in Women." *Journal of the American Medical Association* 257 (April 17, 1987): 2074–2076.

Worth, D. and R. Rodriguez. "Latina Women and AIDS." *SIECUS Report* 12 (January/February 1987): 5–7.

Zikmund, Barbara Brown. "The Struggle for the Right to Preach." In *Women and Religion in America,* Vol. I, edited by Rosemary Radford Ruether and Rosemary Skinner Keller. San Francisco: Harper and Row, 1981.

———. "Winning Ordination for Women in Mainstream Protestantism." In *Women and Religion in America,* Vol. III, edited by Rosemary Radford Ruether and Rosemary Skinner Keller. San Francisco: Harper and Row, 1986.

American Women Today: A Statistical Portrait

NOTE: The Current Population Reports of the Bureau of the Census are listed in ascending order by series and publication numbers. Thus, a report in the P-20 series precedes a P-60 report.

Bureau of the Census. Current Housing Reports, Series H-150–83. *Annual Housing Survey: 1983, Part A, General Housing Characteristics*. Washington, D.C.: U.S. Government Printing Office, October 1984.

———. Current Population Reports, Series P-20, No. 218. *Household and Family Characteristics: March 1970*. Washington, D.C.: U.S. Government Printing Office, March 1971.

———. Current Population Reports, Series P-20, No. 366. *Household and Family Characteristics: March 1980*. Washington, D.C.: U.S. Government Printing Office, September 1981.

———. Current Population Reports, Series P-20, No. 405. *Voting and Registration in the Election of November 1984*. Washington, D.C.: U.S. Government Printing Office, March 1986.

———. Current Population Reports, Series P-20, No. 411. *Household and Family Characteristics: March 1985.* Washington, D.C.: U.S. Government Printing Office, September 1986.

———. Current Population Reports, Series P-20, No. 416. *The Hispanic Population of the United States: March 1986 and 1987* (Advance Report). Washington, D.C.: U.S. Government Printing Office, August 1987.

———. Current Population Reports, Series P-23, No. 112. *Child Support and Alimony: 1978*. Washington, D.C.: U.S. Government Printing Office, September 1981.

———. Current Population Reports, Series P-23, No. 136. *Lifetime Work Experience and Its Effect on Earnings*. Washington, D.C.: U.S. Government Printing Office, June 1984.

———. Current Population Reports, Series P-23, No. 152. *Child Support and Alimony: 1985*. Washington, D.C.: U.S. Government Printing Office, August 1987.

———. Current Population Reports, Series P-25, No. 917. *Preliminary Estimates of the Population of the United States, by Age, Sex, and Race: 1970 to 1981*. Washington, D.C.: U.S. Government Printing Office, July 1982.

———. Current Population Reports, Series P-25, No. 1,000. *Estimates of the Population of the United States, by Age, Sex, and Race: 1980 to*

1986. Washington, D.C.: U.S. Government Printing Office, February 1987.

———. Current Population Reports, Series P-60, No. 127. *Money Income and Poverty Status of Families in the United States: 1980*. Washington, D.C.: U.S. Government Printing Office, August 1981.

———. Current Population Reports, Series P-60, No. 149. *Money Income and Poverty Status of Families and Persons in the United States: 1984*. Washington, D.C.: U.S. Government Printing Office, August 1985.

———. Current Population Reports, Series P-60, No. 155. *Receipt of Selected Noncash Benefits: 1985*. Washington, D.C.: U.S. Government Printing Office, January 1987.

———. Current Population Reports, Series P-60, No. 156. *Money Income of Households, Families, and Persons in the United States: 1985.* Washington, D.C.: U.S. Government Printing Office, August 1987.

———. Current Population Reports, Series P-60, No. 157. *Money Income and Poverty Status of Families and Persons in the United States: 1986*. Washington, D.C.: U.S. Government Printing Office, July 1987.

———. Current Population Reports, Series P-70, No. 9. *Who's Minding the Kids? Child Care Arrangements: Winter 1984–85.* Washington, D.C.: U.S. Government Printing Office, May 1987.

———. Current Population Reports, Series P-70, No. 10. *Male-Female Differences in Work Experience, Occupation, and Earnings: 1984*. Washington, D.C.: U.S. Government Printing Office, August 1987.

Bureau of Labor Statistics. *Marital and Family Characteristics of Workers, March 1960*. Washington, D.C.: Bureau of Labor Statistics, April 1961.

———. *Handbook of Labor Statistics*. Washington, D.C.: U.S. Government Printing Office, June 1985.

———. *Employment and Earnings.* Washington, D.C.: U.S. Government Printing Office, January 1976, January 1986, January 1987, June 1987, July 1987.

———. "Usual Weekly Earnings of Wage and Salary Workers: Fourth Quarter 1987." *News*, USDL 88–43, February 1, 1988.

Equal Employment Opportunity Commission. *Annual Report on the Employment of Minorities, Women and Individuals with Handicaps in the Federal Government, Fiscal Year 1985*. Washington, D.C.: U.S. Government Printing Office, 1987.

Mellor, Earl F. "Workers at the Minimum Wage or Less: Who They Are and the Jobs They Hold." *Monthly Labor Review* 110 (July 1987): 34–38.

National Center for Health Statistics. "Advance Report of Final Natality Statistics, 1985." *Monthly Vital Statistics Report* 36, 4, No. (PHS) 87–1120. Hyattsville, Maryland: U.S. Public Health Service, July 1987.

Social Security Administration. *Social Security Bulletin, Annual Statistical Supplement, 1986*. Washington, D.C.: U.S. Government Printing Office, December 1986.

———. "AFDC: Number of Families and Recipients, by State, October-December 1985." *Social Security Bulletin* 50, (November 1987): Table M-27.

U.S. Department of Education, Office of Educational Research and Improvement, Center for Education Statistics. *Digest of Education Statistics 1987*. Washington, D.C.: U.S. Government Printing Office, May 1987.

Notes on the Contributors

Mary Barberis is a senior research associate at the Washington, D.C.-based Draper Fund, which conducts policy analysis and public education on international population issues. She has written or edited over 200 articles and reports related to demographic trends and socioeconomic development.

Rebecca M. Blank is an assistant professor of economics and public affairs at Princeton University. Her work has focused on the effect of transfer programs and labor market constraints on the behavior of low-income households.

Jane Roberts Chapman is president of the Center for Women Policy Studies, which she cofounded in 1972. The author of books and articles on policy issues affecting women, Ms. Chapman is also executive editor of *Response to the Victimization of Women and Children.* She has served as a consultant and expert witness in a number of class action cases on behalf of female offenders.

Karen Davis is chair of the Department of Health Policy and Management in the School of Hygiene and Public Health at Johns Hopkins University, where she holds a joint appointment as professor of political economy. Dr. Davis, who earned a Ph.D. in economics at Rice University, is the author of numerous books and articles on health economics and policy analysis, including *Medicare Policy: New Directions for Health and Long-Term Care* and *Health and the War on Poverty: A Ten Year Appraisal*.

Cynthia Diehm is a former director of the National Woman Abuse Prevention Project in Washington, D.C. Before turning to domestic violence issues, she spent seven years in program development at the local level and three years providing technical assistance to county officials on criminal justice policies and practices. Ms. Diehm holds a master's degree in criminal justice from George Washington University.

Trish Donahue is executive director of the Criminal Justice Council of San Mateo County. Before moving to the council, she was the criminal justice specialist for the Human Rights Resource Center in San Rafael, California. Ms. Donahue has worked with police departments on numerous issues of concern to women, including domestic violence, sexual assault, sexual harrassment, and affirmative action.

Betty Parsons Dooley has been director of the Women's Research and Education Institute since 1977. An early Texas feminist, she was active in state politics before moving to Washington, D.C. In 1964, she was a candidate for the U.S. House of Representatives from the 16th congressional district of Texas. She served for several years as director of the Health Security Action Council, an advocacy organization that worked for comprehensive national health insurance.

Wava Gillespie Haney is an associate professor of sociology at the University of Wisconsin-Baraboo. Her research interests are women, work, and family. She has published articles on rural women in the United States and Latin America and on small town businesswomen. She chaired the planning committee of the Second National Conference on American Farm Women in Historical Perspective. With June B. Knowles, she is the coeditor of *Women and Farming: Changing Roles, Changing Structures* (1988).

Cynthia Harrison received her Ph.D. in American history from Columbia University. She was a research fellow at the Brookings Institution from 1979 to 1980. Between 1982 and 1988, she served as deputy director of Project '87, a joint effort of the American Historical Association and the American Political Science Association to enhance education about the United States Constitution. She is the author of *On Account of Sex: The Politics of Women's Issues, 1945–1968* (1988), as well as several articles on women and politics.

Wendy Johnson is executive director of the Southeast Women's Employment Coalition and former project director of the Women's

Opportunity in Road Construction Project, a national advocacy and organizing campaign to increase the number of women in federally funded road construction jobs.

Barbara B. Kennelly (Democrat-Connecticut, 1st District), who is in her fourth term in the U.S. House of Representatives, serves on the Ways and Means Committee (of which she is currently the only female member) and the Select Committee on Intelligence. Rep. Kennelly is a member of the executive committee of the Congressional Caucus for Women's Issues.

Kate McGuinness, a 1983 graduate of Barnard College, is a part-time research assistant with the Women's Research and Education Institute. She is doing research to compile an annotated bibliography on women in the American peace movement.

Ruth B. Mandel is a professor at the Eagleton Institute of Politics, Rutgers University. She teaches courses in the English and political science departments and is director of the Center for the American Woman and Politics (CAWP). Dr. Mandel has written and spoken widely about women as political candidates and officeholders, women's political networks, the "gender gap," and about women and power. Her book, *In the Running: The New Woman Candidate* (1983), describes women's experiences campaigning for political office in recent years.

Margaret W. Newton is assistant director of education and communications with the Employee Benefit Research Institute (EBRI) in Washington, D.C. At EBRI (a nonpartisan public policy organization that conducts research on retirement, health, and welfare issues), Ms. Newton helps develop and manage the sponsor, press, and general consumer education and communications program. She regularly writes on employee benefit issues, including child care, parental leave, and pension reform.

Barbara F. Reskin is a professor of sociology at the University of Illinois. She served as study director for the National Academy of Sciences' Committee on Women's Employment, and has written extensively on women's employment. She is currently studying the factors that facilitate and hinder women's progress in traditionally male and mixed-sex occupations.

Michael Rose is editor of two biweekly newsletters, *Workplace Health Report* and *Fair Employment Report*. Mr. Rose has written extensively on occupational health and safety in the United States.

Margo Ross, project associate at the National Woman Abuse Prevention Project (NWAPP), has more than six years experience as a writer and researcher on issues affecting public policy and human service programs. Before joining NWAPP, she worked with Abt Associates, CSR Inc., and the Brookings Institution.

Claudine Schneider (Republican-Rhode Island, 2d District) is in her fourth term in the U.S. House of Representatives. She serves on the Merchant Marine and Fisheries Committee, the Science, Space and Technology Committee, and the Select Committee on Aging. Rep. Schneider is also a member of the executive committee of the Congressional Caucus for Women's Issues.

Anne J. Stone has been a research associate at WREI since 1981, having previously served on the Washington staff of then-U.S. Representative Elizabeth Holtzman. Ms. Stone has authored and coauthored policy analyses on various subjects, including the federal budget, employment issues for women, and tax reform legislation.

Judith Tick is an associate professor of music at Northeastern University. She is the coeditor of *Women Making Music: The Western Art Tradition 1150–1950* (1986) and the author of *American Women Composers Before 1870* (1979), and "Women and Music" in *The New Grove Dictionary of American Music* (1987).

Rafael Valdivieso is vice president for research at the Hispanic Policy Development Project in Washington, D.C. He is a coauthor of *Make Something Happen*, the report of the National Commission on Secondary Schooling for Hispanics, and the author of *Must They Wait Another Generation? Hispanics and Secondary School Reform*, published by the ERIC Clearinghouse on Urban Education at Teachers College, Columbia University.

Donna F. Ver Steeg is a nurse sociologist and associate professor of primary ambulatory care nursing in the School of Nursing, University of California, Los Angeles. She has published in the areas of interdisciplinary practice and organizational influences on professional decisionmaking. Dr. Ver Steeg is a past president of the California Nurses Association. She is a fellow of the American Academy of Nursing and holds membership in Sigma Xi and Sigma Theta Tau.

Gloria Weissman is a public health analyst with the Community Research Branch of the Division of Clinical Research of the National Institute on Drug Abuse (NIDA). She directs a number of national demonstration projects on AIDS prevention for intravenous drug abusers and their sexual partners and coordinates NIDA's activities on women and AIDS. Ms. Weissman, who is a coeditor of the forthcoming monograph, *Women and AIDS: Promoting Healthy Behaviors*, writes and speaks on women, drug abuse, and AIDS.

Margaret B. Wilkerson is professor of theatre in the Department of Afro-American Studies at the University of California at Berkeley, where she also served for nine years as director of the Center for the Study, Education and Advancement of Women. She is the author of *9 Plays by Black Women*, as well as many articles on educational equity and on women and work. In 1985, she presented a report on the educational status of black women in the U.S. at the U.N. Decade of Women conference for nongovernmental organizations in Nairobi.

Barbara Brown Zikmund is a professor of church history and dean of the faculty at the Pacific School of Religion, Berkeley, California. She received her Ph.D. from Duke University. She was ordained in the United Church of Christ in 1964 and has written extensively on the history of women in the church and the struggle for ordination in mainstream Protestantism. In 1986 she became the first woman to be elected president of the Association of Theological Schools in the United States and Canada.

About the Women's Research & Education Institute

Betty Parsons Dooley, *Executive Director*
Sara E. Rix, *Director of Research*
Anne J. Stone, *Research Associate*
Alison Dineen, *Fellowship Program Director*
Terry A. Walker, *Office Manager*
Kate McGuinness, *Research Assistant*

The Women's Research and Education Institute (WREI) is a nonprofit (501[c][3]) organization located in Washington, D.C. Established in 1977, WREI provides information, research, and policy analysis to the bipartisan Congressional Caucus for Women's Issues, as well as to other members of Congress.

From its inception, WREI has sought to facilitate and strengthen links between researchers and policymakers concerned with issues of particular importance to women. WREI gives high priority to:

- Encouraging researchers to consider the broader implications of their work, especially as it relates to public policy;

- Fostering the exchange of ideas and expertise between researchers with technical knowledge and policymakers familiar with the realities of the legislative process and political constraints; and

- Promoting both the informed examination of policies from the perspective of their effect on women and the formulation of policy options that recognize the needs of today's women and men and their families.

WREI's activities include publishing research reports and preparing briefing papers, holding conferences and symposia, and undertaking individual research projects. WREI sponsors the Congressional Fellowships on Women and Public Policy, a program open to graduate students with strong academic skills and proven commitment to equity for women. The fellowship program has a dual purpose: to enhance the research capacity of congressional offices, especially with respect to the implications for women of existing and proposed legislation, and to provide promising women hands-on experience in the federal legislative process.

WREI's research coordination and dissemination efforts are by no means restricted to federal policymakers, however, and WREI receives an increasing number of requests for information from the press, state and local officials, other organizations, and the public.

Board of Directors

Index

About the Editor

SARA E. RIX is Director of Research at the Women's Research and Education Institute (WREI), where she specializes in policy research and analysis. Her primary research interests are employment policy, retirement policy, and the economics of aging. She holds a Ph.D. from the University of Virginia.

Dr. Rix is chair-elect of the research, education, and practice committee of the Gerontological Society of America, a member of the board of directors of the National Coalition on Older Women's Issues, and a member of the American Sociological Association's ad hoc committee on federal standards for the employment of sociologists. She is, or has been, an adviser on or consultant to projects of the PREP (Preretirement Education Planning for Midlife Women) program at Long Island University, the General Accounting Office, Working Women, the Office of Technology Assessment, the National Senior Citizens Education and Research Center, the National Council for Alternative Work Patterns, and the 1981 White House Conference on Aging.

Dr. Rix has studied, written on, and spoken about the work and retirement income needs of middle-aged and older women and men for over ten years. She is the coauthor of *The Graying of Working America* (with Harold L. Sheppard) and of *Retirement-Age Policy: An International Perspective* (with Paul Fisher). Before she came to WREI, she was a research scientist at the American Institutes for Research.